American Politics 001

American Politics 001

✦

The whole nine yards

Ndyfreke Nenty

iUniverse, Inc.
New York   Bloomington

American Politics 001
The whole nine yards

iUniverse books may be ordered through booksellers or by contacting:

iUniverse
1663 Liberty Drive
Bloomington, IN 47403
www.iuniverse.com
1-800-Authors (1-800-288-4677)

ISBN: 978-0-595-52220-0 (pbk)
ISBN: 978-0-595-62278-8 (ebk)

Printed in the United States of America

iUniverse Rev. 10/20/08

Dedication

The writer dedicates this book to all the military veterans, the fallen heroes, the true conservatives in America and their leaders, Barry Goldwater, Bill Buckley, Rush Limbaugh, Tom DeLay, Sean Hannity and Rick Santorum

Credits

Thanks to God In Three Persons
Thanks to family members, best of friends and the five mentors from East 99th Cleveland, Ohio
Thanks to neighbors

Table of Contents

Chapter 1

Rupert Murdoch: One of the Most Powerful People in America

Rupert Murdoch is an Australian born United States citizen. He is the controlling shareholder and CEO of News Corporation.

As a young promising entrepreneur, Rupert had the support of his late father. His father was a pivotal figure in newspaper industries across Australia. Murdoch first began with newspaper ownership and then moved on to television ownership in his native country. In the early fifties, he became the managing director of New Limited. Murdoch developed an interest for the newspaper business. And he began to expand and obtained a number of newspaper companies. Although his business was booming locally, Murdoch went through tribulations. For instance, Rupert was charged with sedition, "A conduct or language that incites rebellion against a state." Murdoch somehow escaped prosecution and was vindicated from the charges.

In the early sixties, Murdoch launched the Australian first national daily newspaper. The paper was said to have had a rough start. Murdoch had wielded the axe by constantly replacing his editors, in order to improve the paper's sales. Murdoch also obtained the Sydney morning tabloid, 'The Daily Telegraph.' Murdoch had the incentive for the business so he expanded his investments into The United Kingdom. [1]He was in good financial terms with international banks. And this was a huge advantage for his business deals. In 1969, while in Britain, he obtained the News of the World. It was probably the biggest acquisition of his life.

News of the World is the most popular English-language newspaper in the world.

Rupert also acquired the Sun, Britain's daily newspaper. He changed the formation of the paper into tabloid format. This increased the sales and profits of the paper. In order to increase his investment, Rupert got involved in politics in his native country and in Britain.

The News of the world and the Sun were very supportive of Margaret Thatcher and other political leaders in Britain. Murdoch's investments in Britain were booming with less government interference. Prime Minister Margaret Thatcher and her successor, John Major were believed to have accepted millions in advance from HarperCollins, for the publication of their memoirs.

HarperCollins is a publishing house owned by Murdoch.

At the end of John Major's Conservative Party era, Murdoch flip-flopped and expressed his support to the Labor Party and its party leader, Tony Blair. In 1997, Mr. Blair was eventually elected as the replacement to Major. Rupert and Tony were very close. Rupert was said to be closer to Blair than he was to other past prime ministers.

Murdoch bought the Times in London. This paper was his flagship British paper. He had since expanded the Times newspaper worldwide. He quickly established himself as a pivotal entrepreneur in Britain's media industry. He also secured the British- based station network SKY Television.

SKY Television is Europe's first 24 hour news channel. [2]

Murdoch worked toward advancing his business investment when he moved to America. In the early seventies, his first acquisition was the San Antonio Express-News. The paper was nothing compared to his first acquisition in Britain. Toward the end of the seventies, Murdoch obtained the New York Post. [3]

In 1985, Murdoch bought seven television stations in American markets. The following year, Murdoch's News Corp launched Fox broadcasting company (Fox Television Network). He was fearless and bold enough to create Fox, a fourth national television network.

The other national television networks are ABC, CBS, and NBC. [4]

FCC Rules

There are rules established by the FCC that limit how much foreigners are allow to own in the media.

Since Murdoch wasn't an American citizen, he had to comply with the foreign ownership rules. This was a setback for Murdoch because he wouldn't be able to increase his investment. He thus worked on becoming a citizen of the United States. His dream came through around the mid-eighties when Murdoch became a naturalize citizen. Rupert Murdoch hurdled his first obstacle. [5]

In 1987, Murdoch first experienced the difference between ownership regulations in America and that of UK/ Australia. Senator Kennedy and Senator Hollings prevented Murdoch from increasing his financial interest. Murdoch had to abide with an FCC ownership rule that prohibits the ownership of newspapers and television stations in the same market. When Murdoch launched FOX Network in 1986, he bought local television stations in New York City and in Boston. Therefore, Murdoch had violated the FCC's cross ownership rule because of his ownership of Boston's newspaper, 'Boston Herald' and his New York newspaper, 'The NY Post.'

Murdoch tried to have the cross ownership rule revoked. And in 1988, Ted Kennedy sponsored a legislation that prevented the cross ownership rule from being repeal. Murdoch sacrificed his Boston TV station WFXT, for his Boston Herald. And he grudgingly sacrificed the New York Post for his local New York TV station, WNYW. Senator Kennedy had been known to target Murdoch's news media outlets because Murdoch had been using the Boston Herald to attack the senator from Massachusetts. Five years later, Murdoch's animosity towards the senator vanished when Senator Kennedy backed his right to re-purchase the Post. [6]

In 1994, a year after Bill Clinton took office; Murdoch had to report to the Clinton- appointed FCC, the conditions that led him to acquired local television stations to create FOX Network. This was simply a slap to the face for Murdoch. He was forced to go back eight years in time. When Clinton was campaigning to become the 42nd U.S. president, Murdoch did his best to ensure Clinton wasn't elected.

FCC was investigating whether FOX was foreign own or American own.

Even though Mr. Murdoch became a U.S. citizen, his company, News Corp. was still registered in his native country. Fortunately for Murdoch, the Committee looking into the case had a Republican majority. Hundt, the FCC Chairman was censored by Republican lawmakers. The Committee voted in Murdoch's favor. "They lambasted me for the audacity of having looked into the question" Reed Hundt said. [7]

The Federal Communication Commission (FCC) is an agency run by the United States government. The United States President only appoints the Commissioners who must get confirmed by the US Senate. However, the President chooses the Chairman from amongst the senate approved Commissioners.

The FCC was established in 1934; they have jurisdiction over television and radio licensing. Before the end of Clinton's tenure, Reed Hundt was succeeded by William Kennard as the FCC's Chairperson. [8]

Murdoch also acquired Fox news Channel. The 24-hour cable network was launched into the world of cable news in October of 96. Liberal bias in American media led Murdoch to acquire the Fox News channel as a counterbalance. After the launch of the heavily-funded Fox News, liberal critics immediately accused FOX of promoting a Republican (right-wing) point of view. Murdoch appointed Roger Ailes as the Chief executive officer. Rupert Murdoch considered Fox News Channel (FNC) as 'fair and balanced' to counter the liberal media. He responded to bias allegations from the Left (Liberals and Democrats): "Given room to both sides, whereas only one side had it before," commented Murdoch's. [9]

Murdoch categorized himself as a Libertarian. With Fox News channel, a new fresh wind just blew in and the cable channels of the country's media changed. Murdoch challenged CNN's founder Ted Turner, probably saying "Sir, there is a new chief in town." Fox News immediately became the most-watched cable news channel in the nation with the signatures of television's most-watched talk show host Bill O'Reilly, Sean Hannity, and Brit Hume. Murdoch considered Hume as his beloved talk show host and the most conservative talk host in America. [10]

In the mid 1990's, the Newt Gingrich (R-Georgia) led Congress allowed broadcasting networks like Murdoch's FOX to expand. Congress increased media companies' national audience size to a maximum of 35 percent. This changed happened in the wake of a 4.5 million book advance offered by Murdoch's HarperCollins to Newt Gingrich. FCC gave Murdoch the green light to buy more local television stations, but his company's national audience must not surpass 35 percent. But Murdoch acquired additional stations and eventually his company's national audience reached more than 35 percent of American homes. [11]

And in 2003, Murdoch overcame yet another hurdle when some congressional lawmakers wanted media companies that reached more than the 35 percent of American's households to conform to the rule. Murdoch's clients had to lobby Congress to pass a law that would increase the ownership cap. With Newt Gingrich no longer in control of Congress and Senator Trent Lott's stance as an anti media consolidation advocate, it was looking like doom and gloom for Murdoch. Senator Lott, the former Senate Majority Leader, was one of the Republican leaders that wanted to limit the ownership cap. Murdoch hopes was hanging by a thread until Senator Lott and other congressional leaders, without a hitch, agreed to increase the ownership cap to

39 percent. Immediately the news came out that Senator Lott (R-Mississippi) agreed to raise the cap because Lott signed a book deal with HarperCollins for his memoir.[12]

Michael Powell, the first FCC chairman in the Bush administration, wanted to raise the limit up to 45 percent. But Lott didn't agree to Powell's proposal and the damage was done when a Federal appeals Court in Philadelphia killed the proposal. After Powell's appeal decision was rendered, Michael Powell noted that "The decision perversely may make it dramatically more difficult for the commission to protect against greater media consolidation. It sets near-impossible standards for justifying bright-line ownership limits."

Kelvin Martin, Powell's successor, is said to be proposing Congress to redraw the media ownership rules. In a meeting at Seattle, Washington about the media conglomerate plan, Martin said jokingly "This year I can say I'm actually thrilled to be here. In fact, if I weren't at this dinner, I'd still be testifying before Congress."

Mrs. Rhodes, a staunch opponent of media conglomerate claimed that "Sam Zell, Rupert Murdoch, and Kelvin Martin want to kill news media. Martin, the FCC Chairman, wants to get rid of the rule that bans conglomerate to own the media" (a paraphrase.) Rhodes continued, "FCC regulates the industries it wants to work for; they want to allow media giants to run the American media. Martin wants to grant Murdoch and Zell media ownership wishes, so that once Martin is done as Chairperson, he will get hire by Murdoch" (a paraphrase.) [13]

Sam Zell is the chairman of equity group investment. In 2007, Zell bought the company that publishes the Los Angeles times, the Chicago Tribune, and other newspaper media outlets. Like Murdoch, Zell donates to both the Republican and Democratic members of Congress. [14]

Big six media conglomerates

In 2004, Murdoch announced that he was moving New Corp's flagship headquarters from Australia to the United States.

Murdoch's News Corp is among the so-called 'Big Six' corporations that control the American's mass media. News Corp in terms of market capitalization is the world's largest media conglomerate company. Time Warner and General Electric own Murdoch's immediate cable news competitors, CNN and MSNBC respectively. General Electric, in terms of market capitalization, is the world's second largest company. General Electric, unlike News Corp, is not a media conglomerate company. General Electric's news media holdings include NBC Universal, CNBC, Telemundo, Sci Fi channels, and other television stations. It has owned NBC Universal since the mid eighties. MSNBC is a joint venture of Microsoft and General Electric.

Time Warner is the world's second biggest media conglomerate. It owns Cable News Network (CNN). Time Warner also owns Court TV, TNT, HBO, TBS, and other stations.

In 2006, Time Warner was the largest media conglomerate in the world.

American media oligarchy also included Walt Disney. In 1996, Walt Disney acquired American Broadcasting Company (ABC).

Disney also owns ESPN, The Disney Channel, SOAPnet, and other stations. Walt Disney is the third largest media conglomerate corporation in the world.

News Corp also faced industry competition from traditional media companies Viacom and CBS, the rest of the so-called 'Big Six.' Murdoch doesn't have to worry about competing with CBS and Viacom; they would only be a concern for him if they merged back together.

On the last day of 2005, the firm was split off. The original Viacom was named CBS Corporation while the new Viacom retained its original name, 'Viacom.' Its major by-product included CBS Television Network, MTV, BET, and the CW network, a joint venture with Time Warner. [15]

Murdoch's American properties include HarperCollins (book publisher), the New York Post, the Weekly Standard, TV Guide, National Geographic, Fox Broadcasting, Fox News Channels, Twentieth Century Fox (film production company), Fox Sports Net, and local television stations in all the major cities in America.

In 2004, a rating showed that FOX cable channel had nine of the top ten programs in the cable news category.

Fox's shows featuring Bill O'Reilly and Sean Hannity are the two most-watched programs in the nation. Murdoch has been successful in every investment that he has undertaken. That is why Murdoch, a media tycoon, is considered one of the most powerful men in our country. [16]

The 2008 presidential election (February 07-December 07)

The 2008 presidential elections are right at the corner. Will Murdoch turns his back on the GOP?

In Britain, once John Major was about done as prime minister, Murdoch threw his support for the other party.

Is that what is going to happen in America now that the media mogul is donating and fund-raising for Senator Hillary Clinton? The New York senator is likely going to win the nominee for the Democratic Party.

Previously, Murdoch did his utmost to prevent the Senator's husband from winning the presidential election of 1992. An evidence of Murdoch's zeal was the Post's relentless and in-depth coverage of the Lewinsky scandal. In 2006, during Hillary Clinton run for reelection in the senate, the New York Post endorsed the Senator. The New York junior senator even attended the 10th anniversary of Fox News channel.

So, does Murdoch foresee the end of the Republican power center in D.C.? Mr. Murdoch will not allow his personal politics get in his way of increasing his business ventures.

Apart from campaign contributions, Murdoch also acquires jobs for former government officials; those that will do his bidding and increased his financial interest. [17]

For the Republican 08 candidates for president, Fox News is said to be favoring the election of former New York Mayor, Rudolph Giuliani. He frequently appears on their programs.

In 1997, Time Warner opted for MSNBC instead of Fox News to partner CNN and be carried on Time Warner's New York local cable system. Fox News challenged Warner's decision. Time Warner then filed a lawsuit and FOX countered with their own suit. Giuliani, then mayor of NYC, lobbied for News Corp. Giuliani had a big influence on the case. This hub-bub led to a feud between Time Warner's Ted Turner and Rupert Murdoch. Tuner ended up comparing Murdoch to Adolf Hitler. The two companies eventually reached a deal permitting Fox News Channel with a slot on Warner's local cable system. [18]

In the presidential and congressional elections, who gives the best and most complete coverage of the elections? Diane Sawyer, Charles Gibson, and 'This Week With' George Stephanopoulos lead ABC's presidential/congressional election team coverage. Brian Williams, David Gregory, and 'Meet the Press' with Tim Russert lead NBC's team coverage. Katie Couric and 'Face the Nation' with Bob Schieffer lead CBS team coverage. FOX provides America with 'Fox News Sunday' hosted by Chris Wallace. And New York Times' David Brooks and syndicated columnist, Mark Shields, make weekly appearances on NewsHour with PBS host Jim Lehrer.

Paper of Record

Murdoch is a jack of all trades. He also has investments in the Internet and the film industry. He has been criticizing British Broadcasting Company (BBC). Rupert probably wishes he is able to acquire the company.

However, in late 2007, he acquired the Dow Jones's World Street Journal (WSJ). Before Murdoch stake his claim as the owner of WSJ, the

Bancroft family, which controlled Dow Jones, had pushed to preserve the independence of the World Street Journal's news coverage. There were a lot of doubts that Murdoch would accept their proposal. The media magnate said "I can't put down $5 billion of my shareholders' money and not be able to run the business." Murdoch refuted the claims that he was going to object to the Bancroft family's proposal, "no plans to change anything" he concluded. The deal take over materialized and an agreement was reached between the two parties to preserve the editorial independence of the Journal.

After Murdoch finally bought the World Street Journal, various newspaper headlines read: "Murdoch Seizes Wall St Journal in $5 Billion Coup" - Washington Post.

"Dow Jones Deal Gives Murdoch a Coveted Prize." - New York Times.

"Rupe Takes the Prize. Wall Street Journal Owner Selling out to Peddler of Post."- Daily News.

With the settlement now over, Dow Jones & company became a subsidiary of Rupert Murdoch's News Corp.

Mr. Limbaugh, a millionaire and a leading conservative activist, talked about the New York Times being the 'paper of record.' And he also talked about how Murdoch will fight to push World Street Journal to become the paper of record: "One of the objectives that Murdoch has is to take on the New York Times as the paper of record." Limbaugh continued,

> "The problem with the New York Times is not really the New York Times. It's the rest of the media. The rest of the media adopts the New York Times agenda. Whatever is on the front page of the New York Times is what television cable news networks decide is news at least the networks, CBS, NBC, the liberal networks. The New York Times always was called 'the paper of record'. Stories on the front page throughout the front section, determine what agenda is in the press."

In 2003, when FCC increased its national audience cap to 39 percent, Limbaugh played a big role. Limbaugh recalled an encounter he had with a news director in Sacramento, California. The big shot said "I remember my first day, (the news director) was strolling through the newsroom one morning, and all he found was the Los Angeles Times, the Sacramento Bee, and the San Francisco Chronicle. He blew up. He started shouting, 'Where's the New York Times? You can't do news anymore without the New York Times.'"[19]

Murdoch has been lampooned and referred to as a union buster, a local media crusher and a warmonger. He argued strongly for the war with Iraq.

His 175 newspaper editors around the world supposedly backed the war in Iraq. One of his editors went on the record saying "Twelve years of defiance by Hussein show that the old policies of containment no longer work. Appeasement is not an option when it comes to dealing with Hussein. Failure to disarm Hussein would make the world a much more dangerous place."

Murdoch had also backed the Bush administration stands against the Iraqi dictator Saddam Hussein: "We can't back down now, when you hand over the whole of the Middle East to Saddam… I think Bush is acting very morally, very correctly, and I think he is going to go on with it," Murdoch said. He also praised Tony Blair for supporting the war in Iraq. The philanthropist believes that ousting Saddam Hussein will lead to cheaper oil worldwide: "The greatest thing to come out of this for the world economy would be a $20 a barrel for oil. That's bigger than any tax cut in any country." Murdoch concluded, "Once Saddam is behind us, the whole world will benefit from cheaper oil which will be a bigger stimulus than anything else." [20]

Murdoch has promoted his own financial interest in the continents of Australia, Europe, Asia, and America.

He publishes about 40 millions papers a week. And he dominates the newspaper markets in Australia, New Zealand, and Britain. Time will tell if he will completely dominate American news media.

Italian media proprietor, Silvio Berlusconi, who later became the county's prime minister, once owned 90% of the Italian media.

Murdoch is sandwiched in between Silvio Berlusconi and Sam Zell in the Forbes World Riches Billionaires. He is ranked among the top 100 Forbes's world wealthiest people. Murdoch is the epitome of a 21st century successful entrepreneur.[21]

Chapter 2

Randi Rhodes: One of the most Powerful People in America

Randi Rhodes is one of the original rank and file liberal activists left in America. She is featured in a progressive news talk radio station flagship at New York City. Randi is ranked as the number one progressive talk show host in America. Many radio affiliates record her show live, 'The Randi Rhodes Show,' just to be broadcasted later in the evening. Some stations airs her show twice in a day.

Randi was part of the U.S. Air force personal. She wasn't involved in combat operation. And she never took credit for her experience in the United States Air Force.

Randi Rhodes started her radio career after she was discharged from the Air Force. After the September 11th 2001 attacks in the country, she gained enormous fame. She was very critical of President Bush's administration and how they handled the situation before the terrorist attacks. Right from the commencement of her show, she has been very suspicious of the entire Bush administration. Her research and findings have made her label the President's administration as incompetent.

She is also a vocal opponent to the right-wingers and neoconservatives. [22]

Her show has the largest audience in progressive talk radio in America. Seldom does she conduct interviews.

She has interviewed John Dean, author of 'Conservative Without Conscience' and 'worse than Watergate,' Bruce Fein, former Deputy

Attorney General, Scott Ritters, former Marine and weapons inspector, Brent Budowsky, a counter pundit and Democratic strategist, Greg Palast, author of 'Armed Madhouse,' and Cindy Sheehan, an anti war advocate, who has been smeared by both the Democrats and the Republicans. She constantly tells her listeners "Never trust any commentary that you hear on the radio, not even me." She tells her audience to do their own findings, and she normally littered her audience with homework. Absolutely nobody can pay attention to the Randi Rhodes show and not have a change of attitude. Some pundits have compared Randi to conservative big shot Rush Limbaugh. Others have a different measurement in comparing Randi to Rush. [23]

Randi's radio career began in Seminole Texas. She worked at several radio stations in various American markets for over a decade. In the mid nineties, she was designated to West Palm Beach, Florida, to work at the WJNO am station. The General Manager of WJNO praised Ms. Rhodes. He acknowledged, "She's very talented. I think she'll be a positive addition." The Famous O.J. Simpson case gave her fame in American media. 'The excellence of radio' was anointed upon her during her coverage of the trial. Her next major assignment was her coverage of the first 21st century presidential election.

In 2004, Randi originally joined AA2.0 Media, a liberal radio network station in New York City. Randi said that before WJNO station was bought by Clear Channels in 2000, she was in the 12noon- 3pm time slot on the local radio in West Palm Beach. And she was in serious competition with Mr. Limbaugh for ratings. She claimed that she repeatedly beat Limbaugh in ratings; that it was so bad that Clear Channels bought out WJNO and changed her time slot to the evening drive. And she was offered a lot of money. However, Limbaugh had way more national audiences than Ms. R hodes.

Florida's West Palm Beach is one of the controversial districts where voters complained of disenfranchisement in the 2000 presidential election. [24]

'Talking back, the coming rise of liberal talk radio' was largely referring to Randi and the AA 2.0 Media Station. Randi was highly responsible for the 2004 presidential election that almost witnesses Senator John Kerry (D) winning over the incumbent. Two years passed and this time around a due was paid; she guided the Democrats to win back both the U.S House of Representatives and the U.S Senate. [25]

Unfair party treatment

Regardless of everything Ms. Rhodes has done for the Democratic Party and it member's reelection bid, liberal senators and blue dog congressional lawmakers are nervous to be a guest on her show. Randi screamed "They avoid me like a plague. Most politicians love me but avoid me because I can either hurt them or win them an election" (a paraphrase.) Nobody wants to take the heat that she brings. So maybe the kitchen's entrance should be left open.

For instance, a certain U.S. congressman hung up the phone on Randi when he made his debut on her show. The congressman refused to answer a particular question.

Ms. Rhodes tells her listeners that U.S. Senator and presidential candidate Joe Biden (D-Delaware) dislikes her because of one encounter they had in 2003 on the senate's floor. "In public he intimidates me, he yelled at me" Randi recalled. Randi said to Sen. Biden, "Why can't you call the President what he really is, a liar?" Randi recalled that Biden's response was, "Why do you have to pick the hardest thing to do?" Randi admitted that she likes the Senator. [26]

One of the reasons that Ms. Rhodes has been categorized as so powerful is her ability to stand up to her challengers. Any time Rhodes decides to go to any of the cable television networks as a national pundit, it is always fair but not balanced. They always have Randi debating two or three conservative pundits, who will not let her talk; eventually she always comes out victorious. She does appear on CNN's Larry king live.

When conservative commentators get excoriated by the mainstream media, the Republican Party will stand up for them. Randi Rhodes never gets such treatment. Any time Randi gets in trouble as a talk show host, no elected Democrats in Congress stand up for her, adopting a "you on your own" attitude. The Democrats are living scared; they are too soft to even protect their own real mouthpiece. [27]

When a University of Florida student was tasered, Ms. Rhodes severely lambasted Senator John Kerry (D-Massachusetts) for not preventing the harsh treatment of the victim. The next day, Ms. Rhodes reported that "she took a lot of hits" from the Democratic Party leadership; not because she was reporting the truth but because she was trashing a fellow Democrat. The Democratic Party called for the bloodletting within the party to cease. Ms. Rhodes explained to her audience "I'm not a party person." Rhodes refused to get syndicated; she chose not to do what the party demanded her to do. The Democratic Party begged to raise money for her but she refused.[28]

In 2005, The Randi Rhodes Show was rumored to be under investigation by the Secret Service when it aired a gunshot sketch warning to the American president. However, she immediately apologized to President Bush and to the Secret Service. Randi addressed her listeners and America "This was just a stupid, stupid bit. But if it crossed the line, then certainly, there must be punishment, and if there is, I want to be punished so that I can actually say 'Equal justice under law' Anybody that has stepped over this line of law needs to be prosecuted, including me." The controversial bit played on her show was: "A spoiled child is telling us our Social Security isn't safe anymore, so he is going to fix it for us. Well, here's your answer, you ungrateful whelp: {sound of four gunshots fired} just try it, you little bastard {sound of a gun cocked}" Ms. Rhodes further apologized incessantly for the skit. She made it clear that the bit was organized by Air America Radio producers without her knowledge. Randi reiterated that she would not have aired the skit, had she heard it before the program began. Nevertheless, she was ready to face the penalty. Randi concluded before her show went off the air

> "I also feel bad there could be a perception that I would be advocating violence against anybody, let alone the President of the United States of America. It's no secret that I think he is a terrible president, but I don't think that anybody should have violence advocated against them in any way, shape or form ever. That skit (bit) will never see the light of day again. It was bad." [29]

Randi Rhodes doesn't anticipate running for Congress, her friend Cindy Sheehan may motivate her, since Cindy is said to be running for the House of Representatives in the California 8 district. Randi prefers the U.S House of Representatives better than the US Senate because the Senate is like a "white men's club," compared to the House that is diversified. Randi can run either in the State of Florida or New York. She still has a home in Florida, although it was damaged by a hurricane. [30]

Bill O'Reilly led the Republican smeared on Ms. Rhodes. O'Reilly frequently trashed her by playing clips of Randi's radio show commentary on his program; which O'Reilly viewed as unacceptable dialogue. Mr. O'Reilly also demeaned her looks on cable television. She felt undervalued when MSNBC and PBS anchormans listening to her radio show and plagiarizing her ideas without giving her credit. Randi complained, "The Democrats are not being courteous to her." Randi Rhodes always chastised the point of views of Limbaugh, Hannity, and O'Reilly. She said she can't stand their propaganda; and she referred to them as "The chief propaganda masters." One of Randi Rhodes' favorite sound bites was a statement from President Bush: "See, in my line of work, you got to keep repeating things over and over again for the truth to sink in, to kind of catapult the propaganda." One reason Ms. Rhodes stopped writing her book was because all the findings about the Bush's administration made her sick to her stomach. Her book was to be titled 'The Big Encyclopedia of Republican Hypocrites.'[31]

Occupation in Iraq

Ms. Rhodes constantly in session and out of session criticized the Bush administration. The Randi Rhodes Show skit: "You are listening to the Randi Rhodes show that means that you probably didn't vote for George Bush, {Bush's voice "You did not vote for failure."} Randi said the outgoing Bush's administration was full of fear and war mongers, and they tried six ways to Sunday to accomplish a way with Iraq.

On May 1st, 2003, President Bush declared the end of combat operation from the flight deck of the USS Abraham Lincoln: "My fellow Americans: Major combat operations in Iraq have ended. In the battle of Iraq, the United States and our allies have prevailed. And now our coalition is engaged in securing and reconstructing that country." Randi scoffed at Bush's statements; Randi said yes, the war was over and now the occupation had begun. Ms. Rhodes said, "Bush doesn't listen to people, when will Bush start to listen to the Iraqis people who wants us out of Iraq."

In Iraq we keep on losing soldiers in the occupation. Democrats in Congress have tried on a number of occasions to pass legislation that would bring the occupation to an end. Ask Madam Rhodes how long the bloody occupations in Iraq will last, and former "goodness gracious" Defense Secretary Donald Rumsfeld will say "It could last six days, six weeks. I doubt six months."

Madam Rhodes has always accused the Bush administration of lying to the American people. She stated there were only in two instances when Bush told the truth regarding the war in Iraq. One Bush statement: "There is no evidence that Saddam was involved in September the eleven." And the other was "So I don't know where he is. You know, I just don't spend that much time on him, (Osama Bin Laden) to be honest with you." Randi acknowledged it took only 2 seconds for Bush to tell the truth. Ms. Rhodes has called for Bush to end the occupation in Iraq because the sectarian violence in Iraq had escalated and has crossed a threshold to an Iraqi civil war.

How long will collateral damage be focused on Iraq? "American foot print should end in Iraq, our military is broken" Rhodes intoned. The country is in the throes of military collapse. [32]

Rhodes poked fun at Bush when the President said "We are trying to figure out how best to make the world a peaceful place. There's an old saying in Tennessee I Know it's in Texas, it's probably in Tennessee -that says, fool me once, shame on... shame on you. It fools me. We can't get fooled again."

Randi, the leading Democratic activist, believed that, "Wars of choice are not winnable. Iraq didn't declare war on America, unlike Germany. Bush has lost the fight (battle) with reality and also the fight in Iraq as well. And there is no connection but he doesn't know." Randi truly said, "Iraqis are guilty until proven innocent."

She brings to our attention the fact that the Iraqi people's business in Iraq is to stay alive. Their businesses are always close. But when a United States congressman visits Iraq, they open up their business just for show (pretense), to get paid and will closed it back once the congressman is gone. Another sound bite "First, let me make it very clear, poor people aren't necessary killers. Just because you happen to be not rich doesn't mean that you are willing to kill," Bush stated.[33]

The Story of Blackwater USA

Ms. Rhodes said that she knew about the private security firm and its activities long before the story reached the mainstream media or the beltway media establishment. But she refused to comment about the story until it was out.

In 2005, a military contractor for defamation sued her. Rhodes had accused contractors of murdering Iraqi civilians at Abu Ghraob prison.

Ms. Rhodes was still the first liberal international radio talk show host to comment on the deeds of the Blackwater merchants. Blackwater security was reported to be banned from Iraq after they were blamed for some civilians' deaths. In September of 07, Associated Press reported, "Eight civilians were killed and 13 were wounded when contractors believed to be working for Blackwater USA opened fire in a predominantly Sunni neighborhood of western Baghdad." Blackwater denied any wrongdoing, claiming self-defense. The people of Iraq complained about the private firm on two fronts. One, Blackwater guards were often too quick to shoot and they were seldom held responsible for their deeds. When the story broke, Maliki, the Prime Minister of Iraq, said he would kick Blackwater out of Iraq. However, State Secretary Rice called Maliki and apologized, and she said Blackwater was not going anywhere. Randi Rhodes said "Rice is the President of Iraq." Maliki's office immediately yielded to Secretary Rice's request and also lauded Blackwater guards for the protection that they have provided. The FBI came to Iraq to investigate the killings that were reported involving Blackwater USA. But the FBI was being protected by the same Blackwater securities that the FBI was investigating.

Blackwater USA is a private military contractor, formed in 1997 by Erik Prince, a right-wing billionaire. Cofer Black, once the Coordinator for

CIA's Counterterrorist Center from 2000 to 2004 is Blackwater USA's vice president. [34]

"I was to find bin Laden, kill him, and bring his head back to the United States in a box on dry ice." Those were orders from Cofer Black to one member of a seven-man CIA team. Gary Schroen, a former senior CIA agent, said, "The gloves were off and that we were there to really go after this guy (bin Laden) and his lieutenants and to kill them." Schroen continued, "Mr. Cofer Black really wanted to demonstrate to us that this was very, very serious." Schroen added that his seven-man team was only given five days to prepare to go into Afghanistan and catch Osama bin Laden. Cofer's orders were triggered by the horrible events of September the eleven.

Randi Rhodes said "the Blackwater mercenary is the rise of the world's most powerful merchant. They have trained the NYPD. They confronted criminals and stopped looters in Iraq." She asked, "Under what authority are they arresting people? The US authorities don't know how many of them are in Iraq, and whom do they report to?"(a paraphrase) The security contractors made money in the devastating area of New Orleans during Hurricane Katrina.

Rhodes later found out that Blackwater operates under the U.S. State Department, even though it is a private security firm. But they are exempt from US military regulations. Randi concluded, "Let Blackwater USA be the military force for the Republicans and our US military troops will be the military force for the Democrats."[35]

Hurricane Katrina

Probably one of the most important achievements in Randi's resume is her partnership with Habitat for Humanity. This agenda is in rebuilding the Gulf Coast, one home at a time. Habitat for Humanity is a charity program.

Her partnership with Habitat for Humanity started in 2005 after Hurricane Katrina. Randi, when reporting the disaster that occurred in New Orleans, literally cried on the airwaves. It was extremely emotional, the heartrending stories that she was reporting on Katrina, how people were losing their lives. Phone calls from affected listeners in New Orleans made her shed tears.[36]

A breakdown of the horrible events Ms. Rhodes reported

Randi said Governor Blanco asked the Bush administration for federal troops, and her request was delayed. Days after, some Bush administration officials claimed that Gov. Blanco never declared a federal state of emergency.

Before the hurricane struck, Homeland Security was warned that the levees wouldn't be able to hold a category 5 hurricane, but no efforts were made to strengthen the levees. A day before the levees gave up, National Guard asked for 700 buses from FEMA, but only 100 buses were dispatched.

Homeland Security Secretary Michael Chertoff and FEMA Director Michael Brown didn't know diddly–squat about emergency management. They had no prior experience in disaster relief before they were appointed by Bush. Brown was an estate-planning lawyer. A day after the levee broke, Homeland Security Boss Michael Chertoff of all people wasn't even aware that the levee had failed. White House staffers showed Bush a DVD to experience the horrific situation before the President visited the Gulf Coast States. Michael Brown had no knowledge that a Convention Center existed until four days after the levees collapsed. Bush applauded Michael Brown "Brownie, you're doing a heck of a job." Bush acknowledged, "I don't think anybody anticipated the breach of the levees." However, the senior senator from Louisiana countered Bush's statement: "We Know the president said, quote, 'I don't think anybody anticipated the breach of the levees,' everybody anticipated the breach of the levees, Mr. President, including computer stimulations in which this administration participated," Senator Landrieu said on the Senate floor.[37]

Anti-Defamation League brought a case against Ms. Rhodes. They had a fit when she commented on the disastrous event. Rhodes's commentary on Katrina:

> "I think about it this way. People were taken one place. Their children were taken another place. This is so much like the Holocaust. I can't even-you know, it's like; you're not supposed to forget the Holocaust so that it can't happen again. And here you have people being loaded onto transportation vehicles, not being told where they're going, and their children are being taken someplace else,"

Randi commented. The Anti-Defamation League wrote to Ms. Rhodes "By comparing the Katrina relief effort to the Holocaust, you (Randi) demean decent Americans and the memory of six million Jews and others who died at the hands of the Nazis."

23,000 and more exhausted Superdome refugees from New Orleans were transported to Texas' Astrodome. Barbara Bush, President Bush's mother, went on a tour to the Hurricane relief center at the Astrodome arena and acknowledged, "This is working very well for them." Although she held a fundraiser for the evacuated victims from Louisiana, she wasn't pleased about the refugees' intentions to remain permanently in Texas "They all want to stay in Texas. Almost everyone I've talked to says we're going to move to Houston." Barbara Bush concluded: "What I'm hearing which is sort of scary is they all want to stay in Texas. Everybody is so overwhelmed by the hospitality. And so many of the people in the arena here, you know, were underprivileged anyway, so this is working very well for them." [38]

President Bush urged officials to stop referring to the victims as refugees. And Bush was saddened about Senator Trent Lott losing his home. "Out of the rubbles of Trent Lott's house- he's lost his entire house- there is going to be a fantastic house. And I'm looking forward to sitting on the porch," Bush said. A majority of citizens from New Orleans were poor and after the devastating storm, the poor had become poorer. The aftermath of the disaster made New Orleans appear as if the city was in a third world country. Bush was severely blamed for the lethargic federal response in the rescue of New Orleans. But without hesitating, Bush took the blame. "To the extent the federal government didn't fully do its job right, I take responsibility," President Bush said.

A year after the calamity, people who live in New Orleans have long felt "abandoned and forgotten." BBC News stated that hurricane Katrina exposed how in the United States, too many African Americans were "at the bottom of the pile."

They have lost everything, their possessions and their homes and they have been left in limbo. The effects of Hurricane Katrina will linger for months, if not years, to come. New Orleans is a local issue not a federal issue, so Americans should cut Bush some slack.[39]

Ms. Rhodes returned in August 2007 from an Alaskan Cruise. Rhodes successfully carried an enormous number of her supporters with her. Although, there were tips that two highly influential conservative commentators sent spies to the Alaskan Cruise. The so-called Senator Ted Stevens' earmarks Alaska labeled 'Bridges to Nowhere' actually went somewhere with Ms. Rhodes and her followers. Ted Stevens, a former president *pro tempore* was the subject of criticism when he threatened to resign from Congress if funds for two local bridges in the state of Alaska were diverted to help the recovery effort in Hurricane Katrina.[40]

Filibuster

Rhodes stressed on her radio program that in the 110th Congress, "We don't have the majority, we need 60 votes to overcome a filibuster, and just one person is needed to stand up for a filibuster, because of that tool" (a paraphrase). Rhodes explained to her audience "We need 60 senators before we (Democrats) can claim to be the party that has the majority." And the Republicans kept on denying a simple up-or- down vote.

Filibuster is a technique used in the senate to prevent a bill from coming to a vote. A senator who opposes a bill can talk the bill to death by holding the floor of the senate, and can prevent the senate from moving forward with a vote. So a senator has to filibuster a bill in order to defeat a bill.

Storm Thurmond, a former President *pro tempore* of the senate, uttered the longest filibuster in the history of the US Senate. The South Carolina senator attempted to prevent the passage of the Civil Right act of 1957. He spoke against the bill for over 24 hours.

The Senate can only overcome a filibuster by invoking a cloture. A cloture is a vote to end a filibuster and limits debate. An approval of 60 votes or three-fifth of the senators' votes is needed to stop a filibuster. Cloture is rarely invoked because it's difficult to muster.

In the 110th Congress, Republican leaders like Sen. Lott allegedly obstructed legislations brought by the Democrats and then ran against the Democrats has "a do- nothing Congress."

The 110th Congress is very polarized, so it makes it difficult to reach bi-partisanship agreement. [41]

Randi is a C-Span junkie and is friends with the owner, Brian Lamb. Ms. Rhodes sometimes referred to herself as a 'black journalist,' thereby confusing her listeners. Another of Randi's skit is "The Randi Rhodes Show', your daily inconvenient truth teller."

The 2008 presidential election (February 07-December 07)

In the ongoing 08 election, Ms. Rhodes said she would not endorse any Democratic candidates for president until after the primary. But the activist has been galvanizing strong support for Albert Gore. In late 2007, the former VP hosted Ms. Rhodes as an invited guest in the Live Earth concert.

Albert Gore hasn't announced any intention for running. And Ms. Rhodes will surely urge her listeners to support Vice President Gore.

A secret lobbying campaign has been launched to draft Mr. Gore. Rhodes noted "Mr. Gore is best qualified, best minded and he won the election before" (i.e. the 2000 presidential election). Randi said that "America doesn't realize how toxic the whole Bush administration is."

She predicts that Republican voters, even the ones that always stay home and vegetate may have to hold their noses and vote for a Democrat for president in the 2008 presidential and congressional elections. The Democratic voters, or according to a Republican senator, "The mythical little guys," will support Albert Gore if he runs. Randi also wants Joe Biden to be our next president. However, she said in the 2008 election, Joe Biden is running for Hillary Clinton's secretary of state.

Randi takes pride in attacking the Republican candidates. With no end in sight, she attacks her former NY Mayor, Rudy Giuliani. The former mayor is connected with Vulture fund mogul, Paul Singer. The Billionaire is believed to have donated heavily for Giuliani's election bid. But Singer is also believed to have engaged in allegedly siphoning off funds assigned to poor African countries.

Ms. Rhodes has been called all sorts of names: Tokyo Rhodes, Osama bin Rhodes, Hussein bin Randi. Talker Magazine named Randi Rhodes 'Woman of the year' for 2007.

Who will be the next set of first tier candidates to replace Ms. Rhodes, the goddess of American talk radio, when she is done with radio commentary? "Has anybody ever heard of Rachel Maddow?" Others are Stephanie Miller and of course Laura Ingraham. Randi Rhodes is one of the most powerful people in America.[42]

Chapter 3

Tom DeLay, one of the most powerful people in America

Tom DeLay was a former member of the US House of Representatives. He represented the 22nd district, Sugar Land, Texas. DeLay was the most powerful lawmaker in Capitol Hill. He was known for pressurizing political adversaries, mainly the Democrats and moderate Republicans. DeLay was referred as the 'Hammer' because he was a no-nonsense disciplinarian. He frequently made the headlines in America politics. In the early eighties, Tom was first elected to the US Congress thanks to presidential candidate Ron Paul, who resigned his seat for a run in the US Senate. After four years in Congress, Mr. DeLay became a prominent conservative figure and was also a ranking member for the GOP. When the Republican Party took over Congress after the midterm election of 1994, he was elevated to the position of a House majority whip for the role that he played in the elections.

Grand Old Party (GOP) is another name for the Republican Party. [43]

Congressional leaders

Vice President is the chief presiding officer of the Senate.

Speaker of the House is the presiding officer in the US House of Representatives and the second in line to the presidency.

President *pro tempore* of the Senate is the acting chief presiding officer of the Senate and the third in line to the presidency.

Majority Leader manages and plans the legislative agenda of the majority party in Congress and its chief spokesperson. The majority leader chooses which bills the Senate/ House will consider.

Minority Leader serves as the chief legislative strategist for the minority party in Congress, and also the party's floor spokesperson.

Majority Whip is charged with informing its members with the plans of the party leadership. And the whip is also charged with gathering its party members to vote on bills and setting the legislative schedule.

Minority Whip is the assistant to the minority leader. The whip's main duty is counting and assembling votes. And the whip also informs its members of the plans of the party leadership. [44]

Headliner 1

In late 1998, DeLay was the driving force behind Clinton's impeachment. During Clinton's second term in office, his main adversary was Tom DeLay. Since Newt Gingrich had announced that he was resigning from Congress, DeLay took on the leadership role and time after time he assailed the President and publicly condemned Clinton's behavior. He became more powerful than before especially after his party's poor performance in the 1998 midterm election. DeLay urged the GOP not to put a dismal 1998 election performance behind them until Clinton was impeached. He pressurized the House Judiciary Committee to speed up the impeachment proceeding. DeLay believed that William Clinton's ungentlemanly behavior was clearly an impeachable offense: "I do what I believe. I believe in the Constitution, I believe in this institution, and I believe in the office of the presidency and I'm doing what I think is the right thing to do." And he demanded the other GOP leaders to take a stand against censure, the motion sponsored by the Democratic Party as a substitute for an impeachment. DeLay, then the majority whip, knew that a censure resolution would have attracted the undecided GOP members. He was said to have allegedly applied pressure on the undecided members to follow the GOP leadership and denounce the president's unmoral attitudes.

DeLay unrelenting campaign to impeach the President was finally over when two articles of impeachment were approved. After the House approved the articles of impeachment, DeLay was accused by Democrats of forcing anti impeachment Republican members to vote on impeaching Clinton. DeLay defended the criticisms: "This fits in with the pattern of conduct that the president is in trouble for—lying, covering up, stonewalling and demonizing their enemies." DeLay's effort was successful;

Unfortunately, it is only the Senate that can convict a president. Impeachment is the House's most powerful tool for oversight of the presidency while a trial and a possible dismissal of office is a tool for the Senate. [45]

After the midterm election in 2002, DeLay was elected House majority leader, a position he held up until 2006. He urged House Republicans to bond together especially in support of Bush's agenda. His position as the majority leader overshadowed the Speaker of the House Dennis Hastert. DeLay was described as a shrewd politician; he personally picked Dennis Hastert to be nominated to the speaker of the House position. And he worked to seal Dennis Hastert the role of speaker. Hastert's appointment was the main reason DeLay didn't vie to be the Speaker of the House. DeLay was a complete 100% true conservative. Tom DeLay, Senator Rick Santorum and Grover Norquist started the famous K Street Project. The project's goal was to fill lobbying firms with former congressional staffers. The project favored Republican members. [46]

Headliner 2

Six months before the 2004 elections, Texas Democratic legislators tried to prevent the Texas state House from establishing a quorum of members when over 40 state legislators flew to Oklahoma. The state House was scheduled to act on a Texas redistricting plan. Tom DeLay, a major proponent of the Texas redistricting plan, again made headlines. DeLay flexed his political muscles when he allegedly used his federal powers to contact federal agencies to track down the plane that was heading to the neighboring state. CBS News reported that: "Democrats say a powerful Republican in Congress got Homeland Security personnel involved in a politicized search that had nothing to do with homeland security. It appears they were used to track down some Texas Democratic legislators who left the state to prevent a vote that could help elect more Republicans to Congress." DeLay's office claimed they had nothing to do with contacting and requesting assistance from the Justice Department and Homeland Security.

Federal assistance was needed to track the plan and locate the so-called 'missing legislators'. CBS reported again that: "Democrats say House Majority Leader DeLay's redistricting Texas power play is designed to add as many as seven more GOP seats to a state congressional delegation Republicans already control." The runaway Texas state legislators' action was due to the redistricting bill that would enable the Republicans in Congress to gain more seats in the 2004 election. The Texas Department of Public Safety received an urgent call from an official, and they dispatched the message to an agency under Homeland Security.

The agency deals with monitoring air traffic and guarding the United States' skies for terrorist activities.

A Texas official told the Homeland Security personnel the following: "We got a problem and I hope you can help me out. We had a plane that was supposed to be going from Ardmore, Oklahoma, to Georgetown, Texas. It has state representatives in it and we cannot find this plane."[47]

A recap of the Midterm election of 2002

The Founding Fathers set the term of the 435 members of the US House of Representatives at two years; with all the seats up for reelection in every two years. And the term of the 100 members of the US Senate were set by the Founders at six years; with only one-third of the 100 seats up for reelection in every two years.

After the elections, the Republicans controlled both houses of Congress and also the presidency. In the House, the Republicans secured their majority with a gain of six seats; bringing the margin in the House to a 24 seat difference. And in the Senate the GOP won 2 seats and they won back the majority. The war on terrorism exceedingly overshadowed the elections. And that was the platform that the Republican ran on. Bush, the Republican President, was very popular; he had a 70% approval rating. His high approval rate was a substantive advantage for all of the GOP incumbents.

108th -109th United States Congress: January 2003 to January 2007

Dennis Hastert was the speaker of the House; he wasn't as effective as Newt Gingrich largely due to the presence of Majority Leader Tom DeLay. It wasn't until the latter part of the 109th session, when DeLay resigned from Congress, that Hastert was noticed. The other bicameral leaders included Roy Blunt (R Missouri) and John Boehner (R-Ohio). They were the new faces for the Republican's leadership. They both took Tom DeLay's GOP leadership position. The two politicians vied for the Majority leader position. Rep. John Boehner was elected to the helm of the party and Rep. Roy Blunt accepted the majority whip position. Nancy Pelosi (D-California) and Steny Hoyer (D-Maryland) were the Democratic minority leader and Democratic minority whip respectively. Deborah Pryce, a promising congresswoman from Ohio, was the House GOP conference chairman. [48]

In the Senate, two new faces in the GOP leadership field were also introduced. They were Bill Frist (R-Tennessee) and Mitch McConnell (R-Kentucky). Tom Daschle (D-South Dakota), previously the majority leader, became the senate minority leader. After the election of 04, Daschle was replaced by Harry Reid (D-Nevada). Senator Daschle lost his reelection bid thanks to Senator Bill Frist's vigorous campaign against the ex Democratic leader. Daschle was left mulling over his future. The Senator was eager to return to Congress, but Frist derailed his ambition. Another new introduction in the senate leadership was Illinois senior senator, Dick Dublin. He was elevated to the minority whip position. He replaced Harry Reid. The Republican Conference Chairman was Rick Santorum. The conservative senator from Pennsylvania was the third ranking GOP leader. Senator John Edwards (D-North Carolina) vacated his senate seat for a run for the presidency. At the end of that particular congressional session, three GOP lawmakers Rep. Cunningham, Rep. Foley, and Rep. Ney all resigned in disgrace from Congress. This setback projected the end of the "Republican revolution" era. [49]

DeLay worked on the 2004 Bush reelection campaign and he masterminded a plan for the Republican Party to gain more seats in the House. DeLay overlooked the consequences and the repercussions, and helped to redistrict the congressional district in Texas. Texas Republicans gained more seats in the US House of Representatives. And in 2005, a grand jury in Texas indicted DeLay on criminal charges. The charges included conspiring to violate election law. DeLay said a prosecutor with close ties to the Democratic Party in Texas brought the case against him. Tom denied any wrongdoing. But House's rules forced him to resign temporarily from his seat as the party's leader. The charges that were pending and his ties with a certain lobbyist had hastened his resignation.

DeLay has not been convicted of any crime.[50]

One man's fight

In the late seventies, DeLay won the election for an open seat in the Texas House. Before his political career, he owned a Pest control company. While operating the company, the government banned a certain pesticide that was used in extermination work. This action provoked Tom. And from then onward, he opposed government regulation of businesses. He carried that mentality with him throughout his political career. DeLay had close ties to the Christian Right.[51]

In only his third year as a congressman, DeLay was appointed to the powerful House Appropriations Committee. In the 1994 midterm elections, DeLay played a major role for his party winning back the majority in Congress after 40 years in the hands of the Democrats. Back in 1989, the cordial relations between Gingrich and DeLay deteriorated when Gingrich competed for the minority leader position. DeLay supported Ed Madigan (R-Illinois) over Gingrich. And in 1995, House GOP leaders, Speaker of the House Newt Gingrich (R-Georgia) and Majority Leader Dick Armey (R-Texas) weren't in support of his appointed as the majority whip.

DeLay twice attacked Gingrich. First, during the impeachment proceeding against Clinton, Gingrich had his own extra martial affair. And he also attacked Gingrich on the 1995-96's government shutdown. Tom DeLay recounted the following in his book 'No Retreat, No Surrender: One American's Fight,' he wrote that:

> "He (Gingrich) told a room full of reporters that he forced the shutdown because Clinton had rudely made him and Bob Dole sit at the back of Air Force One. Newt had been careless to say such a thing, and now the whole moral tone of the shutdown had been lost. What had been a noble battle for fiscal sanity began to look like the tirade of a spoiled child. The revolution, I can tell you, was never the same."

In a passage in DeLay's book, he revealed Dick Armey's ambitions:

> "He resented me for being the other Texan on the leadership team, and he resented anyone he thought might get in the way of his becoming speaker of the House. Beware the man drunk with ambition. I think the rest of us were eager to drive a conservative agenda. Dick was eager to get to the top, and this lesser motivation made him a lesser figure on our team."

DeLay wasn't finished yet. He also singled out President Bush: "He has expanded government to suit his purpose, especially in the area of education. He may be compassionate, but he is certainly no conservative in the classic sense."

Apart from being one of the most powerful Americans, DeLay also established himself as a Born again Christian. [52]

Headliner 3

Bill Frist and George Bush weren't the only headliners when the Schiavo case was brought to light; DeLay got the most media attention. Terri Schiavo had sustained a heart attack and she fell into a coma. For over 15 years, Terri Schiavo had been kept alive by a feeding tube. Her parents pushed to continue keeping the feeding tube on, while her husband opted for the removal of the feeding tube. After a heated legal and political battle, the brain damaged Terri

Schiavo's feeding tube was removed. Tom called the feeding tube removal "an act of barbarism." DeLay and other GOP members of Congress, stood for what they believed in and they became like moonlighters for that intense period, as they worked all night even through the weekend to draw up a bill to force doctors to reinsert the feeding tube. House committee supervised by DeLay, successfully filed an urgent request to the U.S. Supreme Court. They asked the Judges to order Mrs. Schiavo's feeding tube be reinserted. However, the Supreme Court turned down the House's request to reinsert the feeding tube. This provoked DeLay to call the Court's action: "A moral and legal tragedy. A death row inmate has more of a process to go through than Terri Schiavo does." After the loss of Terri Schiavo, Tom DeLay lamented, "This loss happened because our legal system did not protect who need protection most, and that will change. The time will come for the men responsible for this to answer for their behavior, but not today. Today we grieve, we pray, and we hope to God this fate never befalls another." Still unable to keep his composure, DeLay continued, "I never thought I would see the day when a U.S. judge stopped feeding a living American so that they took 14 days to die." DeLay later publicly apologized for the eyebrow-raising remarks he made. He was accused of rationalizing violence and threatening the Supreme Court Judges. [53]

After Newt Gingrich resigned from Congress, DeLay built a solid relationship with GOP House members. Under DeLay's watch, more partisan than ever before was the talking point in Capitol Hill. DeLay was the most valuable tool for the whole GOP Party. DeLay made it extremely difficult for the Democrats to pass bills in the House floor for a vote. DeLay was called the hammer largely because of his leadership abilities, his extensive fund-raising abilities, and his unprecedented whipping abilities. In just his first term as majority whip, DeLay, the third-ranking Republican leader, was the master of squeezing out votes to pass important bills. Throughout his tenure as the majority whip, he delivered victories for the GOP House regardless of the small majority in the 106th and 107th Congress. He had a habit of winning votes congressional lawmakers thought lost. Both the Democrats and the Republicans were amazed and they marveled at DeLay's ability of swaying the votes of his party. No past minority or majority whips in the history of Congress had been able to accomplish what DeLay achieved in swaying the votes. DeLay was the most effective whip leader in the history of Congress. [54]

After he was elected majority leader, the Hammer scenario continued, and the party discipline continued. His staunched efforts to preserve GOP control of the House labeled him as the most powerful name in Capitol Hill. As the second ranking leader in the US House of Representatives, DeLay developed the issues that formed the conservative ideology. Because of his intense partisanship, he appealed to fellow Republican and conservative members. And because of DeLay's 'hardball politics' and the ways in which he tried to referee members of Congress's activities, he was described by opponents as a difficult and challenging leader. He was also accused of blackmailing, threatening, and bribing House members.[55]

Headliner 4

In March of 2005, DeLay led Congress to set limits on Palestinian Authority aids. He blocked direct assistance to that part of the region. DeLay's action restricted Bush and the White House efforts to fully fund the Israeli occupied territories. Supporters of direct aid to the Palestinian authority were very critical of the House leader: "DeLay became more Jewish than the chief-rabbi- if you can twist the phrase that way-and he was not going to let it through," a fellow congressman said. DeLay once contemplated cutting all of the aid before the bill was passed. DeLay's authoritarian attitude angered the White House and some members of Congress that supported direct aids to the Palestinian Authority. Mahmoud Abbas was the leader of the region.

DeLay is an evangelical Christian. He is said to have opposed the creation of Palestinian, but he called for peace with Israel.

During President Bush's first term in office, Bush had been pushing for peace in Hamas led by Gaza and Finah's West Bank, both of which are part of Palestinian National Authority. The President tried to establish the United States as a broker for peace between the people of Israel and Palestine. Because of DeLay's powerful position in Congress, he undermined Bush's executive power. DeLay got all the legislative power in his hands and was tapping away executive foreign affairs power. After Tom DeLay snubbed President Bush regarding the Palestine aid and other piece of legislations, Bush declined to defend DeLay's pending ethics charges. However, Senator Trent Lott turned peacemaker. He called on the two powerful Texans to clear their differences: "I do think the White House needs to remember that people who fight hard for you as a candidate and for your issues as a president. Tom deserves your support, aggressive support," Senator Lott said. [56]

It wasn't until the downfall of Mr. DeLay that the Democrats finally look certain to take control of the House. Democrats in the House targeted wholesale changes after being the minority party for 12 years. If Tom wasn't indicted for an alleged crime, the GOP would not have lost the House in 2006. In his 2007 book 'No Retreat, No Surrender: One American's Fight,' Tom DeLay did address the accusation that he violated campaign finance laws in Texas. DeLay wrote:

"I believe it was Adolf Hitler who first acknowledged that the big lie is more effective than the little lie, because the big lie is so audacious, such an astonishing immorality, that people have a hard time believing anyone would say it if it wasn't true. You know the big lie like the Holocaust never happened; well by charging this big lie about money laundering, liberals has finally joined the ranks of scoundrels like Hitler." [57]

A recap of the Midterm Election 2006

Three factors weighed heavily in the elections; the failed war in Iraq, the scandals that were exposed in the 109th Congress, and Tom DeLay's resignation from Congress. In the House, the Democratic Party forecasted a big win. And, as anticipated, the election resulted in an overwhelming net gain of 31 seats for the Democrats Party. The elections brought the tally to 233 Democratic House of Representatives members while the Republicans were reduced to 202 members. The bad news was the war in Iraq helped the Democratic candidates, as the GOP pandered to the extreme far Right and to other constituents for their reelection bid. Most of the Republicans distanced themselves from Bush. But they were left to reflect on a miserable election campaign.

With a 25-seat majority in the House going against the Republicans, it will be an uphill climb for the Republican Party to retake control of the House in the future.

The Democrat's sweeping victory was credited to Rep. Rahm Emanuel, Sen. Charles Schumer, and Gov. Howard Dean, the DNC leader. They won back the majority in the House after 12 years. In the senate race, two GOP presidential hopefuls, Rick Santorum, the third ranking GOP leader, and Virginia's George Allen, surprisingly lost the incumbency. Former vice president nominee Joe Liebermann lost the Democratic primary ticket in Connecticut. But he was re-elected as an independent, after he bested his Democratic challenger. The outcome of the midterm election brought the total number of 16 female senators, the highest ever in the history of the senate. The Democrats regained control of both houses for the first time since 1994.

110th Congress: January 2007-January 2009

Nancy Pelosi made history, as she was the first woman to be elected into the speaker position. Restoring "integrity" was the promise Pelosi made as she took over the reins of Congress from Dennis Hastert. Rep. Steny Hoyer bested

Rep. John Murtha for the majority leader position. Congressman Murtha, a decorated war veteran from Pennsylvania, had the backing of Rep. Nancy Pelosi. James Clyburn (D -South Carolina) became the second African American in history to be elected as majority whip. He won a fierce challenge from Rahm Emmanuel (D-Illinois). On the other side of the aisle, Rep. Boehner and Rep. Blunt retained their position as the ranking leaders of the Republican Party. Congressman John Lewis from Georgia, the Senior Chief Whip, was another African America in a leadership role for the Democratic Party.

In the Senate, Bill Frist declined to run for reelection and his party lost the right to organize the senate. Even though the Republicans had an equal number of senators like the Democrats, the two independent senators caucused with the Democrats. Bill Frist resigned from Congress to make a possible run for the presidency in 2008. Democratic senator Harry Reid was elected the majority leader and Richard Dublin became the majority whip. In the Republican leadership, Mitch McConnell took Bill Frist's place as the new leader of the Republican Party. The party did shine a ray of light into the gloom of the party's election defeat when Senator Trent Lott was nominated to a leadership position. The former Majority Leader had a second chance and took the initiative as he won over Lamar Alexander for the minority whip position. President Bush and Senator Mitch McConnell were in favor of Sen. Alexander while rank and file Republicans favored Sen. Lott. New York senior senator Charles Schumer became the third most powerful Democratic senator. In the latter part of 2007, Schumer later became the fifth overall in the US Senate after Senator Lott announced his resignation from Congress. Senator Lott, a Mississippi statesman, was rumored to accept a lucrative lobbying job. His minority whip position was handed to John Kyl (R-Arizona) instead of Lamar Alexander, the Republican Conference Chairman and former presidential candidate from Tennessee. [58]

Although the GOP preparations of the 2006 election had been hampered by DeLay's resignation, their defeat and DeLay's resignation would be an incentive for the party to work harder for the next elections.

The state charge of conspiracy to violate campaign finance laws had been dismissed outright against DeLay, but a second grand jury indicted him on charges of money laundering and conspiracy to launder money. President Bush ran to DeLay's side by defending the Majority Leader. Bush said DeLay was innocent of criminal charges in Texas. DeLay was simply set up and railroaded by his opponents. Despite the charges, DeLay continued to be viewed in many circle as the most powerful U.S. member in Congress.

On the development in the Iraqi region, Tom DeLay argued that: "It's the fault of the liberals, the media and the Democrats that from the very beginning have tried to undermine the will of the American people to fight this…The media calls the shots." Tom DeLay is highly well respected.[59]

Pardon and culture of corruption

Jack Abramoff, one of D.C.'s most prominent lobbyists, was a close friend to Tom DeLay. Abramoff held fundraisers for DeLay. He arranged for the Majority Leader to accompany him on a golf trip to Scotland and a business trip to the Northern Mariana Islands. Abramoff did maintain close ties with DeLay's aides.

Lobbyists are individuals paid to pressure members of the executive, judicial and legislative branches of government to further the aims of interest groups.

In January 2003, the Washington D.C. lobbyist agreed to plead guilty in a D.C. federal court to conspiracy, tax evasion, and mail fraud. The next day, he pleaded guilty in a Florida federal court to public corruption and tax evasion in his purchase of Sancruz casinos. The Sancruz casino was an offshore gambling business organization. But the purchase hinged on a forged 23 million wire transfer.

Another legal issue claimed that Abramoff overcharged Native American tribes involved in casino gambling. Abramoff allegedly defrauded his clients by collecting tens of millions of dollars from casino rich Indian tribes. He made this possible by allegedly bribing congressional lawmakers and government officials in passing legislations. And he also ordered the tribes to donate millions of dollars to members of Congress. Abramoff's hospitality towards lawmakers was very welcomed. For instance, he sponsored lavish trips, tickets to events, and expensive meals.

Abramoff will go down in history as one of the most influential lobbyists in D.C.

Abramoff's right hand partners also pleaded guilty and were asked to testify against him. Abramoff had a personal connection with Republican leaders DeLay and Bush. Two of DeLay's former staffers pleaded guilty on November of 2005 to related charges. [60]

Who will Bush Pardon?

Will Bush pardon Abramoff? A pardon is an "Exemption of a convicted person from the penalties of an offense or crime by the power of the executor of the laws."(Answer.com Search) Article II, Section 2 of the Constitution stated: "The President shall have power to grant reprieves and pardons for offenses against the United States."

There were reports that Abramoff had visited the White House and took family pictures together with the President. After Abramoff pleaded guilty, he was said to have agreed with federal investigators to rat out other corrupt government officials. Abramoff's cooperation with investigators led to a sentence reduction. Reports even had it that Abramoff once had an office space in the FBI's Justice Department building. The extensive corruption scandal led to the conviction of the President's administration deputy U.S. secretary of the interior, Steven Griles. Other convictions were made involving members of the executive and legislation branches of government. Abramoff had special relationship with Grover Norquist, the president of a conservative lobbying group, and Ralph Reed, the former director of the Christian coalition.

Abramoff is serving a six-year sentence in prison. [61]

Bob Nay was the chairman of the House Administration Committee. Nay, a Republican congressman from Ohio did outstanding favors for Abramoff. He put statements into congressional records, introduced legislations, and used his chairmanship title to influence other members' decisions. In return, Nay was said to have accepted bribe offers from the lobbyist. Ney was first subpoenaed by a federal grand jury investigating the Abramoff scandal. And he was under scrutiny until his arrest. In October of 2006, he pleaded guilty to charges of conspiracy. And in January, 2007, he was sentenced to 30 months in prison.

Former Chief of staff to the vice president **Lewis Libby** was charged with leaking Valerie Plame's name to the media. Plame was a covert CIA operative. Libby's action was seen as retribution on Ambassador Joe Wilson.

Duke Cunningham, a representative from California, was a GOP member of Congress until November 05. He pleaded guilty to bribery, wire fraud, tax evasion, and mail fraud. After entering the pleas, he resigned from Congress. In March of 06, he was sentenced to 8 years and 4 months in prison for taking bribes from defense contractors. He sat on the House subcommittee that approves and oversees defense contract spending. He was believed to have purchased a million-dollar mansion. The judge reduced his sentence largely because he served in the Vietnam War as a Navy fighter pilot.[62]

Jeffrey Skilling was the CEO of Enron Corporation until 2001. He was indicted on 35 counts of fraud, inside trading, and conspiracy. And in 2006, he was convicted on 19 counts of multiple federal charges relating to Enron's financial collapse. He was sentenced to 24 years in prison and was ordered to pay millions of dollars to the victims of Enron's collapse. About a month after quitting Enron, and before the firm declared bankruptcy, Skilling sold millions of shares of his stake in the company. Authorities said he knew the company was going to face an economic depression. When Enron pronounced bankruptcy, thousands of Enron's employees lost their jobs and life savings. Mr. Skilling was supposed to be sentenced alongside Enron's founder, Kenneth Lay. However, Lay passed away.

The last culture of corruption was **Rep. Jefferson.** On June 4, 2007, a federal grand jury indicted the nine-term Democratic congressman from Louisiana, William Jefferson, on 16 charges related to corruption. The FBI launched an investigation into Jefferson's alleged corrupt business deals in Africa. The prosecutor asserted that Jefferson received over $400,000 in bribes and had his hands in a number of illegal deals in Africa. If convicted, he could be sentenced to a maximum of 235 years. The charges included racketeering, wire fraud, money laundering, soliciting bribes, obstruction of justice, and conspiracy. In May 2006, his congressional office was raided by the FBI and some of his documents were seized. The raid of Jefferson's office set off a series of bitter political events. In August 05, before his office was invaded, FBI agents raided Jefferson's house and they found $90,000 in cash in Jefferson's freezer. It was a setup by the FBI. The serial number found on the $ 90,000's currency matched the serial number given by the FBI to an informant. Agents told the Judge in charge of the case that a corruption probe had been launched against the congressman from Louisiana. And the cash found in his freezer was part of a $100,000 payment from investigators that had been delivered by a cooperative informant.

Congress contends that the raid on a congressional office in Capitol Hill might have breached the constitutional separation of powers between the legislative and executive branches of government.

During that period, the Speaker of the House and the House Minority Leader were outraged against the heads of the Justice Department. The Attorney General and FBI Director were adamant that the raid was constitutional. And they threaten to quit if the documents were asked to be returned to Rep. Jefferson. Legal experts said the raid violated the U.S. Constitution. The raid was the first time FBI agents searched a congressional office. Rep. Jefferson has denied any wrongdoing. [63]

DeLay was a hard-nosed leader; he appealed to fellow conservatives and Republicans in America. Veteran columnist Robert Novak claimed that, "DeLay was the most conservative congressional leader I have witnessed in 50 years covering Capitol Hill. I rate him with Lyndon B. Johnson as a dominant legislator." Tom DeLay's resignation from Congress caused a huge detriment to the Republican Party. Throughout his career in Capitol Hill, media speculation had centered on DeLay. He shepherded the Republican Party for a decade. Tom DeLay was a consummate leader. [64]

Chapter 4

Richard Cheney, one of the most powerful people in America

Cheney is the most unapproachable officials in America. He is the most feared American politician. Dick Cheney has the most impressive and extraordinary American government resume in the modern day era. Cheney is a former White House chief of staff to President Gerald Ford, and a former member of US House of Representatives from the state of Wyoming.

During Cheney's time in Congress, he was the second ranking Republican leader in the House.

Cheney is also a former United States Secretary of Defense in Walker Bush's administration. And finally, since the dawn of the new millennium, Cheney has been the Vice President of the United States. Richard Cheney is also the president of the United States Senate.

On two occasions, he took on the role of acting President of the United States. Cheney was also the CEO of transnational corporation, Halliburton. [65]

After becoming vice president, Cheney was immediately asked in early 2000 if he was considering running for the Oval Office. Cheney said he has no intention to run for president. Again in 2004, after the Bush-Cheney ticket won reelection, he was asked that same question on Fox News Sunday. Cheney said: "I will just say just as hard as I possibly know how to say, if nominated, I will not run, if elected, I will not serve, or not only no, but hell no, I have got my plans laid out I'm going to serve this president for the next four years, and then I'm out of here."

Cheney had received five draft deferments; he was a supporter of the Vietnam War. He had other priorities in the sixties so he could not serve. It wasn't just meant for Richard to be a Veteran, but at least he has paid his dues to the American people with his impressive resume. [66]

Quid pro quo

Cheney's political career began in President Nixon's administration and continued in the Ford administration. Cheney worked as a staff member for Donald Rumsfeld. They both work hand-in-hand, culminating in President Ford Administration. Ford's presidency was an administration that was divided; Cheney and Rumsfeld waged political war against Henry Kissinger and Nelson Rockefeller, the secretary of state and the vice president respectively. President Ford had to choose between Cheney's side and that of Kissinger. After the period of political infighting ceased, Cheney became the new White House Chief of Staff. [67]

In 1978, while taking exile from Democratic president Jimmy Carter, Cheney returned back home to Wyoming. He represented Wyoming's At-large congressional district in the US House of Representatives. Cheney as a congressman rose to the rank of minority whip. He succeeded former congressman/ Senator Trent Lott (R-Mississippi). Cheney was also the ranking Republican in the House Intelligence Committee. While serving as a congressman, his voting records had been lampooned by the media. Cheney voted against the override of President Reagan's veto of a bill imposing economic sanction on the apartheid regime in South Africa.

A president veto is a presidential power use to prevent a Congress approved bill from moving forward. The veto can be overrode by 67 votes from members of the senate and a two-thirds majority in the House. If a two-third vote in both houses of Congress is achieved, then Congress will be able to pass a law against the wishes of the president.   Probably the most important vote Cheney cast during his tenure as a congressman was against the released of Nelson Mandela from prison. He voted against a congressional resolution along with 145 Republicans and a number of conservative Democrats. Cheney was severely criticized. He later addressed his criticism by saying he opposed the resolution because the "ANC (African National Congress) at that time was viewed as a terrorist organization and had a number of interests that were fundamentally inimical to the United States." [68]

Toward the end of the Reagan regime, the Iran-Contra Affair was uncovered. Members of the Reagan administration were reported to have sold weapons to Iran, an avowed enemy. Cheney at that time was the head of House Intelligence Committee; he blocked the Democrats from questioning Vice President Bush when the U.S. Congress was trying to investigate the Iran-Contra scandal. [69]

Cheney served the U.S. Congress for a decade until President Walker Bush came looking for a Secretary of Defense. Cheney relinquished his post as the minority whip to serve the Executive branch. In retrospect, Cheney, during the Halloween Massacre, was one of the main players in appointing Walker Bush as the CIA Director in the Ford administration. Cheney's appointment as Secretary of Defense raised questions about a quid pro quo.

Halloween Massacre was a term used to describe significant changes that occurred in President Ford's cabinet.

As Secretary of Defense, Cheney worked alongside Paul Wolfowitz and Colin Powell. He was responsible for the appointment of Colin Powell as the Joint Chiefs of Staff Chairman; a step that would cease critics who lambasted Cheney for his vote concerning Nelson Mandela. [70]

After the Democratic Party again took over the executive branch, Cheney made the American people aware of his political future while on CNN. He was asked whether he has any future ambition to run for the presidency. He said, "Obviously, it's something I will take a look at. Obviously, I've worked for three presidents and watched two others up close, and so it is an idea that has occurred to me." Cheney took another exile back to his private sector of Halliburton. He probably gave up political ambitions. And in 1995, Cheney spoke to journalists in a press conference "When I made the decision earlier this year not to run for president, not to seek the White House, that really was a decision to wrap up my political career and move on to other things." Cheney then became the CEO of Halliburton. In the latter part of 2000, Gov. George Bush, who was the Republican presumptive nominee for the 2000 presidential election, asked Richard Cheney to head his election of a search committee for vice president. All the names that had been bandied about for vice president and the ones that were being vetted; were all surprised like a deer caught in headlights when Bush announced that the person heading the vetting process was the nominee. Well the rest was history; Cheney resigned from his CEO position in Halliburton and put his work into becoming the vice president.[71]

The 12th Amendment vs. Cheney

Before Cheney resumed office as the vice president, angered opponents questioned if Cheney was a Texan or a Wyomingite. Lawsuits were filed by Gore-Lieberman supporters from Texas charging that the vice presidential nominee was a residence of Texas. So its 32 Electoral College votes should not count for a Bush-Cheney ticket. Cheney rubbished suggestions that the lawsuit could affect the outcome of the election. His aide dismissed the lawsuit as frivolous. The federal court in Dallas, Texas, where Cheney resides, intervened in the matter. But eventually the case against Cheney didn't hold water. The 12th Amendment to the constitution that was ratified on June 15th, 1804 stated: "The electors shall meet in their respective states and vote by ballot for president and vice president, one of whom, at least, shall not be an inhabitant of the same state with themselves; they shall name in their ballots the person voted for as president, and in distinct ballots the person voted as vice president:" According to the Constitution, either Bush or Cheney must be an inhabitant of another state. Cheney, a seasoned politician, had lived in Texas. His Halliburton Co. operated in Dallas. But when he was elected as a congressman, he represented the state of Wyoming, not Texas. Cheney also owned a property in Wyoming. Five months before the general election, Cheney was said to have changed his voter's registration card from Texas to Wyoming. If Cheney didn't change his voter's card back to the state of Wyoming, the 32 Texas electoral votes would not have registered for the Bush- Cheney ticket.

Despite his Wyoming voter's registration card, Cheney is a resident of Texas and an inhabitant of Wyoming. As for Bush, he is a full-blown Texas cowboy. The 12th Amendment uses the phrase 'Inhabitant,' not resident.[72]

Electors are representative who are elected in the state to formally choose the American president. State legislators select these electors, who must pledge to support the presidential candidates of their party. In the Electoral College, each State would have a number of electors or total number of votes equal to its total number of congressional representatives. For example, the state of Texas in 2000 had 30 congresspersons and 2 senators. [73]

Fighting the war against terrorism

After the attacks on the World Trade Center (WTC), Cheney and Bush were kept in distant locations. They were kept out of the public eyes, not seen together in tandem for security reasons. "You've got a situation in which you don't want to provide the terrorists with a target of being able to, in effect , decapitate, the U.S. government by striking at both the president and the vice president at the same time," Cheney said. Cheney communicated with the White House via secure videophones.

Cheney did capitalize on that precaution. For a long period of time, Cheney was not seen in public. He remained at undisclosed secure locations. Catapulting the liberal talk radio hosts with one of their most played sound bites, "We also have to work, though, sort of the dark side, if you will. We've got to spend time in the shadows in the intelligence world. A lot of what needs to be done here will have to be done quietly without any discussion" -Cheney's comment on Meet the Press. [74]

Rush Limbaugh, the conservative leader, asked Cheney why "Bill Clinton's administration officials are attempting to defend themselves in all of this hubbub, are trying to create the impression that this whole al Qaeda and modern era terrorist problem began on January 22nd of 2001 (the first day Cheney began serving)." Cheney responded rightly

> "Well, I go back to the first attack on the World Trade Center in 93, when the man named Ramzi Yousef, together with others, tried to bomb the WTC then. Remember they took a truckload of explosives and set it off in the parking garage underneath the WTC. It didn't do what they hoped it would do. He eventually was captured. He is now doing 240 years in the federal pen. But what we know, I think, looking back at that, nobody realized it at the time, but looking back at that, was that was perhaps the first al Qaeda attack on the U.S. homeland. Ramzi Yousef turned out to be Khalid Shaykh Muhammad's nephew. Khalid Shaykh Mohammad is the guy who came up with the idea of using airliners to strike the WTC in about 1996, we believe, when he first suggested that, and who later supervised the attack of 9/11."

Another question was asked to the vice president concerning Richard Clarke, the chief counter-terrorism coordinator during the Clinton administration, in his statement about why terrorists hate us. "Mr. Clarke said that actually if we would just take some more time and talk to these people, understand why they hate us, we might be able to forge some kind of peace with them." Cheney answered,

> "I think that's totally unrealistic. At least, I fundamentally disagree with his assessment both of recent history, but also in terms of how to deal with problem. As I say, he was the head of counterterrorism for several years there in the 90's, and I didn't notice that they had any great success dealing with the terrorist threat. I think what we've done since, going into Afghanistan, taking down the Taliban, closing the camps, killing al Qaeda, wrapping up a significant

percentage of the total leadership of al Qaeda, that is an effective policy."

Cheney, a statesman from Wyoming, defines a success against al-Qaeda in terms of "Our ability to wrap up major parts of the organization, to prevent further attacks against the United Sates, obviously. I think all of that-all of those are hallmarks of success." [75]

Whether in Iraq or Afghanistan, Congress voted on a war with the terrorists. The Bush administration acknowledged that we must fight them over there so that the terrorists would not come and attack us again, since oceans no longer protect us.

In 2005, Cheney was interviewed by CNN Larry king Live. He was asked about the progress made in the ongoing war in Iraq and his response was another sound bite that the liberal talk radio frequently played "I think they're in the last throes if you will of the insurgency." What the Vice President meant by the insurgency being in its last throes had been interpreted carelessly by the mainstream media; it doesn't mean ending right away.

Living in the last days on earth doesn't necessary mean this year or next year before the world comes to an end. From an anti-terrorist standpoint, the insurgency will definitely come to an end. [76]

Presidential line of succession

In 1985, Ronald Reagan went under the knife and temporarily transferred the powers of his office to his deputy, Walker Bush, under the seldom invoked 25 Amendment. In 2002, George Bush temporarily transferred authority to Cheney and in July 2007, Bush again relinquished power of his office to Vice President Cheney.
Amendment 25 section 3 stated

> "Whenever the president transmits to the president *pre tempore* of the Senate and the speaker of the House his written declaration that he is unable to discharge the powers and duties of his office, and until he transmits to them a written declaration to the contrary, such powers and duties shall be discharged by the vice president as acting president."

After the president took back power from Vice President Cheney, Bush wrote to the Speaker of the House and the President Pro *tempore* of the Senate. "This letter shall constitute my written declaration that I am presently able to resume the discharge of the Constitutional powers and duties of the office of the president of the United States." Cheney said he used the two hours as acting president to write letters to his loved ones. [77]

February 27, 2007, a suicide bomber tried to change Cheney's schedule for a meeting with the president of Afghanistan. There was an assassination attempt when the attacker bombed the surrounding area to the main entrance of the U.S. military base in Bagram, Afghanistan. 23 people were killed and 20 Afghan workers were wounded. The Taliban immediately claimed responsibility for the attack. And they acknowledged that the Vice president was their main target. For a short period of time, Cheney was rushed by the Secret Service to one of the base bomb shelters: "I heard a loud boom, and shortly after that the Secret Service came in and told me there had been an attack on the main gate, apparently a suicide bomber" Cheney said. Cheney was never in danger; he wasn't near the site of the explosion. The explosion happened near the first of many checkpoint gates. Because of the intense security, reports said the attack came as a surprise. A spokesperson for American coalition force told reporters "We maintain a high-level of security here at all times. Our security measures were in place and the killer never had access to the base. When he realized he would not be able to get onto the base, he attacked the local population." Cheney concluded "I think they clearly try to find ways to question the authority of the central government, and striking at Bagram with a suicide bomber is one way to do that. It shouldn't affect our behavior." A day after he met with Pakistani president Pervez Musharraf, Cheney visited President Hamid Karzai of Afghanistan. [78]

After the assassination of President Kennedy, the 25th Amendment was signed into law.

According to the amendment, temporary or even permanent presidential powers can be given to the Vice President if the President is unable to fulfill the duties of his office. Any disability on Cheney will lead to the temporarily appointment of Speaker of the House, Nancy Pelosi (D-California). Looking over the shoulder of Cheney, she is next in the presidential line of succession. She will hold that position until Bush appoints a replacement for vice president. The appointee has to be confirmed by Congress. Looking over Speaker Pelosi's shoulder in the presidential line of successions will be the president *pro tempore* Senator R Byrd (D-West Virginia) and the Secretary of State, Madam Rice, the numbers 4 and 5 respectively.

The presidential line of succession also recognized the Secretary of Treasury, Secretary of Defense, and the Attorney General in that order. [79]

As Vice President, Cheney has taken an unprecedented policy role within the administration and he earned a reputation as an extremely "hands-on" deputy. He has also taken an active role in cabinet meetings and policy formation.

Cheney is not only referred to as the real president of the United States, but he is often described as the most active and powerful vice president in American history. "You talk to Cheney and things happened, and he doesn't necessarily take credit. There is a connection between going to Cheney and getting action, Sen. Lott said about Cheney. The Veep is believed to be the last voice the President seeks advice before he makes major decisions.

Some pundit said since Cheney took office, the Defense and State Departments had been sidelined. In the beginning of 2007, on Juan William's NPR show, Bush claimed he viewed Cheney as a "Person reflecting a half glass full mentality." [80]

Towards the end of the 07, Cheney was rumored to be resigning as vice president. His resignation would give Bush a chance to name a replacement that will be in the race for the 2008 presidential election. But the replacement was going to be a mere makeweight.

Over the years as secretary of defense and as vice president, Cheney has been in good relationships with the Saudis and most part of the Middle East. He has frequently met with their leaders. [81]

Impeachment of a 20th century president

A federal Impeachment is when the lower chamber of Congress brings federal charges against a member of the executive branch of government that may or may not culminate in removal from office by the upper chamber of Congress.

Article 2, section 4 of the United States Constitution stated: "The President, Vice President… shall be removed from Office on impeachment for, and Conviction of, Treason, Bribery, or other high Crimes and Misdemeanors." In 2007, Vice President Cheney had been penciled down for impeachment.[82]

A Recap of The last Impeachment of a United States President

In September 1998, Independent Counsel Ken Starr reported to Congress and asserted that there was "Substantial and credible information that President William Jefferson Clinton committed acts that may constitute grounds for an impeachment." Kenneth Starr's investigation led to evidence that the sexual harassment lawsuit brought by an Arkansas government employee and the Monica Lewinsky scandal concluded that the President committed an act of perjury by lying under oath.

The U.S. House of Representatives

In the Legislative Article, Clause 5, section 2 stated: "The House of Representatives…shall have the sole power of impeachment." After the Republican controlled House Judicial Committee reviewed Ken Starr's reports, they asserted that there were sufficient grounds for impeachment. The Democratic Party wanted a censure resolution against Clinton. Democrats pleaded to the Republicans to adopt their resolution as an alternative to impeachment. The Republicans reproved the Democratic Party alternative to impeachment. The Democratic leadership in the House asked its members to grandstand and walked out of the chamber "We walked to demonstrate our deep displeasure at the action of the majority party; they disregarded the clear will of the majority of the American people," said Dick Gephardt, the minority leader. Gephardt's assistant, David Bonior, House minority whip, said: "This House is out of touch. It is out of control. And it is so consumed that they have just denied us a chance to vote on the one option--the one option--that commands the support of the American people, and that is censure." After too much grandstanding, intensely partisan debates were the outcomes. The Democrats kept pushing for a censure resolution. They pointed out that Bill Clinton was not a dictator or a tyrant leader. After the debate, the Democratic Party efforts failed. The GOP blocked a floor vote on censure and thus the GOP passed House Resolution 611. And they voted out four articles of impeachment. Out of the four articles of impeachment that were recommended, only two were approved. The impeachment proceedings were largely party line; only five Democrats voted for impeachment. The President was impeached on grounds of perjury and obstruction of justice. Article one charged that the President "Willfully provided perjurious, false and misleading testimony to the grand jury" in the sexual harassment lawsuit. And article three charged that the president "Has prevented, obstructed and impeded the administration of justice."

The Upper Chamber

Legislative Article: Clause 6, section 2, stated, "The Senate shall have the sole power to try all impeachment. When the President of the United States is tried, the Chief Justice shall preside: And no person shall be convicted without the concurrence of two thirds of the members present." The impeachment trial in the US Senate commenced, as the Democrats in America faced a nail biting wait to hear the final verdict from the Senate.

The Chief Justice at that time was Rehnquist. Before the trial proceeding began, he had sworn in all the 100 senators as Jurors. The President's fate was at stake as the allegation of the president committing high crimes and misdemeanors while in office was in full effect. The Jurors then voted on the two articles of impeachment.

President Richard Nixon denied Congress a chance for an impeachment trial when the Watergate scandal broke out. The Watergate scandal was when alleged associates of Nixon illegally broke into the Democratic National Committee at the Watergate hotel. Their actions immediately prompted a federal investigation. The FBI, the Senate, and House Judiciary Committee all conducted an investigation. The break-ins occurred a few months before the 1972 presidential election, when Richard Nixon was preparing for his reelection bid. In a nutshell, tape records showed that Nixon and his staffers had attempted to cover up the break-in. Nixon's tenure came to an unceremonious end when Congress presented articles of impeachment against him. The next president, President Ford, issued a pardon for Richard Nixon.

President Nixon resigned from office but President Clinton did not resign. Clinton refused to heed to the calls for his resignation from big shot Tom DeLay and other GOP ranks. DeLay uttered "I'd say that the President is in real trouble. Things are rather sad right now, solemn. This is a very serious thing that the institution of the United States has only done one other time. And it a tragedy that this president has brought us to this point." Bob Livingston (R-Louisiana) stepped down as the designated speaker. He resigned from Congress because he had his own extramarital affairs. He also called for the president to step down.

After the senators voted, two thirds or 67 senators were required to convict the president but that wasn't achieved. President Bill Clinton, like President Andrew Johnson in 1868, was acquitted largely due to bipartisanship. No Democratic senators voted to convict Clinton and moderate Republicans also voted for acquittal. At the end of the process, Bill Clinton addressed the nation with the following statement: "Now that the Senate has fulfilled its constitutional responsibility bringing this process to a conclusion, I want to say again to the American people how profoundly sorry I am for what I said and did to trigger these events and the great burden they have imposed on the Congress and on the American people." [83]

One of the 2008 Democratic candidates for president presents articles of impeachment against Cheney as House resolution 333. Whether the effort from the congressman is for his presidential hopeful or not, the article remains in the House Judiciary Committee.

However, in late 2007, the Republicans in the House surprisingly voted not to table the impeachment. First, Majority Leader Steny Hoyer introduced a call to table House resolution 333(take the impeachment resolution off the table) and of course the Republicans voted to table the resolution. Then, according to CSPAN, the Republican leadership led by Roy Blunt and John Boehner, the minority whip and minority leader respectively, directed their Republican members to switch their votes from tabling the resolution, to vote not to table the resolution. There were twice as many Republicans than Democrats that voted not to table the resolution. So the resolution was not tabled.

What is the Republican Party's plan? America will wait and see. The resolution now goes to the Judiciary Committee. Nancy Pelosi and with Steny Hoyer are against the impeachment of the Vice President.[84]

Quid pro quo continues

On June 20, 2004 a fight of the statesman occurred between Senator Leahy and Vice President Cheney, with the latter using unorthodox language against the former. The senator had been accusing Cheney of using his position as the vice president to help Halliburton Corp. obtain major defense contracts, specifically in the ongoing war in Iraq. The Vice President acknowledged "Part of the problem here is, that instead of having a substantive debate over important substantive policy issues, he had challenged my integrity and I didn't like that. But most of all I didn't like the fact that after he'd done so, then he wanted to act like everything was peaches and cream." Leahy responded, "I think he was just having a bad day. And I was kind of shocked to hear that kind of language on the Senate floor." Cheney claimed that his congressional colleagues "felt that" the obscenity that he directed towards Leahy "Badly needed to be said, that it was long overdue." Cheney added that he felt better after cursing at the senior senator from Vermont. Neil Cavuto of Fox News asked Cheney if he had any regrets uttering the epithet. Cheney said, "No. I said it. That is not the kind of language I usually use." But he was not pleased with the conduct of the Vermont's statesman. [85]

Fourth branch of government

Because of his powerful position inside the Bush Administration, some pundits labeled Cheney as American's Prime Minister.

America should consider having a Prime Minister like Great Britain, only if Dick Cheney is our first. A Prime Minister cannot be categorized as a dictator. Some anti Bush-Cheney Americans consider Bush to be our one and only dictator, especially when President Bush joked that "A dictatorship would be heck of a lot easier, just as long as I am the dictator." Others do consider Cheney as the leader of the country while Bush as American's spokesperson. Maybe that is what Cheney was trying to inform the American people in mid 2007 about the Fourth Branch.

There are three branches of government: the Judicial, Executive, and Legislative branches. The executive branch of Bush, Cheney, and the president's cabinet executes the laws. The legislative branch is made up of the U.S. Congress (Senate and the House); they are the lawmakers. And the judicial branch of government, that is the Supreme Court, interprets the law. [86]

Cheney's story raised red flags; every major news media outlets were talking about the story. It made national headlines until Congressman Rahm Emmanuel threatened to cut funding the executive branch of Cheney's VP office "The vice president has a choice to make, if he believes his legal case, his office has no business being funded as a part of the executive branch." The Vice President's office asserted that it was not required to be in accordance with a presidential order requiring agencies under the executive branch to report to the National Archives on the number of documents they classify or declassify. Cheney maintained that he primarily work in the legislative branch; therefore, the rules governing agencies within the executive branch doesn't apply to him.

Constitutionally, Cheney serves as the president of the Senate, with the power granted by the Constitution to vote in the Senate as a tie-breaker. But a tie break seldom occurs in the Senate, therefore the Vice President rarely presides over the upper chamber of Congress "I have a foot in both camps, if you will," Cheney claimed.

> "As vice president, obviously, I'm next in line to succeed the president if something happens to him. I have an office in the West Wing of the White House. I advise the president, I'm a member of the National Security Council. Those are all executive functions granted to me basically by the president. At the same time, I have responsibilities under the Constitution for certain things on Capitol Hill. In the Senate, I am president of the Senate, I am the presiding officer in the Senate, and I cast tie-breaking votes there. My paycheck actually comes from the Senate"

Cheney concluded. With the absence of Cheney in the Senate chamber, the duty of the senate presiding officer will be presided over by the president *pro tempore* of the senate. These events prompted Dianne Feinstein, the senior senator from California to call it the "height of arrogance." And Senator Wyden (D-Oregon) said, "The vice president is saying he's above the law, and the fact of the matter is, legal scholars are going to say this is preposterous."

An AA2.0 media top commentator said Cheney's executive branch office should be outsourced to India.

Cheney has a total of three offices in the legislative branch. In 2001, Dennis Hastert, the former Speaker of the House, gave Cheney an office near the House floor. And Cheney also has two offices in the senate chamber. So Cheney can claim to be a member of both branches of government. Dennis Hastert's successor, Nancy Pelosi, might seize Cheney's lower chamber office.[87]

Cheney, an honoree, was awarded the Presidential Medal of Freedom.

During his tenure as vice president, Cheney was having heath problems; however, those health problems never involved Cheney being rushed to the hospital. Cheney has served America to his last breath. He has done a superb job and he should be given all the credit.

As Richard Cheney looks forward to a new phase in his career, most people are unsure about his idea of attacking Iran, but he is one of the most powerful people in America. There you go, SIR.[88]

Chapter 5

Rush Limbaugh, the most powerful person in America

Rush Limbaugh is the leader of the Conservative Establishment. He is also a veteran American radio talk show host. Rush Limbaugh is the originator of talk radio. "In the beginning was the Word, and the Word was with God, and the Word was God" (John chapter 1 verse 1). "The beginning of talk radio was Rush. And God gave Rush the Word, and the Word was with Rush, But the Word was God" -Nndy Nenty.

For over nineteen years, Rush mostly discussed the politics and economic issues of the day on his program, 'The Rush Limbaugh Show.' Limbaugh began his career on radio as a teenager in the mid-sixties. Rush was determined to join the US Army but didn't, because he had medical problems that at that time would disable him from enrolling. Rush had been up and down in the radio industry, struggling trying to secure fame. In the late eighties, the revoked Fairness doctrine played a big role in Rush's career.

Now the fairness doctrine benefits any talk radio commentator in the country. The Fairness doctrine is a policy that states that radio and television stations must provide contrasting point of views.

Limbaugh finally got the monkey off his back when he moved to California. He then moved to New York WABC EIB –AM, his flagship station.

It is a fact that Rush has been the one-man army that brought AM Radio in America back to life. According to reports, The Rush Limbaugh Show has more listeners than any other talk radio show in the nation. And according to thousands of citizens, "The Rush Limbaugh's show is the best three hours of the day." [89]

Rush was highly congratulated by the Republican Party for their monumental victory in the midterm election of 1994. Most of the credit was given to Rush. Why? He did what no one in talk radio had ever done before. He informed the people of America the reality of the situations at hand. For instance, Rush commented on all the corruption that was going on in the U.S. Congress and the benefits of the Contract with America. All the events were documented on his program.

Any one that doesn't know Rush Limbaugh doesn't know diddly-squat about American politics. Mr. Limbaugh is rarely seen on television.

In 2007, he did a cameo appearance on Fox News Channel's the ½ hour News hour.

Rush confessed that after the Fairness Doctrine was revoked, the Feds tried to shut him down. Rush said that was one of the most ridiculous experience. He continued "If you don't give it up (problems), it will always keep you in prison." [90]

In the early nineties, Rush hailed President Walker Bush and dealt with President Clinton. And in the new millennium, he hailed President George Bush. When W. Bush won the election of 1988, the media said that Rush wouldn't have anything to talk about. And when President Clinton won the 1992 presidential election, they claimed that Clinton's election made Rush a megastar.

So in 2008, if a Republican wins the White House, the media will have a new narrative on him. It has always been a never-ending process for Rush. Sometimes he loses and sometimes he wins. Rush put it this way

> "I remember 1988. Bush 41 wins the election, and the media says, well, that's it for Limbaugh! There is nothing more to talk about. His guy won. There's going to be nothing for him to talk about here. I'd only been on the air for three months. In 92, Clinton wins election. The Drive-By Media says, well, that's it for Limbaugh! Clinton won the White House. A Democrat is in the White House. Limbaugh's been discredited. Who's going to want to listen to him? He lost. Now they say Democrats in the White House made me a Mega star." [91]

Rush, for 2 decades, had been very critical of the incoming and outgoing Democratic lawmakers in Capitol Hill, especially the 110th United States

Congress. Rush joked about the five non-cancerous polyps found when Bush was having a medical checkup. He joked that they were Sen. Reid, Speaker Pelosi, Rep. Murtha, Sen. Schumer, and Sen. Lewis.

On the topic of the 2003 Iraq war, Rush conducted a mouth-watering interview with one and only Cheney. Limbaugh asked "You and Bush have derided the theatrics of Harry Reid and Nancy Pelosi and other Democrats. Is this who they really are? Is this what they really intend to lose this war, to make sure we come home defeated?" Cheney replied,

> "I think that the policies that they are recommending would in fact produce that result. I've got some friends on the other side of the aisle, and I don't want question everybody's motives. I do believe that a significant portion of the Democrats including I think, Nancy Pelosi are adamantly opposed to the war and prepared to pack it in and come home in defeat, rather than put in place or support a policy that will lead to victory."

Limbaugh's dialogue with Cheney continued, "Can you share with us whether or not you understand their devotion, or their seeming allegiance, to the concept of US defeat." Cheney responded

> "I can't it seems to me so abundantly clear, that we really need to prevail in this conflict, that there is an awful lot riding on it. They seem to think that we can withdraw from Iraq and walk away from it. They ignore the lessons of the past. Remember what happened in Afghanistan. We'd been involved in Afghanistan in the eighties, supporting the Mujahideen against the Soviets and prevailed. We won. Everybody walked away, and in the nineties, Afghanistan became a safe haven for terrorist, an area for training camps where they launched attacks on the United States on 9 /11. So those are real problems, and to advocate withdrawal from Iraq at this point, it seems to me, simply would play right into the hands of al-Qaeda." [92]

Prosecution and Doctor shopping

A Florida Palm Beach State attorney launched an investigation to determine if Rush had violated Florida's doctor shopping laws. In 2003, desperate prosecutors stumbled upon Limbaugh's private medical records, seized them, and searched for proof of evidence to convict the conservative big shot. These prosecutors illegally seized his medical records. Limbaugh's constitutional right of privacy had indeed been violated. Palm Beach's court records show that 'doctor shopping' charges have been brought to the court only once in five years. Limbaugh's lawyer said because of the court's record review, "Rush Limbaugh has been singled out for special prosecution because of who he is. We believe the state attorney's office is applying a double standard." On the record, Limbaugh had been advocating against the use of illegal drug on his show. He added that if a person was found guilty, they should be sent to jail. So was Rush guilty? In any case, Limbaugh practiced what he preached. A judge issued a warrant out for Rush's arrest. However, Rush and his entourage went to Palm Beach County jail. He was charged with doctor shopping. No Palm Beach County police officers, not even the sheriff, wanted to be responsible for handcuffing Mr. Limbaugh. Although he went through an arrest routine, the bottom line was that at no point was he handcuffed. And he was immediately asked to go after bail money was issued. A police officer attested to the astonishing event that took place in the county jail. On his show in October 2003, Rush admitted he was a prescription drug addict. He bettered himself by taking few weeks off work to enter a rehabilitation program. A Rush aide reported that over Rush's duration in the program, Mr. Limbaugh had no relapse.

According to Palm Beach County law, doctor shopping is illegal. It's the act of duping two or more doctors to prescribe the same prescription medication.

Rush was accused of getting prescriptions of both Oxycodone and hydroquinone within a 30 day period. The doctor shopping case was a headline news story for the mainstream media. They finally thought they'd nailed Rush. New York Times headlines "In Legal Deal, Limbaugh Surrenders in Drug Case," and Washington Post "Rush Limbaugh Turns Himself In On Fraud Charge In Rx Drug Probe."

Because he was innocent, Rush didn't wait to make a court appearance. He filed for a not guilty plea to the rarely prosecuted charge. And on April 29 2006, he was ordered to pay a fine of $30,000 to cover the cost of the investigation. Rush's lawyer asserted that the state's agreement resulted from a lack of evident supporting the charge. The deal finally ended the investigation. However, Rush didn't get off scot-free. The single charge would not be completely dropped until Limbaugh entered a treatment program lasting 18 months. The prosecutors' dossier of evidence against Rush was insignificant: "Mr. Limbaugh and I have maintained from the start that there was no doctor shopping, and we continue to hold this position" Limbaugh's attorney said. Once the investigation that he circumvented the law to obtain prescription painkillers was over, Limbaugh was extremely relieved: "This is the first day of the rest of my life" his spokesman said on his behalf.

Limbaugh has never had any blemishes on his record; they attempted to smear his credibility as a law abiding "general all around good guy."

What is the moral of this story? Every single day, Rush Limbaugh's actions are scrutinized. The media is waiting for Rush Limbaugh to make the smallest mistake, so as to charge him with a case or a complaint. He is always being talked about; the whole of mainstream media can't stop mentioning Mr. Limbaugh's name. They get their talking points from his show. It's only logical that the Democrats would want a conservative magnate like Rush in their ranks. Rush Limbaugh is in a class of his own. He is undeniably and undoubtedly the most intelligent and wisest person in the United States. It's difficult for Rush to maintain the equilibrium with any great or famous Americans. [93]

The Limbaugh Institute for Advanced Conservative Studies, a study that exceeds all audience expectations, is the only way to hear Rush speak. It costs an arm and a leg to see Rush Limbaugh live in person.

Limbaugh's program has nurtured and educated millions of his supporters with the conservative ideas, principles and values.

Apart from meeting and surpassing all audience expectations on a daily basis, Rush's audience is approximately 25 millions, for crying out loud, that is the whole population of Australia. [94]

Inept Democratic leaders

On June 17th and 18th of 2007, the Senate staged a round the clock session to debate the Iraq war. And Rush was "having fun, more fun than a human being is allowed to have." Through a majority roll call vote, Majority Leader Harry Reid ordered the Sergeant-at-arms to keep senators near the senate chamber and request absent senators to promptly attend the debate. The debate over the war legislation continued throughout the evening and even during the wee hours of the cool morning. Sleeping cots were set up off the senate chamber. The consequence of any senators not appearing for the debate might be an example of what happened to Oregon's Republican senator, Bob Packwood. In 1988, the Sergeant-at-arms roughly carried Packwood into the Senate chamber to attend a debate. The Republicans launched the last all night session to force Democrats to filibuster Bush's judicial nominations. The Bill Frist leadership complained that "Unprecedented obstructionism" was going on in the senate. Well, in 2007, it was the Democrats' turn to force the Republican Party to filibuster all night. After the all night debate, the Democrats fell short of the 60 votes needed to override a filibuster. The

Republican senators remained steadfast in their opposition to the anti war legislation. They rejected measures to bring American troops back home. "I bet I can stay up longer than they can" Senator Coburn, a Republican senator, said regarding the Democratic senate members. Republican leader McConnell gave his take: "Indeed anyone who watched it unfold might have thought they were turning into an episode of 'The Twilight Zone.'" "A political stunt, petty kindergarten games," Lamar Alexander, third ranking GOP leader, opined.

Rush said that he was trying to stay awake to watch the whole event but that he went to bed with Sen. Hillary Clinton and woke up with Sen. Barbara Boxer, meaning the last senator he watched on TV before falling asleep was Clinton and when he woke up there was Boxer on the senate floor. Rush concluded that the all night session was nothing but a fundraiser for the senators. [95]

Rush Limbaugh is also a teacher/ lecturer; he teaches his listener on his show. He talks about conservatives 101. For example, "Conservatives want to examine what stops the suffering of people and determine why he or she suffered; unlike the liberals who feel empathy and sympathy for people. The liberals want to use everyone else's money to fix the problem and that is an incurred way of getting what they want" (a paraphrase).

Rush said "They want equal distribution of misery." He continued, "For conservative is about philosophy, but for the Democrats is about race." One caller cried when she called Rush's program. She said, "Please don't ever go away." Rush has touched so many lives through his commentaries and lectures on his program.[96]

Media Matter for America, a progressive research and information center organization, have been very critical of Rush. One of their duties is to correct conservative misinformation in the U.S. Media.

Over the years, some liberal progressive groups have turned some of the accuracies of the Rush Limbaugh show into inaccuracies. Of course that is conventional wisdom; anything Rush says will always be questioned.

They have launched a broadside against Limbaugh for almost 2 decades. Rush has also been attacked by book writers, most notable 'Rush Limbaugh is a Big Fat Idiot,' written by a candidate for the US senate from Minnesota.

And for almost 20 years now, Rush has been constantly vacuuming away the hates, lies and despises that the Left has uttered against Republicans and conservatives. Rush is a Sacrificial Lamb's representative that absorb the attacks coming from liberals and Democrats. Any attacks on Bush and Cheney by the Left, is actually an attack on Rush. [97]

Apart from Dick Cheney, Newt Gingrich, and a few others, Rush hardly invites any guest on his show. Rush only interviews people of his status.

Karl Rove, the so-called Bush's brain, was the last important figure to be a guest on his show. In late 2007, un-gentlemanly remarks were made against Rush Limbaugh and Karl Rove. The mainstream media were all over Rush and Karl. An MSNBC reporter referred to Rush as a snob.

Mr. Limbaugh doesn't brag when he says "Half of his brain tied behind his back, just to be fair."

Limbaugh proved that notion when he debated Democratic heavyweight, Vice President Al Gore in 1992. They were debating if there was an ozone hole above America or not. It turned out that no hole in the ozone layer opened above the United States. So Rush was right and Gore was wrong. [98]

Remarks ignite firestorm

In late 2007, in the wake of Rush ending his 18 month probation, he made a comment that got the whole news media to attack him. Media Matters spearheaded the attacks.

The controversy over Rush's comments about "phony soldier(s)" went on for months. That proves how powerful Rush's rhetoric is and how it moves the country.

Rush was referring to a man that falsely claimed to be an Iraq veteran. And his dialogue was clearly taken out of context. The excerpt reads:

Limbaugh: "What is really funny is, they never talk to real soldiers,

The Caller: They like to pull these soldiers that come up out of the blue and talk to the media."

Limbaugh responded: The "phony soldier."

Days after the phony soldier comment, Senate Majority Leader Harry Reid called Clear Channels to discipline Rush for the hateful and unpatriotic remark.

Reid is a United States senator from Nevada; and polls in Nevada showed him way lower than the polls for Mr. Limbaugh. By the way, Limbaugh doesn't hold any political office but has a higher approval rating than the leader of the United States Congress.

Senator Harry Reid, on the floor of the senate, condemned Mr. Limbaugh's remarks. Reid said Rush's comment was "So beyond the pale of decency that it cannot be left alone." Senator Reid urged his Democratic colleagues to sign a letter of disapproval to the manager of Rush's Clear Channel to sanction Mr. Limbaugh. The idea was unanimously agreed by members of the Democratic Party and they all signed the letter. Reid believed that Rush was calling our military soldiers- "phony soldiers," Reid has previously assailed Richard Cheney, calling him "the administration's chief attack dog."

Clear Channels syndicated Rush Limbaugh program on radio. The CEO of Clear Channels responded to the Majority Leader's letter:

> "Over the years Mr. Limbaugh has repeatedly praised the dedication and valor of our brave men and women in uniform. Given Mr. Limbaugh's history of support for our soldiers, it would be unfair for me to assume his statements were intended to personally indict combat soldiers simply because they didn't share his own beliefs regarding the war in Iraq,"

Mark Mays wrote. After Senator Reid wrote to Clear Channel, Rush Limbaugh, an activist who has made numerous trips to Iraq since when the war began, weighed in "The effort here is simply to discredit people that they consider effective and powerful on the right (Republicans) ginning up, leading up into the 08 elections."

The Democratic Party is angry at Rush's political effectiveness; they couldn't stand it. [99]

Mr. Limbaugh, a National Treasure and a Prophet, observed that the Senator Reid led modern Democrats in Congress stands for- censorship, subpoenas, and surrender. Rush joked "The Democrats should serve Osama bin Laden a subpoena because Bush can't catch bin Laden" (a paraphrase.) Osama has been labeled "Osama bin Laden (D) Democratic Representative At-large from Afghanistan."

Democratic leaders in Congress had admitted defeat of America in the war in Iraq. Rush had countered and reprimanded the Democratic leaders in the following way: "Liberal is the most godless choice you can make, they are invested in defeat, they look forward for the day the news is bad (in Iraq)." Rush stressed on, "And they're trying to remove our troops in Iraq in the midst of a success. What type of doom and gloom politician are these. Whosoever is the new president come 2008, will still keep our troops in Iraq. As long as Bush is still the president, they will keep on saddling Bush with the loss until the new president is nominated" (a paraphrase). [100]

Republicans Abandoned principles

On June 27, 2007, Senator Lugar, the ranking member of the Republican senate Foreign Relation Committee, called the president's Iraq strategy a failure during a speech on the floor of the senate. The Indiana Senator said it was time to start pulling out American troops from Iraq. But Lugar also said, "The longer we delay the planning for redeployment, the less likely it is to be successful." A redeployment to where? The next day, Ohio senior senator

George Voinovich made the same claim: "We must not abandon our mission, but we must begin a transition where the Iraqi government and its neighbors play a larger role in stabilizing Iraq." -Voinovich's letter to Bush.

Rush was cut to the heart, he trashed both Republican Senators Lugar and Voinovich. He asserted that they were joining the "cut and run" Democrats and they were running for the tall grass. He said "They have joined the Democrats to raise the white flag and surrender in Iraq."

Behind closed doors, some GOP senators have been speaking out against Bush's Iraq policy. But how long will they continue to publicly ignore the elephant in the room?

After Lugar and Voinovich expressed their outraged, the Democratic senators hoped they could capitalized on the tune of the Republicans, and they could muster the 60 votes needed to pass anti war legislation that would call for the president to withdraw our combat troops from Iraq.

Even if the Democrats were able to draw the 60 votes needed to overcome a filibuster, they still have to face a possible veto by the president. They really need 67 votes from its members and a few from the Republican members to override a president's veto pen.[101]

The Bush administration had appealed to Congress for more time and patience with the ongoing war. Limbaugh acknowledged that some Republicans had abandoned their principles and taken a dramatic change on the Republican platform. Some of the Republicans that Rush pointed out were moderate Republican senators like Hagel of Nebraska, Snowe and Collins of Maine, Smith of Oregon and senior senators Warner (R-Virginia) and Specter (R-Pennsylvania). They have all made similar remarks and had been skeptical of the Iraq war strategy.

Some Republicans were trying to derail the Bush administration's legislative agenda. Rush said eloquently, "Republicans are accepting the premise of the liberal agenda. The whole liberal premise is all for government to expand. We can't cave in for the Democrats to compromise on our principles." [102]

The 2008 presidential election (February 07-December 07)

Rush referred to the first tier Democratic candidates for the 2008 presidential election as "Mr. and Mrs. Edwards, Mr. and Mrs. Obama and Mr. and Mrs. Clinton." Because Sen. Clinton challengers Sen. Obama and Sen. Edwards sent their wives to attack Sen. Clinton. Rush said, "Their gloves are about to come off" when one of the wives said that if you can't run your house, then you can't run the presidency. Rush was very critical of Sen. Clinton. Rush said Clinton portrayed herself as a victim in her campaign.

Hillary Clinton has been swift boated by the Obamas and the Edwards and only time will tell once they throw the kitchens sink strategy on Hillary.[103]

Mr. Limbaugh's show, a cutting-edge of societal evolution, is an award winning show. Rush "is a way of life". He is a real Civil Rights activist and the greatest American radio talk host of all time in the history of the country.

Rush proclaimed "Rush Limbaugh, a talent on loan from God."

In 2007, the Landmark Legal Foundation nominated Rush for the Nobel Prize. Rush Limbaugh preached, "The resurrection of Jesus Christ is the key to Christianity. Christianity can't exist without Jesus Christ resurrecting" (a paraphrase.)

The following are Mr. Limbaugh's words to the wise: "If people don't like you, they hate you because they want to be like you. You can't argue with a fool, because people won't know the difference. Those who don't believe in God, they believe anything." [104]

Who politically beget whom?

All the presidents in Rush Limbaugh's lifetime

President Harry Truman/ Barkley Tenure
A talent on loan from God was born.
President Eisenhower/ Richard Nixon Regime
Kindergarten schooling etc.
President Kennedy/ LB Johnson Tenure
Growing up in Missouri, school
President Johnson/ Hubert Humphrey Tenure
Growing up in Missouri, school
President Nixon/ Agnew & Ford Regime
Rush was a working independent.
President Ford/ Nelson Rockefeller Regime
Voting age, military recruit age
President Carter/ Walter Mondale Tenure
Rush was in the local radio business. [105]

President Reagan/ Walker Bush Regime

Rush Limbaugh's first big influence was lobbying Reagan to repeal the fairness doctrine. The Rush Limbaugh radio show commenced in New York City and in only three months, he propelled Vice President Walker Bush to a win. Bush won the presidential election of 1988 and thus became the president-elect. His challenger was Massachusetts governor Michael Dukakis. The Governor tried to capitalize on the Iran-contra scandal against his chief opponent. Dukakis, a far-left candidate, opposed the Pledge of allegiance in schools. Rush started carrying water for the Republican ticket for president. And immediately, Rush galvanized voters and the press attention. Dukakis once had a 20 percent lead over the Vice President. But with Rush on the horizon, the Governor lost his lead. Despite the Iran-contra scandal, President Reagan remained a very popular president and that was also a big plus for Walker Bush. [106]

Bush/ Quayle Regime

Walker Bush as the incumbent lost the 92 presidential election to an unknown governor from Arkansas. Bush 41 didn't keep his pledge against not raising taxes. Bush didn't "Read my lips, no new taxes," But he did raise taxes. "The Congress will push me to raise taxes and I will say no." -Walker Bush's comments during the 1988 presidential campaign. In the wake of the Persian Gulf War, Bush still had a decent approval rating, but he did move away from the conservative base. He was labeled as a moderate Republican. And Bush lost a significant number of Limbaugh's supporters. Ross Perot, a third party candidate and a conservative business man, got 19% of the popular votes. He was labeled a 'spoiler' because he took away votes from Bush. Ross Perot was the main reason Walker Bush lost the presidency. Clinton, the 1992 Democratic nominee, was not a member of Congress and that was a big advantage for the governor. Governors don't get to vote on legislations unlike congressional lawmakers who vote and pass laws and of course presidents, who put some laws into effect. Bush 41 served in World War 2, unlike Clinton who never served the nation. Clinton was also an anti Vietnam War advocate. Clinton had no foreign affairs experience, and no voting (congressional) records. So his votes can't be challenged. Rush Limbaugh brought out all those substantive issues on his program against Clinton, but at the end of the day, Bill Clinton had the last laugh. [107]

Clinton/Gore Tenure

The next presidential election was in 1996. This was a chance for Limbaugh to rectify what went wrong in 92. Again the odds were against Rush. The Republican nominee, Senator Bob Dole and former president, Walker Bush, had a substantive disagreement. And that was a big disadvantage for the Republican Establishment. Some of Rush's supporters were considering Pat Buchanan or Steve Forbes as a possible party nominee. Dole, like Walker

Bush, served the country in World War 2. Although Limbaugh was leading the conservative movement, all the odds and all the dead weights within the Republican Party led to Dole's big loss to the incumbent president. Senator Dole's running mate Jack Kemp, a representative from New York, did cave in to Al Gore. During an encounter with Gore, Kemp threw the whole Republican Party under the bus. Limbaugh recalled Al Gore's words to the Republican nominee: "You are not racist like the rest of your party," and the Republican nominee answered "Thank you." General Colin Powell, the Chairman of the Joint Chief of Staff, didn't run for president. The Clinton camp was scared of Powell because if he did run, he would draw African American votes away from Clinton which would probably deny Clinton the presidency. Ross Perot was also back to assume his position as the 'spoiler' for the Republican nominee. However, Perot was not as effective as he was in the 1992 presidential election.[108]

They always say three strikes and you are out; well, that didn't apply to Mr. Limbaugh.

In the 1st presidential election of the 21st century, Rush finally pleased the conservative- Republican Americans. For months, Limbaugh fired on all cylinders and eventually got a Republican into the White House. It was a long and hard-earned battle, equivalent to that of the 1994 midterm congressional election.

Even though the chances look dim for the Republican Party, they still overcome all odds.

Fresh new GOP breeds were introduced to the field of presidential candidates, most notable the senator from Arizona, John McCain, and President Walker Bush's son, Governor George Bush. Rush cried for all the old seasoned politicians like Dan Quayle, Forbes, Alexander, and Perot not to explore a presidential bid and Limbaugh rallied around Governor Bush. Towards the end of Vice President Gore's pedestrian tenure, he got the Democratic nominee for the 2000 presidential election. But Gore lost the general election to Texas's governor, George Bush. After the loss, the Democratic Establishment tried to appease their party by blaming 3rd party candidate Ralph Nader for Albert Gore's loss. They also blamed voting irregularities in Florida, the Monica Lewinsky scandal, and the impeachment of William Clinton. But they didn't add to their laundry list that Albert Gore lost his home state of Tennessee to Gov. Bush. And his running mate, Senator Lieberman, was the first prominent lawmaker in the senate to chastise Bill Clinton on the Lewinsky scandal.

Rush had to choose between Governor Bush and Senator McCain for the Republican nominee. After viewing which of the two records was most in line with the conservative principles, Rush picked Gov. Bush and urged his millions of supporters to support the governor from Texas.[109]

Bush/ Cheney Presidency

The next presidential election was in 2004. The presidential campaign came on the heels of Bush's decision to keep the troops in Iraq after declaring the end of combat operation. Again Rush had to put in work by galvanizing millions of conservative voters to stand by Bush and Cheney. After Bush's lack-luster performance in the first presidential debates against Sen. Kerry, Bush bounced back and was leading in the polls. Rush lambasted the John Kerry/John Edwards Democratic presidential ticket for first supporting the war in Iraq and later disapproving funds for the troops.

The flip-flop by the Democratic ticket speaks volumes about the challengers.

Rush had to defend the Bush-Cheney ticket from the surrogates dispatched by the Democrats to attack the Republican ticket. When all was said and done, the incumbent president was re-elected and Rush Limbaugh, the genius, once again came out victorious. The seasoned conservative leader exposed the political inexperience of Kerry's running mate; a message that resonated with the American voters. [110]

The 2008 presidential election (February 07-December 07)

The presidential election of 2008 is in effect. Rush has made it clear that he is no longer going to carry water for the Republican Party.

On November 8th 2006, after the GOP loses the House and the Senate, Rush managed to "put a punctuation point" on a sad morning by looking at the future and ensuring Americans that the defeat would not spell the end of conservatism

> "I feel liberated, and I'm just going to tell you as plainly as I can why. I no longer am going to carry the water for people who I don't think deserve having their water carried. Now, you might say, well why have you been doing it, because the stakes are high. Even though the Republican Party let us down, to me they represent a far better future for my beliefs and therefore the country's than the Democrats Party does and liberalism."

Regarding the 2008 presidential campaign, Rush hasn't endorsed or supported any of the GOP candidates. Mitt Romney has flip-flopped on his position; Mayor Rudolph Giuliani supported gun control laws and gay rights.

John McCain and Mike Huckabee were big problem for conservative voters. Fred Thompson might have been the only candidate that Rush would have supported prior to November 8th, 2006.

Real conservative politicians like Tom DeLay, Rick Santorum and Newt Gingrich are politicians that Rush would support regardless of his "no longer… carry the water" comment. So if a Democrat wins the 2008 presidential election, Rush will not be held to blame.

Rush was responsible for the Bush 41, Bush 43, and Bush 43 reelection as president of America. And Rush did finish on a high note when he said he was no longer going to carry water for politicians.

In the beginning continues

Rush resigning and resting on his laurels will make Mr. Hannity assume the position as the leading conservative activist. Conservatives in America should seek an alternative if Rush decides to retire to private life. They have to prepare for that eventuality. Hannity will be set to spearhead the challenge, he has been an understudy to Rush for many years now. And has deputies for Rush in the past.

Rush's *versatility, plus his professionalism* have been a major factor *for the Republican Party and it can never be replaced.*

On the other hand, when you have a situation where DeLay, Gingrich and Limbaugh are no longer high up on the pecking order for the Republican Party, the party would definitely be sidelined. [111]

Rush is an American legend and he has cemented his place as one of the greatest conservative figures in the history of the country; like Goldwater and Reagan. Rush's die-hard supporters are scared of Rush's future on the radio because of the Congress push to re-repeal the 'fairness doctrine.'

Rush said if the fairness doctrine should be reversed, his voice would still be heard even if he has to use a loud speaker to spread his message in public.

The big shot thanks his followers for their steadfast support. Despite all the struggles Rush has been through, he has never been an opportunist, nothing has ever fallen invitingly for him.

Rush Limbaugh did his utmost to be where he is, to lead the conservative movement. He is a candidate for a Nobel Prize award. Somebody said what hasn't Rush Limbaugh achieved in his lifetime; president of the United States? Rush Limbaugh's power is stronger than simply being the president of a country.

America will definitely be a better place if Rush Limbaugh's program is next on every American's menu. The substance that Rush brings to the table is beyond measure.

Rush is the man that runs America. Just like one caller on his program said "Rush you are the most powerful person in America, if not the most powerful person in the world." Let's applaud for Mr. Rush Hudson Limbaugh. Give respect when it is due. It doesn't matter if your political ideology is conservative or liberal. [112]

Chapter 6

21st Century: Condoleezza Rice for American president

The 2008 presidential election (February 07-December 07)

Rice is American's foreign president. If she becomes the United States president, America will have a leader who has in-depth experience on foreign policy. Condoleezza Rice is the first woman from the minority race to be appointed as secretary of state. And she is only the second woman in American history to hold that position.

Civil Right movement

Condoleezza was born in Birmingham, Alabama, in the height of the segregation era. During the violent days of the Civil Rights Movement, Rice's father had been passionately protective of Condoleezza. Rice's father was a Presbyterian minister. He was in support of the Civil Rights movement's goals, but feared being counterproductive if his support for the movement would put Condoleezza in harm's way. [113]

Civil Rights were constitution guaranteed rights granted by the government. The modern day civil rights movement began in the 1950's. President Johnson signed the Civil Rights Act of 1964 into law. It granted equal protection under the law, equal treatment of every American, and equal citizenship to all social groups. It also outlawed discrimination in public places and in employment. The Civil Right Act of 1964 achieved a substantial number of rights for African Americans since the 19th century's Reconstruction. President Kennedy first proposed that Congress considered a legislation that prohibits segregation in public places. However, when the president died, his successor LB Johnson signed the proposal into law. Passage of the act was difficult. In Congress, the House Committee left the Civil Rights bill dead in the water until a majority of supporters threatened to send the bill to the House floor without House committee approval. In the Senate, the bill was filibuster by some Southern senators. However, the Democratic leader of the senate, Hubert Humphrey, worked with the Republican leader to support the bill and brought an end to the filibuster.[114]

In 1963, a bomb took the lives of Rice's friend and three other young girls. Rice said, "The crime was calculated to suck the hope out of young lives, bury their inspirations. But those fears were not propelled forward, those terrorists failed." Five years had elapsed, and the President had fight to reduce discrimination in America. The 1965 Voting Rights Act was put into law, and after King's death in 1968, President Johnson also put to law a Civil Rights Act that banned housing discrimination. [115]

Rice's biography

Rice enrolled at the university of Denver Colorado. And at the tender age of 21, she received her B.A. in political science. She later obtained her Master's Degree in political science from the university of Notre Dame. In the early eighties at the age of 26, she earned her Ph.D. in political science from Denver's Graduate school of International studies. Rice had an interest in the politics of Soviet Union and foreign relations. [116]

In the late 1970's, Rice changed her party affiliation from Democrat to Republican because of President Carter's foreign policy stance. Rice served in the administration of President Walker Bush. She was the Soviet and East European affair Director, and she was also a Special Assistant to the President. After the Bush 41 administration ended, she pursued an academic career. Dr Rice was hired as a professor of political science at Stanford University. And for six years, she served as provost. Dr Rice made history during her tenure as provost. She was the first female to ever occupy that position. And the University record showed that she was also the youngest, and the first minority provost at Sanford. [117]

American case against a dictator

Rice assisted then Gov. George Bush in the Governor's 2000 presidential campaign. She worked as Bush's foreign policy advisor. During Bush's first term as president, Condoleezza Rice was appointed as National Security Advisor. Unfortunately for Condoleezza Rice, nine months after her appointment, the tragedy of September 11th occurred. Before the attacks on the WTC, Rice frequently met with George Tenet, the CIA director, and Cofer Black, the Counterterrorism chief, about the threats posed by al-Qaeda. The CIA director was reported to be demanding immediate attention from Rice to clear the counterterrorism policy. Federal officials revealed that presidential orders called 'findings' would have given the CIA full authority to carry out covert actions against al- Qaeda and bin Laden. Tenet said "Rice was polite, but they felt the brush-off." Rice was believed to be less forthcoming with the meetings with Tenet.

Rice claimed that the president's daily brief, 'Bin Laden determines to strike in US,' was old information presented to her. However, Rice said she did not recall any so-called emergency meetings with the CIA Director.

> "What I am quite certain of, however, is that I would remember if I was told, as this account apparently says, that there was about to be an attack in the United States. And the idea that I would somehow have ignored that I find incomprehensible, especially given that in July when we were getting a very steady stream of quite alarmist reports of potential attacks." [118]

On May 6, 2004, Rice refused to testify before a commission on 'Terrorist Attacks upon the United States.' She was later asked by Bush to appear before the commission, but only on certain conditions. [119]

Before the World Trade Center attacks and before Rice assumed office as the National Security Adviser, she told a foreign affair magazine,

> "As history marches toward markets and democracy, some states have been left by the side of the road. Iraq is the prototype. Saddam Hussein is isolated, his conventional military power has been severely weakened, his people live in poverty and terror, and he has no useful place in international politics. He is therefore determined to develop WMD. Nothing will change until Saddam is gone, so the United States must mobilize whatever resources it can, including support from his opposition, to remove him."

Rice was making comments about Saddam's dictatorship. Rice was one of Bush's main advocates for the invasion of Iraq. After Iraq went to the United Nations on issues involving weapons of mass destruction, Rice wrote a column published by the New York Times entitled *"Why We Know Iraq is Lying."* Condoleezza Rice also declared: "He already has other weapons of mass destruction (WMD), but a nuclear weapon, two or three or four years from now. I don't care where it is." Rice continued, "When it is to have that happen in a volatile region like the Middle East is most certainly a future that we cannot tolerate." On January 10th, 2003, National Security Adviser Condoleezza Rice stated the following in an interview on CNN: "The problem here is that there will always be some uncertainly about how quickly Saddam can acquire nuclear weapons. But we don't want the smoking gun to be a Mushroom cloud." This ominous statement made headlines worldwide. [120]

In the 2004 presidential election, Rice rallied to gain America's support for the reelection of President Bush. Rice finally banished any talk of Saddam's link with the 9-11 attacks: "While Saddam Hussein had nothing to do with the actual attacks on America; Saddam Hussein's Iraq was a part of the Middle East that was festering and unstable, and was part of the circumstances that created the problem on September 11th." And on issues of weapons of mass destruction she said, "U.S. officials never expected that we were going to open garages and find weapons of mass destruction."

The final montage about Iraq and Saddam Hussein coming from the National Security Adviser was:

> "Iraq, is one of the most dangerous regimes, I think the most dangerous regime in the world's most dangerous region, in the middle East, is a big reason or was, under Saddam Hussein a big reason for instability in the regions, for threats to the United States. He had used weapons of mass destruction. He had the intent and was still developing the capacity to do so. Saddam Hussein's regime was very dangerous"

–Rice's report on CBS's 60 minutes. [121]

The first United States Secretary of State was Thomas Jefferson, who later became a United States President. In 1996, Madeleine Albright made history; she was the first women to be appointed U.S Secretary of State. Colin Powell, a retired 5 star US army general was the 65th US secretary of State. Powell made history, as he was the first African American appointed to that position. A Gift for all Rice's efforts in assuring Bush reelection was given: Bush picked Rice to be his new secretary of state. And the Senate overwhelmingly confirmed her nomination. [122]

Middle East reformer

Rice became the 66th United States secretary of state; Bush couldn't wait to put her in that limelight. She was the second African American ever to be state secretary. Rice became the number one US chief diplomat. "Right off the jump," she immediately reformed the US diplomacy and the whole State Department. Her goal was titled 'Transformation Diplomacy' which she described as "Working with our many partners around the world and building and sustaining democratic, well-governed states that will respond to the needs of their people and conduct themselves responsibly in the international system." The newly minted Secretary said that the goal would build strong security, fight poverty, and make democratic reforms. Her main focus was democracy in the Middle East. Rice stated that her 'Transformation Diplomacy' is in part about "changing people's lives." She also focused on finding solutions to problems like drug trafficking, disease, education, and the defeat of violent extremism. Rice caused a sea change in the nation's foreign policy.

After the death of Yasser Arafat, Rice pushed for a peaceful and democratic election in Palestine. She asserted that "There should be the ability of Palestine people to participate in the elections" because it will "Represent a key step in the process of building a peaceful, democratic Palestine state." In the same address she denounced the Palestinian terrorist group Hamas.

The group doesn't recognize Israel's right to exist.

Rice proved herself as a world diplomat. Rice called for international support in demanding that Hamas recognize Israel's right to exist. However, Hamas agreed under their terms that Israel would have to fully withdraw from disputing territories, namely Gaza, the West Bank, and East Jerusalem. [123]

In early 2005, Rice used the term 'outpost of tyranny' to refer to countries suspected to be a threat to human rights. Apart from Iraq, which other countries was Secretary Rice referring to? Iran might just be one of them, although she had been pushing hard diplomatic strategy with Iran.

Rice played a major role in ending the conflict between Israel and Lebanon. Rice, while attending to questioning, stated that status quo would not be the right path for the two countries. She suggested instead "The birth pangs of a new Middle East. And whatever we do we have to be certain that we're pushing forward to the new Middle East not going back to the old one." [124]

After the mini war began, she negotiated a 48 hour halt on Israel air-raids. The ceasefire began to take shape. The ceasefire was an opportunity to create a new environment in which Israel, Lebanon, and the party of

Hezbollah could all live in peace. On Fox News with the magnificent Bill O'Reilly, she elaborated,

> "We think it's very important that after these events are over that we will not have a return to the status quo ante, and so the United States is working for a ceasefire, for an end to the hostilities. And if we don't work for a ceasefire that will be lasting and enduring, then we're going to be right back here in several months talking about another ceasefire."

Finally, Rice shepherded the United Nations to pass a UN Security Council Resolution 1701 to officially end the conflict. [125]

The 2008 presidential election (February 07-December 07)

The mainstream media recognized Dr Rice as a powerful leader specifically because of her 'Transformation Diplomacy' policy. Throughout her service as the secretary of state, Condoleezza Rice has shown the utmost diplomacy.

Will President Bush put her in an even higher limelight? Can President Bush announce to America that Rice will be appointed vice president before the end of 2007? But there will only be one problem. Will Cheney be willing to give up his seat? Since Vice President Cheney and Sec. Rice don't really get along. Speculation has been rife that the Vice President will retire before the end of his term. If Rice is appointed as vice president, it will give her an advantage in becoming the 2008 GOP nominee. Rice will take African American votes from both Senator Clinton and Senator Obama. [126]

Apart from Thomas Jefferson, past presidents like James Monroe, John Adams, and James Madison were some of the state secretaries that occupied the White House in the 18th and 19th century.

If Sec. Rice runs for president and be successful, she will be the first secretary of state in the 21st century to occupy the White House. America knows that if Rice were elected president, America will be on top of the pile when it comes to terrorism. Rice brings vast experience in that area. She popularizes the notion that counterterrorism involves, in part, countering the extremist ideologies that drive global terrorism. Rice is the type of future president America needs in this era of terrorism.

Rice lectured: "We must defend ourselves against shadowy networks of stateless enemies. Securing America from terrorist attack is more than a matter of law enforcement. We must also confront the ideology of hatred in foreign societies by supporting the universal hope of liberty and the inherent appeal of democracy." [127]

For two consecutive years as the national security advisor and as state secretary, she was ranked as the most powerful woman in the world by Forbes magazine; and in 2006 she came up second in the same reading. When Rice became a Provost, she made it her goal to balance the budget at Stanford University. The school at that time was running a deficit of $20 million; and before the end of Rice's tenure, she announced that the deficit has been eliminated and the school was now holding a record surplus. For the past four years, Time magazine had endorsed her as one of only three people, more than three times, to be ranked among the world's most influential people. [128]

African Americans in all sections of the country have reprimanded Dr. Rice. Unprecedented attacks as been uttered against Rice. What is Secretary Rice's take on this? Well, Rice was a guest on Bill O'Reilly's program. O'Reilly asked "Does it hurt your feelings when some anti-Bush people say that you're a shill for him and sold out your race?" The secretary responded "Oh, come on. Why would I worry about something like that? Bill, the fact of the matter is I have been black all my life. Nobody needs to tell me how to be black." [129]

Prominent women in America

Rice is probably the most prominent woman in America; Hillary Clinton will give her more of a challenge for that honor than the junior senator from California.

During her confirmation hearing before the US Senate for the secretary of state position, Sen. Boxer wanted to hold Rice and the Bush's administration accountable for their failures in Iraq and in the war on terrorism. Boxer said that Rice's support for Bush and the war in Iraq "Overwhelmed her respect for the truth." Rice responded, "I have to say that I have never ever lost respect for the truth in the service of anything."

Madam Boxer, whose voting records in Congress was very consistent, eventually voted against Dr. Rice's confirmation. Senator Boxer (D-California) was the most popular female senator until the arrival of Hillary Clinton. Barbara Boxer had been in the US Senate since 1993.

In early 2007, Rice's second public criticism from Sen. Boxer came in a hearing before the senate Foreign Relations Committee to discuss the administration's position on Bush's Iraq surge plans. The California senator verbally attacked Madam Rice:

> "Now, the issue is who pays the price, who pays the price? I'm not going to pay a personal price. My kids are too old,

and my grandchild is too young. You're not going to pay a particular price, as I understand it, with immediate family. So who pays the price? The America military and their families, and I just want to bring us back to the fact."

White House Press Secretary Tony Snow considered this an attack on Rice's status as a single, childless female: "I don't think she was intentionally that tacky, but I do think its outrageous Boxer is sort of throwing little jabs because Condi doesn't have children, as if that means that she doesn't understand the concerns of parents. Great leap backward for feminism." Whether Rice fully comprehended the price of sending our troops to war or not, she responded to Boxer's cutting remarks: "I thought it was okay to be single. I thought it was okay to not have children, and I thought you could still make good decisions on behalf of the country if you were single and didn't have children." The senator from California responded by saying that her comment was taken out of context.[130]

After her appointment as Secretary of State, Condoleezza Rice sought to withdraw her commitment to the war in Iraq. A tiresome question was asked on how long U.S. troops would stay in Iraq. Sec. Rice hypothesized, "I think that even to try and speculate on how many years from now there will be a certain number of America forces is not appropriate." Rice proceeded, "I do believe that we are moving on a course on which Iraqi security forces are rather rapidly able to take care of their own security concerns." [131] Rice on NBC's Today Show said keeping Iraq stable would be "A long process of dealing with what the president called a long time ago a generational challenge to our security brought on by extremism, coming principally out of the Middle East." Another California Democrats, Rep. Nancy Pelosi weighed in. And she stressed that this kind of rhetoric coming from Secretary Rice meant that the White House was endorsing a 10 year "Open-ended commitment."

For many years to come, the United States will occupy Iraq.

The House Speaker said, "We need a new direction that redeploys our troops from Iraq, rebuilds our military, and refocuses on fighting terrorism across the world." It was fascinating that when Rice was appointed as the Secretary of State, it was an historical moment, but she wasn't really given that honor like Nancy Pelosi (D-California). Madam Pelosi became the first female in United States History to be elected as the Speaker of the House. She became the second in line to be president, overtaking Rice, who remained fourth in line to be president. [132]

Speaker Nancy Pelosi will not be the most powerful woman in the nation if Senator Clinton, Secretary Rice or Barbara Boxer becomes a president.

There is no doubt that President Bush and Secretary Rice are very close personal friends.

A question was asked to President Clinton as to how much effort the Bush administration made in going after Osama bin Laden before the September 11th attacks. Bill Clinton responded by accusing President Bush and other Republicans of ignoring Osama bin Laden until the actual attacks. Rice immediately came to Bush's defense. In an interview she stated that "What we did in the eight months 'before the terrorist attack' was at least as aggressive as what the Clinton administration did in the preceding years." Then Senator Clinton came out defending her husband:

> "I think my husband did a great job in demonstrating that Democrats are not going to take these attacks. You know, and I'm certain that if my husband and his national security team had been shown a classified report entitled 'Bin Laden determined to attack inside the United States' he would have taken it more seriously than history suggests it was taken by our current president and his national security team." [133]

Rice chafed at the Senator's statement and she countered, "The notion that somehow for eight months the Bush administration sat there and didn't do that is just flatly false." The back and forth then continued. "They had eight months to try. They did not try. I tried. So I tried and failed," Bill Clinton confessed. The former President further acknowledged that his administration's effort to capture al-Qaeda's Osama bin Laden before September 11th was practically more effective than that of his successor's administration.

The buck stops here. Bush made the following statement when asked to weigh in: "I've watched all this finger-pointing and naming of names and all that stuff but our objective is to secure the country." Bush continued, "And we've had investigations, we had the 9/11 commission, we had the look-back this, we had the look-back that. American people need to know that we spend all our time doing everything we can to protect them. I'm not going to comment on other comments." [134]

The 2008 presidential election (February 07-December 07)

So will Secretary of State Condoleezza Rice run or not? Dick Morris and Eileen McGann wrote a book in 2005. 'Condi vs. Hillary: The Next Great Presidential Race triggers our expectation for them to run.' Both Clinton and Rice have degrees political science. Hillary is already running but will Condoleezza run?

The Republicans would not be surprised in the least if Rice was nominated to take Cheney's place. In late 2007, Rice poured scorn on suggestions that she could run for the Oval Office when she was interviewed by highly influential commentator Sean Hannity.

Sean: Now I have the toughest question. You know, I know you don't want to talk about the political side of things, but you do know and you are aware and you read everything I'm sure you can get your hands on, that your name often comes up as somebody that -- at the top Republican candidates for president next year would consider as a vice presidential running mate. Would you ever consider that if asked by any of those candidates?

Rice: Sean, I think we've had this conversation a few times. I'm going to do everything --

Sean: That's why I saved the question for last.

State secretary Rice said her ambition was not the presidency. She tried to swerve away from the question but Mr. Hannity stuck to his question Sean continued: Would you rule it out completely if asked?

Rice: Sean, it's really not for me.

Sean: It's not -- being vice president?

Rice: It's not for me.

Sean: Well, that means under no circumstances?

Rice: Sean, we've had this conversation before. It's not for me. (Laughter.)

Sean: You can't blame me for trying. I mean that's my --

Rice: I know. I always expect you to try.

Rice eventually won't run for President 44, but will certainly be short listed as vice president for the 2008 Republican presidential nominee. And if the 44th president of America is a Democrat, Rice may be in the running for president 45. [135]

Chapter 7

21st Century: Newt Gingrich for American president

The 2008 presidential election (February 07-December 07)

Newt Gingrich will be a potential candidate for President 44 or 45; whether he will run for his country most prestigious position is still not a fact. Newt knows what it takes to be a top-ranking official of the United States. He is one of the modern day's most brilliant thinkers of the 20th-21st century. Newt is a Doctorate degree holder.

Newt was a history professor for eight years at University of West Georgia in Carrollton. And as a professor in the 1970's, he ran twice for the U.S House but was unsuccessful. In his third attempt, Newt finally won a seat in Congress. He overcame Representative Jack Flynt's choice to choose a state senator to run against Mr. Gingrich. Jack Flynt, a conservative Democrat decided not to run for reelection. When Congressman Flynt successfully ran twice against Gingrich, he felt the pressure coming from Mr. Gingrich. Newt became a member of U.S. House of Representatives from Georgia's 6th district. [136]

Ethics violations in Congress

Newt grew popular in the face of the Republican House members and had a big influence on the Republican Caucus. Newt and other House GOP members brought charges against Jim Wright, the Democratic Speaker of the House. The Speaker was believed to have used a book deal to evade House ethics rules: "It is vital that the Ethics Committee hire outside counsel and pursue these questions thoroughly. The trust of the public and the integrity of the House will accept no lower standard," was Newt Gingrich's comment on the charges brought against Speaker Jim Wright. Wright was prompted to resign from the speakership position. And Newt Gingrich was given all the credit for his effort in the inquiry that led to the resignation of the Speaker. [137]Towards the end of the eighties, Dick Cheney vacated his position as the minority whip. Newt's influence within the party enabled him to succeed Cheney. Newt as minority whip was the second most powerful Republican in the U.S. House. His growing popularity continued in the House and he was viewed in many circles as the GOP leader.

Because of the sense of an alleged corruption going on in Congress, Newt and a few other Republicans foresaw a deterioration of Congress and a serious tilt at winning the House. Following the resignation of Speaker Wright, the GOP uttered bitter complaints against the Democrats. In 1992, the Democrats were losing faith in the eyes of the American people because of the House banking scandal and the Congressional Post Office scandal. The two scandals led to a few convictions. In the House banking Scandal, over two-third of the members of the House of Representatives had overdrawn and abused their House checking accounts. And the Democratic Speaker of the House, Tom Foley, didn't effectively penalize its members. [138]

In early 90's the GOP envisioned a change of House takeover and they made Clinton's health care plan a major campaign issue during the forthcoming election. Gingrich was a co- author of the famous Contract with America. The Contract was a document detailing a major reform of the federal government. The contents of the contract included welfare reform, term limits, tougher crime laws, a balance budget law, restriction on American military participation in UN mission, and more. The Contract with America eventually turned out to be the answer for the Republicans taking over Congress. Gingrich was the main architect of his party's dramatic success in the 1994 midterm congressional election. Big shots like Tom DeLay and outside Capitol Hill support from Rush Limbaugh also had a big role in the Republican revolution. [139]

A Recap of the 1994 Congressional midterm elections

Senators are elected for six years while Representatives are elected for two years. All the 435 seats in the House of Representatives are up for reelection while only 33% of the 100 senators are up for election.

After the 1994 Midterm Election, the Republicans saw a net gain of 54 seats in the House. The election had become a major debacle for the Democratic Party. The "Republican revolution" gave the GOP 230 of the 435 House members while the Democrats ended with 204 House Members.

The Democrats might have to summon the genie out of the bottle, if they want to retake the House in the next election.

In the Senate, the upper chamber of Congress, the Republican Party won 8 seats and to the dismay of the Democratic Party, Richard Shelby changed his party affiliation from Democrat to Republican. The Alabama senator's defection left the Republican Party with 54 senate members with the Democrats settling with 46 members.

104th -105th United States Congress: January 1995 to January 1999

Newt Gingrich became the first Republican Speaker of the House after 40 years.

He finally broke a hoodoo that had been looming for 4 decade. He was the chief architect of the historical Republican revolution. The bicameral leaders of Congress were Dick Armey (R-Texas), who was elected as the majority leader and Tom DeLay (R-Texas), the majority whip. On the other side of the aisle, Richard Gephardt (D-Missouri) and David Bonior (D-Michigan) were the ranking leaders for the Democratic Party. The senate leadership was headed by World War II veteran Bob Dole (R-Kansas) and the majority whip position was occupied by Trent Lott (R-Mississippi). For the Democrats, Tom Daschle (D-South Dakota) was elected minority leader; he replaced Maine's George Mitchell. And Senator Wendell Ford (D-Kentucky) was elected as the minority whip. Senator Lott later replaced Bob Dole as the majority leader while Sen. Don Nickles (R-Oklahoma) replaced Sen. Lott as the majority whip. Bob Dole was forced to resign from Congress after he won the Republican nominee for the 1996 presidential election. [140]

Greatest Speaker of all times

Newt was elected as the 58th Speaker of the House of Representatives because Minority leader, Bob Michel (R-Illinois), did not run for reelection. This left Newt as the highest ranking Republican. Gingrich replaced Tom Foley (D-Washington), who was the speaker of the House before the election. Gingrich as Speaker of the House was the second in line to the President and the number one Republican official in the nation. The Republican revolution ended 4 decades of Democratic Party majority in the House. During Gingrich's time as the Speaker of the House, he ended the corruption in Congress that existed during the Wright-Foley Speakership. He represented the GOP when they opposed some of the Democratic President's policies. And his relationship with Bill Clinton was compared to former Speaker O'Neil political rivalry with President Reagan.[141] The tug of war between President Clinton and Speaker Gingrich led to the Federal government shutdown in the mid-nineties. The government's failure to meet funding measures resulted in the shutdown. After the President accepted the GOP budget proposal, Federal government agencies and departments were reopened. But the damage had already been done because it affected all the sectors of the economy. It was the longest federal government shutdown in the history of the country. [142]

Congress brought all ten of Gingrich's crafted Contracts with America to a vote within the so-called 'first 100 days of the session.' Most of the legislation was stalled up in the senate and of course vetoed by the Democratic President. Eventually most parts of the contract were enacted into law. President Clinton referred to the contract as the 'contract on America.' Newt Gingrich re-developed the policies that formed the Republican agenda and partisan was on the rise in the House of Representatives.

Newt, with his popularity among Republicans and conservatives, was said to be contemplating running for the 1996 presidential election. However, he declined to run and instead focused on keeping the Republican Party in control of Congress.

Speaker Gingrich will be known in American history as the greatest American Speaker of all time.[143]

Gingrich's leadership in the House didn't last long; the Speaker was accused of unethical behavior. He was alleged to have accepted an advance as part of a book deal. Eighty-four ethics charges were filed against Newt following a House Ethics Committee investigation. The Speaker was charged with violating tax laws, breaking House rules regarding favors for contributors, and abusing official resources to promote his political agenda. Gingrich firmly admitted that he had violated House ethic rules. He was punished, but the punishment didn't involve his immediate resignation as speaker of the House. To a great extent, the House Ethics committee didn't want his resignation. The Republican Party was defending Gingrich because he led them to power; he enforced strict discipline and loyalty within the party. But the Democratic Party was conflicted because many of its members had their own ethical shortcomings. And other Democrats also complained that the Republicans were stonewalling on the probe. If the resignation of Speaker Gingrich had occurred, Dick Armey would have been the next Speaker of the House. This could explain the reason why Armey, the Majority Leader, kept Newt in the dark about a coup that was waged against the Speaker.[144]

Coup d'état in Congress

In September 1997, just less than three years after Gingrich became House speaker; some GOP House members conspired against Newt in a coup. New York congressman, Rep. Bill Paxon, and other House GOP backroom members spearheaded the plot. Paxon, the House Republican NRCC chairman, urged the rebels to express their disapproval of the Speaker. They held secret meetings to discuss a rebellion against Speaker Gingrich. The plotters, who tried to usurp power, were to offer the Speaker an ultimatum to either voluntary resign or be voted out. They were also assured to accomplish enough votes if the 'voted out' option was rendered. If the plan succeeded, Paxon would position himself as the new speaker of the House. That eventually didn't happen, because there were disagreements within the coup plotter's inner circle. So the coup went sour and Bill Paxon, the leader of the Coup d'état attempt, was axed from his House Republican leadership position. Congressman Paxon was the scapegoat for the rest of the coup planners. Rep. Paxon won reelection five times in the House and was considered one of Newt Gingrich's lieutenants.

The ranking Republican leaders apologized to Newt Gingrich and to the senior members of the Republican Party for the revolt against their leader. They were informed about the uprising against the Speaker. One of Gingrich's supporters spoke out and said, "The leaders admitted that they sat and listened and some of them entertained hypothetical." Gingrich's supporters advised the Speaker to have a no-confidence vote against Tom DeLay, the majority whip, Richard Armey, the majority leader, and John Boehner, the republican conference chairman. But Gingrich turned down their request and he worked on unifying the party: "Bless those who persecute you. Bless and do not curse them," Gingrich quoted. DeLay's career was rumored to be coming to an end in the aftermath of the coup. When asked again if he was going to strip DeLay, Armey, and Boehner of their leadership positions, Gingrich digressed from the question and said "Let me emphasize; I will not allow another chapter to be written in this tiresome and overwrought saga." In the aftermath of the failed Coup d'état, DeLay and Armey straightened things out with the Speaker and they worked to re-establish trust in the party. [145]

The following year arrived, the year of the Monica Lewinsky scandal and the year of the midterm election. Gingrich had become a highly polarizing figure among his colleagues in Congress and the Republican voters in America. And the Democratic Party capitalized on that scenario. Newt tried to reestablish himself as the true leader for the Republicans. With the election looming, he focused on the perjury charges against President Clinton. The Republicans were adamant they would win more seats in the House. But after the elections, Newt was faulted for his party losing 5 seats in the House, which cumulated in his resignation. Newt Gingrich expected resignation as speaker of the House came right before the dawning of the new millennium. Although he had been reelected to an 11th term in Congress, he declined to serve. [146]

Gingrich was reelected ten times. He was only reelected six times in his original 6th district because of the United States Census. Other than the loss of respect from his colleagues in Congress, Newt knew that there was no support from the GOP caucus; via returning back to Congress as the Speaker. His House peers and the Republican caucus reprimanded him because he wasn't able to lead the GOP to rescale the heights of their remarkable 1994 midterm election victory. Newt took his loss up and out of the speaker's seat, out of the floor of the House, and finally out of the doors of the congressional building. Gingrich's resignation left the GOP facing *a dearth of true leadership*. Time magazine selected Newt Gingrich as the man of the year for his role in the Republican revolution. [147]

A Recap of the 1998 midterm election

After the midterm elections of 1998, the GOP lost five seats to the Democratic Party in the House. It was an alarmingly poor performance from the Republican Party, which had changed the history book of Congress. They still had the majority in the House, but with a narrow margin. The Republicans attacked the morality of the President. But it resulted in a backlash against the Republican Party. Speaker Gingrich announced his resignation from Congress. In the senate, Al D'Amato, the senator from New York, lost his reelection bid.

106th – 107th United States Congress: January 1999 to January 2003

Newt Gingrich stepped down as the Speaker of the House and because the GOP was still in control of the House, fellow Republican Dennis Hastert (R- Illinois) replaced him. Both Dick Armey and Tom DeLay retained their leadership positions. Dick Gephardt of Missouri remained as the minority leader and Michigan's David Bonior as the minority whip. However, in the 2000 elections, Gephardt and Bonior both resigned from their leadership position, giving others a chance to rule. Nancy Pelosi (D-California) and Steny Hoyer (D- Maryland) were the two new faces for the Democratic leadership. Rep. Gephardt was said to have stepped down from his leadership position in order to concentrate on a possible run for president in 2004.

In the Senate, Trent Lott kept his Senate majority leader position seat and Tom Daschle retained his minority leader seat. After the 2000 elections, both parties had 50 senators. But since the Vice President was from the Republican Party, the Vice President had the tie-breaking vote in favor of the Republican Party. However, on June 6 2001, seven months after the start of the 107th Congress, Senator James Jeffords (R-Vermont) changed his party affiliation from Republican to Independent. And he caucused with the Democrats. This change gave the Democratic Party the slim majority of 51 caucus members and the right to control the senate; leaving the Republicans with 49 caucus members.   There was a change of party leadership position from Sen. Lott's senate majority leader to Sen. Lott's senate minority leader. The reverse went for Senator Daschle. Don Nickles started as the majority whip but ended as the minority whip while Harry Reid (D-Nevada) started as the minority whip and ended that congressional session as the majority whip. [148]

The lame duck session for the US president is when a sitting president loses his reelection bid and is due to leave office. For example, President Walker Bush's last two months in office (November 1992-January 1993). The whole presidency of a second term president is also considered 'lame duck,' for example, the 106th and the 107th congressional era of William Clinton as president.

George Bush took over from President Clinton in this particular era. And Senator Lott was forced by President Bush to resign from his party's leadership position because of the pro-segregation comments he uttered at Senator Storm Thurmond's 100th birthday ceremony. President George Bush's displeasure with Senator Lott started when Senator Lott endorsed Rep. Jack Kemp over Walker Bush for president in the 1988 presidential election. And in 2003, their relationship had deteriorated when Lott spoke out against an FCC rule.

In Congress, the 'lame duck' session for House and Senate members who lost their reelection bid only lasts for two months.

Newt Gingrich never officially had a 'lame duck' session because he won his reelection bid and announced his retirement.[149]

Most innovative thinker

After his time in Congress, Gingrich has maintained a career as a political analyst, consultant, and prolific author.

What all Americans are waiting for is his ambition to run for president. Gingrich, the conservatism's brain, has expressed interest in being a candidate for the 2008 Republican nomination for president.

After the released of winning the future, a 21ˢᵗ Century Contract with America book; he made several trips to the early primary electing states to discuss his book. For four decades, the state of New Hampshire had been the first real test of a presidential candidate's legitimacy. The winner of the New Hampshire primary elections from 1952 to 1988 went on to win the presidency.

Iowa and South Carolina are also important early primary voting states. The early primary results indicated how a presidential candidate gets along in retail politics. Retail politics "Is a type of political campaigning in which the candidate focuses on local events and meeting individual voters" and is "The old-fashioned shaking hands and kissing babies" {Reference dictionary .com.}[150]

Newt Gingrich also has another book titled 'A Contract with the Earth,' released in 2007. The book is about his environmental ideas and his take on global warning. Wondering how many more contracts are left in Newt's stash? Maybe his next contract will be called 'Contract to be President.'

Just like in 1996, Newt has been mooted as a possible candidate for president. And in 2006, supporters of Newt Gingrich formed a grassroots movement to support a possible run for the presidency. In Early 2007, when Newt Gingrich was interviewed by Tim Russert on 'Meet the Press,' he further acknowledged that he might be running for president. But in mid 2007, the Speaker remained coy about whether he would run for the Oval Office. [151]

During the Monica Lewinsky scandal, Newt was the Speaker of the House. He was reported to have somehow laid low in the case of impeachment because he was also having an affair. "Let the one without sin cast the first stone." However, he eventually wedded the friend, so we should erase the term 'hypocrisy' on Newt's resume because he married the friend unlike President Clinton, who didn't marry Lewinsky. Newt Gingrich also turned born-again. He said, "There are things in my own life that I have turned to God and have gotten on my knees and prayed about and sought God Forgiveness." [152]

Since Newt's Speakership ended, he supported a guest workers program for Mexican citizens. Mexican citizens would be allowed to come into the United States and work for a period of time, then return back to their country. Newt Gingrich, a statesman from Georgia, emphasized that "The government should quit mandating that various documents be printed in any one of 700 languages depending on who randomly shows up" to cast their vote. Newt Gingrich allegedly compared bilingual education with ghetto language: "The American people believe English should be the official language of the government. We should replace bilingual education with immersion in English so people learn the common language of the country and they learn the language of prosperity, not language of living in a ghetto." He ridiculed government consideration that ballots for voting should be printed in different languages: "Citizenship requires passing a test on American history in English. If that's true, then we do not have to create ballots in any language except English" he said. Supporters of bilingual education criticized the former Speaker. [153]

Newt Gingrich is a senior fellow at the conservative think tank American Enterprise Institute. Newt is also a contributor at Fox news Channel. Newt Gingrich plays very close to influential commentator, Sean Hannity. Gingrich is often featured on Sean Hannity's show. In Atlanta, Georgia, they host a program together called 'solution day' to take back our government. [154]

The former Speaker cited the war in Iraq, "The way we are waging the war, not the war itself," the failed federal government response to Hurricane Katrina in New Orleans and the rise of illegal immigrant due to lack of border control were grounds for the belief that changes in the systems of federal, state, and local government were needed. Gingrich said to reporters, "Now that may or may not make the White House happy. But I think that's the whole point about making a clean break."

Gingrich made it clear that he wasn't calling out President Bush, but he happened to be the leader of an ineffective government. He did called Bush "A very decent man who believes very deeply in what he is doing."

The 2008 presidential election (February 07-December 07)

Newt said in respect to the GOP 2008 presidential candidates, "I believe for any Republican to win in 2008, they have to offer a dramatic, bold change. If we nominate somebody who has not done that, they get to be the nominee but there is very, very little likelihood that they can win." Newt Gingrich has advised the GOP candidates and at the same time, he had voiced criticism against the Republican candidates on many fundamental issues. Acting as the god father for the GOP presidential candidates, Newt Gingrich maintained he wasn't happy with the candidates at his disposal going into the general election. The former Speaker dismissed the Republican presidential field as a "pathetic" group of "pygmies." Mr. Gingrich urged the GOP candidates to master the ideas in his 21st century contract with America. He said that there were circumstances under which he would run. He stressed that those circumstances would be if the GOP candidates don't heed to his platform ideas "They need a bold agenda to overcome Hillary" (a paraphrase.) [155]

By late 2007, Speaker Gingrich may enter the race because it seems the GOP candidates aren't heeding the conservative platform. It will be good news to many Republicans. Newt will be a counterbalance to the Democrats who also wish that Vice President Al Gore would run too.

Gingrich ridiculed the GOP candidates for being subjected to a presidential debate moderated by MSNBC's star Chris Matthews. And he found it absurd for GOP candidates to stand "passively at microphones" waiting to be called upon. Newt refused to "Shrink to the level of 40-second answers, standing like a trained seal, waiting for someone to throw me a fish."

Newt Gingrich is the only GOP potential candidates that can set a high standard for the 2008 election. Other than Rush Limbaugh, no notable political figures articulate the conservative ideas better than the former Speaker.

A Gingrich for president supporter said, "If America wants to judge the competence and substance of a presidential candidate, they should debate Gingrich."

When responding to questioning, Newt rejected the notion that his political baggage will stand in his way to becoming president {Examiner.com July, 2007}. Newt says Senator Hillary Clinton has an 80% chance to win the presidency and that also includes him.

Mr. Gingrich scoffed at McCain's Campaign Reform Act of 2002. Gingrich said eloquently, "I have no interest in trying to figure out how I can go out and raise money under John McCain's insane censorship rules so I can show up to do seven minutes and twenty seconds at some debate." McCain lunched back at the Speaker, "I see the former member of the House of Representatives as a person who has many, many comments to make and he's made many, many comments critical of me in the past. We had a fundamental disagreement about the role of money in politics." If the ex Speaker runs for the White House, McCain would look forward to pitting his wits against Newt for the nod to become the GOP nominee.

The Campaign Reform Act, co-sponsored with Russ Feingold, limits the amount of money that can be raise by candidates running for a federal office.

A big blow for the true conservative voters, Mr. Gingrich finally rejected a 2008 presidential bid that has been looming since 2006.

The Speaker indicated that he is working on a grass roots change in how the nation is governed, with more bipartisanship. But the goal would take about five years to fully develop. This means that Gingrich will definitely run in 2012; depending on which party has the incumbent president. Newt Gingrich is also short-listed as a possible vice president nominee in the 2008 general election.

Speaker Gingrich is one of the most innovative and brilliant thinkers in modern times; a fact that has been admitted by the conservatives and the liberals. By and large, most Republicans label Gingrich as the most engaging and most innovating thinker in America. [156]

Chapter 8

21ˢᵗ Century: John McCain for American president

The 2008 presidential election (February 07-December 07)

What hasn't John McCain achieved? He is a decorated war Veteran, a former US congressman, and a US senator. Could John McCain be a President of the United States of America? Hasn't John reaped? Isn't it time for him to sow?

McCain was born in Panama. His citizenship was assured at birth by jus sanguinis, and jus soli.

Jus sanguinis is "A rule that a child's citizenship is determined by its parents' citizenship" and jus soli is "A rule that the citizenship of a child is determined by the place of his birth" {Merriam-Webster's Online Dictionary}. [157]

28ᵗʰ Amendment in the making

McCain is eligible to be elected to the presidency, unlike made- politicians like California State governor Schwarzenegger and famous former Mayor of Cincinnati Jerry Springer.

Article 2, Section 1 of the US Constitution stated: "No person except a natural –born Citizen or a Citizen of the United States at the time of the Adoption of this Constitution shall be eligible to the Office of President;

neither shall any Person be eligible to that office who shall not have attained to the Age of thirty-five years."

Efforts to guarantee equal right to naturalize citizens have been pushed by lawmakers. In 2003, Orrin Hatch put forward a constitutional amendment that would disable Article 2, Section 1 of Constitution.

Naturalized citizens are prohibited from holding the office of the president. That position is only reserved for natural born citizens. Former secretaries of state Henry Kissinger, Madeleine Albright, and Michigan's Governor Jennifer Granholm are other dignitaries that can't run for president.

Orrin Hatch, a Republican senior senator from Utah, proposed the 'Equal Right to Govern Amendment.' The senator co-sponsor bill was seen as a stepping-stone for naturalized citizens to be able to run for the presidency. Hatch, a close associate to the governor of California, said any foreign-born American citizen should be given the green light for a shot at the presidency. Gov. Schwarzenegger also added "There are so many people in this country that are now from overseas, that are immigrants, that are doing such a terrific job with their, bringing businesses here, that there's no reason why not." Schwarzenegger referred to past secretaries of state Henry Kissinger and Madeleine Albright, and their major contributions to the country. [158]

McCain a POW- Veteran

John McCain started his career as a Navy Aviator. John has this pedigree or family tree associated for serving the country. His father was a U.S. Navy admiral. His grandfather was also a U.S. Navy admiral. John entered the United States Naval Academy and graduated with a Bachelor of Science degree prior to the end of the fifties. McCain went on to be trained as a naval aviator. He later graduated and became a naval light attack pilot. John was part of the trip to Vietnam. In 1967, while serving in Vietnam, he was almost killed. When his crew was preparing to lunch an attack, a rocket struck McCain's A-4E Skyhawk at the coast of Vietnam. He climbed out of the cockpit of the jet and upon looking for safety, a bomb exploded and a fragment from the bomb struck John's chest and leg. The aftermath of the explosion killed many sailors and destroyed a number of aircrafts, but could not kill John. The death toll was reported to be at 200.

Only five months after the first tragedy, death again came toward John's side. An enemy missile shot down McCain's Skyhawk. This time around, John broke one of his legs and both of his arms. John was meant to be a survival of crashing Skyhawks. Unfortunately, he was surrounded by anti-American troops. They roughed him up and stripped him of his clothing.

The enemies, who were soldiers from North Vietnam, had introduced to John to the expected treatment of becoming a prisoner. Thereafter, McCain was severely tortured. They crushed his shoulder with the use of a projected blade in the form of a rifle, and pinned it on his abdominal area and on his foot. After afflicting him with so much pain, he was now taken in as a prisoner of war (POW).

As a POW, he was daily interrogated and rigorously beaten. Time after time, McCain stonewalled the Vietnam soldiers. He refused to provide any information they needed. While he was a prisoner, John's father commanded American forces in Vietnam. McCain turned down an opportunity to return home because he wanted every prior POW to also be released. He continued to be tortured and in the long run, he was unable to raise his arms above his head. In a nutshell, John spent a total of five years and six months as a POW. Two of those five plus years he spent in a solitary confinement. After he was released as a prisoner of war, he still went back to serve his country for another nine years. He finally retired from the Navy in the early eighties as a Captain. During his military career, he received a Silver Star, a Bronze Star, the Purple Heart, and the Legion of Merit. [159]

In the early eighties, McCain served has a member of US House of Representatives from Arizona's first district. He succeeded John Rhodes, a long serving GOP congressman. And toward the end of the eighties, popular US Senator Barry Goldwater stepped down from his senate seat and was replaced by John McCain. John later grew to be as popular as Goldwater.

At least the state of Arizona can boast of having 2 great senators.

In the United States Senate, senators strived for longevity.

Senator John Kerry has more seniority than Senator McCain in Congress. They are both decorated veterans. The senate comprises of many war veterans. Most notable are Arlen Specter (R-Pennsylvania) who served in the Korean War and Ted Stevens (R- Alaska) the former president *pro tempore* served in World War II. Another World War II Republican senator is Virginia's John Warner. And Warner's fellow Virginian senate serving partner Jim Webb is a decorated Vietnam War combat veteran. Webb, the Republican turned Democratic senator, bested popular Republican senator George Allen in the 2006 midterm election. Another Vietnam War veteran in Congress is Chuck Hagel. The moderate Republican senator is said to be making a run as a 3rd party candidate for president in the 2008 election. But he is considering being a running mate to New York City's Mayor, Michael Bloomberg. There are three other World War II veterans in the 110th Congress. [160]

Going back into 20th century, an archive of late Barry Goldwater

Senator Goldwater was a libertarian Republican politician and a true original conservative politician. He served the nation and rose to the rank of Major General. Barry Goldwater differed with the Religious Right on the issue of abortion.

Goldwater was an anti-communism activist. This was during the height of the Cold War between the United States and the Soviet Union. Senator Goldwater was a five-term US senator from Arizona and the Republican Party's nominee for president in the 1964 election. In the primary election of 1964, his chief rival was Nelson Rockefeller, the former moderate governor of New York. His foreign policy stance was attacked by his chief challenger in the 1964 primary election and by the incumbent president in the general election. Because of his foreign policy stance, he lost the 64 election by a landslide to LB Johnson. Senator Goldwater also strongly opposed liberalism; the incumbent president called him a reactionary. [161]

A possible nuclear war was said to be the route taken by Sen. Goldwater if he was elected as president. He was responsible for Nixon's resignation after the Watergate Scandal was uncovered. Goldwater called for Nixon to step down. The former senator from Arizona led the conservative movement in the 1960's. He continued the role vacated by Ohio's senator, Robert Taft. Goldwater redefined the conservative movement. He condemned Jimmy Carter's presidency because Carter was associated with communism. Goldwater praised Reagan's presidency, but wasn't pleased with the Iran-Contra scandal. Goldwater, the three star general, was known as the father of modern day conservatism. [162]

Toward the end of the nineties, Senator John McCain entered the race as a presidential candidate. Reports from his New Hampshire campaign camp asserted that McCain made more than 200 stops during his campaign visit. His efforts paid off and he won the State primary by 49-30 over Governor Bush. However, McCain lost South Carolina, allowing Bush to regain his lead over him. Visualizing McCain winning South Carolina would have definitely given McCain the 2000 Republican presidential nominee.

McCain campaign came abruptly to an end when he lost 9 of the 13 primaries on Super Tuesday. McCain never really recovered from his loss in South Carolina and never recovered from the alleged gimmicks of Karl Rove. The former White House Deputy Chief of Staff, Karl Rove, who was often referred as 'Turd Blossom,' was said to have dispatched false messages. "Would you be more likely or less likely to vote for John McCain for president if you knew he had fathered an illegitimate black child?" The message implied that

John had a black child out of wedlock. The strategy poisoned the minds of conservative voters. [163]

Aftermath of the 2000 primary

Who does the Republican Establishment really want to endorse: a moderate Republican senator like John McCain, or a conservative Republican governor like George Bush?

The result of the 2000 Republican primary had split U.S. senators in the Republican Party. Independent reformers identified themselves with the Arizona statesman, while the conservative Republican senators identified themselves with Gov. Bush. In 2001, there were rumors from Capitol Hill that McCain was on the verge of changing his party affiliation from Republican to Independent. He allegedly held private meetings with Democratic senators Tom Daschle, John Edwards, and Ted Kennedy. Later, McCain rubbished the reports that he was on the verge of switching his party affiliation. The Senator insisted he never entertained the idea of leaving the GOP. [164]

During the next presidential election in 2004, John McCain could not run because the incumbent president was from the GOP. So John supported the incumbent president. McCain's endorsement brought renewed enthusiasm to the Bush-Cheney ticket. McCain turned down an opportunity to be a vice president nominee. Senator John Kerry, the Democratic presidential nominee, repeatedly asked John McCain, a Republican, to run as his running mate (vice president) in the 2004 election. If John McCain had taken that offer, Kerry would have stood a chance to win the 2004 presidential election. After John Kerry was swift boated during the 2004 election, McCain went on 'Amy Goodman's show' and backed the Massachusetts senator by stating: "I have said the campaigning against his war record, the 'Swift Boat' ads on his records in combat was dishonorable and dishonest because I believe he served honorably." [165]

According to McCain's voting records, he has not been consistent.

In early 2000, McCain had a moderate voting record. By the 2002 midterm election, his voting records leaned towards the conservative platform. After the war in Iraq, it seems John McCain was leaning towards the moderate point of view. He loses supports from the conservative base. And after the midterm election of 2006 and the February 2007 'troop surge' in Iraq, the senator voting record was generally conservative. [166]

In February of 07, the maverick senator from Arizona made clear his intention in running for the presidency.

With McCain's popularity among many Americans and all his efforts he put in as a Navy Captain, John McCain should be handed that position as the president of our country. What else do we want him to do?

McCain was the chairman of the senate Indian affairs committee during the D.C lobbying scandal. His Chairmanship helped in exposing Jack Abramoff and others. Conrad burns, a senator from Montana, lost his reelection because of his ties with Abramoff. In 1997 McCain was named by Time as one of the '25 most influential people in America.'[167]

When the host of Daily Show, Jon Stewart, hosted the senator, John McCain joked about an improvised explosive device (IED). After being subjected to severe questioning by the host, McCain jokingly told Jon Stewart that he had a present for him: "I think maybe shopping in Baghdad…. I have something picked out for you, too- a little IEDs to put on your desk." The next day, Rep. John Murtha was furious and he publicly assailed McCain on the House floor. While salivating for an apology from McCain, Rep. Murtha stressed, "Imagine a presidential candidate making a joke about IEDs when our kids are getting blown up." AA2.0's Randi Rhodes, another political figure that has served the nation also severely chastised the senator. McCain responded, "I don't know how to react to that kind of hysteria to a comedy show. All I'm going to say to Murtha and others is to lighten up and get a life."[168]

The 2008 presidential election (February 07-December 07)

As for the 2008 presidential election, McCain may find Bush's endorsement detrimental to his candidacy, but it is vital that John McCain get in touch with the conservative base; that is where he will get his support. McCain needs a support from Rush Limbaugh and Sean Hannity. Any support from one of them may give McCain a chance to win the presidency.

In 2000, Rush Limbaugh supported Bush over McCain. Senator McCain's supporters have called on Mr. Limbaugh to support McCain because McCain supported Bush's surge plan of troops in Iraq. And McCain previously endorsed Bush in the last presidential election.

Rush will be applying a double standard against McCain if he doesn't support the senator in the Republican primaries.

In 2004 McCain referred to Mr. Limbaugh as an "entertainer," completely disrespecting the leader of the conservative movement. [169]

Throughout 2007, John McCain has been campaigning for the coming 2008 election. Being that he is a senator, he hasn't spent much time in Congress as he seeks the GOP presidential nomination. But in a rare Senate appearance, guess who wants to put up a fight with McCain? John Cornyn, the junior US senator from Texas, one of Bush's royalties and one of Karl Rove's breeds.

Cornyn attempted to challenge John McCain during a meeting on immigration legislation. John McCain, who was probably frustrated about the polls that showed him in third place way below Mayor Giuliani and Gov Romney, wasn't in the mood to argue with the senator from Texas. Senator Cornyn started talking loudly to McCain concerning the number of judicial appeals illegal immigrants should get. According to sources, John McCain used unorthodox and obscene language: "…I know more about this than anyone else in this room," shouted McCain at the senator from Texas. Senator Cornyn countered, "Wait a second here I have been sitting in here for all of these negotiations and you just parachute in here on the last day you are out of line." [170]

Do Americans torture?

In 2005, John McCain introduced a bill that passed through the House and the Senate. The Senate voted 90-9 to support the bill. And the President issued a signing statement. Bush accepted the bill because it banned the use of "Cruel, inhuman, and degrading treatment" by U.S. people anywhere in the world. The bill also forbid U.S. Military interrogators from using interrogation techniques not listed in the 'FM 34-52 U.S. Army Field Manuel' on Interrogation. The bill was titled the 'McCain Detainee Amendment.'

No matter how effective John McCain's amendment is, there will always be a loophole.

Over his tenure in the senate, McCain reached across party lines and co sponsored bills with Democratic senators Russ Feingold, Joe Lieberman, and Ted Kennedy.

McCain made it clear that he is against torture. It's conventional wisdom that if we torture, the people that are holding our soldiers captive will torture us more. John McCain is also against rendition. Rendition is surrender or handing over of persons, criminal suspects or terrorists. Rendition is also the act of rendering i.e. kidnapping and sending people to other countries to be tortured, so that we can still maintain that we don't torture. If suspects speak out too much, they may be labeled as terrorists and be immediately rendered to countries where torture during interrogation is still practice; like one of our eastern European prisons that officially don't exist. [171]

John McCain has also called water boarding torture: "I have sought that result for years. Water-boarding is a form of torture. And I'm convinced that this will not only help us in our interrogation techniques, but it will also be helpful for our image in the world." Water boarding was a harsh interrogation method that simulates drowning. Towards the end of 2007, the CIA Director Gen. Michael Hayden had banned the controversial interrogation technique. [172]

The 2008 presidential election (February 07-December 07)

Sen. McCain has already set in motion the 'Straight Talk Express,' the campaign conveyance the senator used during his last presidential race: "I'm still the same candidate I was, little bit older, but still the same candidate. We are still having fun. We are still on the bus, still having the town hall meetings in the same way that we were before, and am convinced we're doing fine." Media big shot Randi Rhodes claimed that "John McCain is the only original candidate from the bunch of GOP candidates that is qualified to be the next president of America" (a paraphrase). "He is the only person that says what he means," Rhodes acknowledged, although over the years Ms. Rhodes had chastised McCain by claming that the "Straight talk express has gone over the cliff." In late September 2007 during his presidential campaign McCain came out with a 'No surrender tour' in the States of Iowa, New Hampshire, and South Carolina. McCain ended his speech by saying, "The transcendent issue of this campaign will be this conflict we are in between good and evil, between the forces of radical Islam and extremists that are trying to destroyed America and everything we believe in. I'm qualified I know the face of war. I know the face of evil. I will win. We will win".

'Straight Talk Express' still remains his number one campaign conveyance.

McCain had been advocating that Americans couldn't lose the war in Iraq. And he made it clear that he criticized President Bush on the war long before the 'surge' was implemented. The senator has visited Iraq on numerous occasions. [173]

Polls show that John McCain is the most famous GOP candidate for the 2008 presidential election. His national name recognition is a huge advantage for him.

He filled the vacancy left by Goldwater, one of the greatest names in our history. For crying out loud, McCain was an American war veteran. He was captured as prisoner of war, and was occasionally beaten to a bloody pulp, yet he denied his captors valid top information.

It is conventional wisdom that John should be the GOP nominee for the presidential election. And how many Americans won't buy that conventional wisdom? Maybe Americans should endorse any war veteran; what more do we want them to do?

John McCain is talking about Alabama governor Bob Riley as a possible running mate in the 2008 election. John, if elected, will make history as the first president of America to be born outside the 50 states. However, he is allowed to serve if he wins. What about a possible running mate with the governor of California?

Governor Schwarzenegger was not born in America; the US Constitution prohibits a foreign born to be a vice president. The12[th] amendment stated: "No person constitutionally ineligible to the office of president shall be eligible to that of Vice President of the United States."

If the 12th Amendment can be reversed, Gov. Schwarzenegger will really be a success for Senator McCain. On the other hand, with support from Rush Limbaugh, Sean Hannity, and John McCain's 'straight talk express', all sales are final; whether it is Hillary or Obama. [174]

Age is nothing but a number. John may be the oldest president ever in the history of the United States if he gets the presidency. McCain is strong and durable, if he can last another eight years in the US Senate, why can't he last four years as president starting from his inauguration? Reports in 2005 showed that McCain's health is excellent, not at all a concern. [175]

Chapter 9

21ˢᵗ Century: Hillary Rodham Clinton for American president

The 2008 presidential election (February 07-December 07)

Clinton is the junior senator from New York State. She is originally from Illinois. The State of Arkansas is also a Democratic stronghold for Hillary Clinton. So in the legislative branch of government, she is allowed to run for office in any of those mentioned states. However, in the executive branch, she can run in any state, whether she is from Bush's Texas or Cheney's Wyoming, for president. Clinton will remain the main Democratic candidate for president 44 pending the primaries. Whomsoever her main challenger is in the Republican Party, she has an edge over any Republican nominee.

What Rodham has achieved on her own without using that famous name 'Clinton' was very mind-boggling.

A perfect role model: some important achievements of Hillary Rodham/ Hillary Clinton

She was the first student speaker in the history of Wellesley College to deliver their first commencement exercises. Arkansas' Rosa law Firm named her as their first female partner. And for two years, she was named by National law journal as one of the most influential lawyers in America. She eventually became First Lady to the then governor of Arkansas. And she made it to the White House as a First Lady of the United States. She was also the one and only First Lady to be elected as a US senator. She opened the gates for prominent women like Laura Bush and Lynne Cheney to ponder about that fact. [176]

Hillary Clinton biography

Hillary was bred in a conservative Christian family. She revealed that she wanted to run to Africa because of her father's conservative beliefs. But she opted to stay and continue in the conservative tradition. And in 1964, she supported the Republican nominee for president. Wellesley College was where she earned her bachelor's degree; her discipline was in the field of Political Science. She was politically involved in college activities while she was a student at Wellesley College. She was converted from a Republican to a Democrat because of two likely reasons. One, she was against the war in Vietnam and became an anti-war supporter for the presidential campaign of Eugene McCarthy. And two, the death of Martin Luther King Jr. She believed in civil right for all Americans. By the early seventies, Hillary was now a leaning Democrat. She again campaigned for the famous George McGovern for the Democratic candidate for President. [177]

Going back into 20th century; an Archive of George McGovern

George McGovern was the grassroots people's choice for president in the 1974 election. The South Dakota statesman served in the House of Representatives and in the US Senate. McGovern was a decorated combat veteran who served in World War II. Govern redesigned the nomination processing system. This was after the disorderly convention of 1968. The 1968 Democratic nomination convention between presidential candidates McCarthy and Humphrey, witnessed an unprecedented primary elections. The presidential nominee didn't win any primaries. These changes were to allow primaries not caucused to decide the conventional delegates to choose the Democratic nomination for president; thus limiting the power of state leaders. The McGovern-Fraser commission established rules that would enable more minority group representatives and activists to participate in party functions. George McGovern surprisingly won the Democratic presidential nominee in 1972. His main opponents in the Democratic primary election were old rivals Senator Eugene McCarthy and Vice President Hubert Humphrey. The Democratic rank and file favored Humphrey, but the anti-war voters favored McGovern. Because McGovern had an experience as a veteran, he was totally against the Vietnam War. He turned his campaign into an anti-war crusade against Nixon. But he eventually lost the general election by a large margin to the incumbent. He supported Amnesty and abortion rights. He also ran for president again in 1984. [178]

After graduating from Wellesley, Hillary enrolled and graduated from Yale Law School and began her career as a lawyer. Hillary was now based at Washington, D.C., and she was a member of the impeachment inquiry staff in DC advising lawmakers on Capitol Hill during the famous Watergate scandal. She was very effective in campaigning for her husband's governor race in Arkansas and for the Democratic presidential campaign of Jimmy Carter. This time around both elections yielded a positive result, in retrospect for her efforts in supporting McCarthy and McGovern. Hillary was Arkansas's First Lady and at the same time she was appointed to the board of directors of the Legal Service Corporation by Carter's administration. She was the chair of the board until the end of President Carter's presidency.

In the early nineties, during the presidential campaign for her husband, Bill Clinton stated that if he were elected, American voters would get 'two for the price of one.' Bill Clinton visualized the role Hillary would assume. Bill Clinton successfully won the election and was America's next president while Hillary continued practicing law. [179]

Greatest First Lady of all times

While she was the country's First Lady in Bill Clinton's administration, Hillary played a prominent role in public policy issues. She was highly criticized by the Republicans because of her unprecedented duties as a first lady. Well, it was the sign of the times that 'two for the price of one' was the talking issue for many conservatives who referred to the Clintons as co-presidents, a co-presidency, or Billary, whichever pleased them. Hillary succeeded in establishing the children's health insurance program. However, the Democratic control U.S. Congress turned down her main initiative, the Clinton health care plan. [180]

If the well-orchestrated health care plan would have pass, it would give employees the privilege of receiving health coverage from their employers through individual health organizations.

When a citizen complained that she didn't want to get pushed into a plan not of her interest, the First Lady lectured, "It's time to put the common good, the national interest, ahead of individuals." When Hillary was told that the health care plan could bankrupt small businesses, Mrs. Clinton sighed "I can't be responsible for every undercapitalized small business in America." She blamed her failed health care plan on her political inexperience.

Is health care a right or a privilege? Conservatives claim that health care is a privilege while liberals claim that health care should be a right, not a privilege. Hillary Clinton might get to decide which is which. By and large, Hillary wants universal health care for all Americans. [181]

The First Lady worked with then Attorney General Janet Reno to create the office on Violence Against Women in the Justice Department. She was one of the well-recognized women in the world. She was very outspoken against radical Islamist groups in Afghanistan on how they treated the afghan women. And Hillary said the US would work to secure the rights of women in Afghanistan. [182]

Toward the end of President Bill Clinton's term as president, there was a senate seat in the state of New York that was going to be vacated at the end of the congressional session. First Lady Clinton looked at the opportunity to advance her political career and she pondered running for the open seat. Well, Senator Boxer, the junior senator from California, and also an in-law relative to Hillary Clinton, 'built a bridge' for Hillary to meet with Sen. Moynihan, the out-going senior senator from New York. On NBC's Meet the Press, Senator Moynihan said, "That New York could uses some of Hillary Clinton's magnificent, young, bright, able, Illinois-Arkansas enthusiasm" in the U.S. Senate and "She would be welcome and she would win." Moynihan praise to Hillary was kind of fascinating; he was one of the most outspoken critics of the health care plan well crafted by the First Lady. [183]

The unsettled First Lady finally found refuge in New York. Rodham Clinton became the first First Lady to be elected into the U.S. Senate. This legally happened after the Clintons purchased a home in Chappaqua., New York. Hillary Clinton was supposed to face Mayor Giuliani, the then Mayor of New York City. But fortunately for Mrs. Clinton, Giuliani sustained a health problem and Congressman Lazio took the spot. At that period of time, Giuliani was more popular in the state of New York than Hillary Clinton. She overwhelmingly won the elections into the U.S. Senate like no man's business. [184]

Senator Clinton was selected to be on the Senate's Committee on Armed Services. After the attacks on the WTC, Clinton joined her fellow senior senator from New York to obtain $21 billion in funding for the WTC site redevelopment. She had previously spoken out against the Taliban and how they treated the women in Afghanistan. Senator Clinton explained unequivocally, "We want to ensure that the women of Afghanistan have the opportunity to define their own future and not to have it defined for them by us, or by men who want to oppress them." Thus, after the World Trade Center attacks, she strongly supported military action in Afghanistan because this might lead to improving the lives of Afghan women who suffered under the Taliban government. [185]

Mistake or not, she voted in favor of the Iraq Resolution, which authorized the United States president to use military force against Iraq. She also voted against a resolution sponsored by Senator Carl Levin (D- Michigan). The Levin Amendment would have first allowed the U.N. to authorize the use of forces against Iraq, before the US Congress gave the green light to invade Iraq. Sen. Clinton later said that she didn't read the National Intelligence Estimate that was delivered 10 days before the vote to all members of Congress. But she claimed that she was briefed on the report.

National Intelligence Estimates are confidential documents prepared by the National Intelligence Council and are given to lawmakers.

Clinton addressed that: "If Congress had been asked to authorize the war, based on what we know now, we never would have agreed." While accepting full responsibility for her error, she repeatedly insisted that she had been misled by false intelligence on Iraq's weapons of mass destruction presented by the President's administration. Clinton lamented that the Bush administration's assurances, that Iraq possessed weapons of mass destruction, turned out to be empty ones. [186]

In 2005, Clinton said although an immediate withdrawal of American troops from the Iraqi region would be a mistake, Bush's pledge to keep our troops in Iraq "Until the job is done" was also a wrong course of action, as it might give the Iraqis "An open -ended invitation not to take care of themselves." She faced criticism from her fellow Democratic colleagues, who favored immediate withdrawal. She lambasted the Bush administration but asserted that "Criticism of this administration's policies should not in any way be confused with softness against terrorists, inadequate support for democracy or lack of patriotism." [187]

Sen. Clinton has worked with GOP senators, Bill Frist, Lindsey Graham and James Inhofe on a number of issues. However, she was very critical of a Republican piece of legislation in the House of Representatives that would make it a felony for any person to come into America illegally. "It is certainly not in keeping with my understanding of the Scripture, because the bill would literally criminalize the Good Samaritan and probably even Jesus himself," Clinton preached. In 2005, Clinton worked briefly with former Speaker Newt Gingrich in support of a proposal for incremental universal health care. [188]

Supreme Court Judges

Sen. Clinton was against Bush's Supreme Court nomination of John Roberts and most especially Samuel Alito. Clinton joined half of the Democratic senators in support of a filibuster against the nomination of Samuel Alito. During Alito's confirmation Clinton said that Alito would "Rock back decades of progress and roll over when confronted with an administration too willing to flaunt the rules and looking for a rubber stamp."

Supreme Court Justices Samuel Alito Jr. and Chief Justice Roberts were nominated by President G. Bush, confirmed by Congress and eventually appointed by President 43. The 42nd United States President appointed Stephen Breyer and Ruth Ginsburg. The 41st United States President appointed Clarence Thomas and David Souter. The 40th United States President appointed Anthony Kennedy and Antonin Scalia. And the 38th President of United States appointed John Stevens. All four Supreme Court Justice appointed by Reagan voted far more conservatively than those appointed by the aforementioned presidents. Sandra O'Connor was a Reagan appointee and the first woman to serve on the Supreme Court. She did flip-flop on some cases. But in the most important political case, Bush v Gore (2000), she stuck with her fellow conservative Justices led by former Chief Justice Williams Rehnquist, to vote in favor of Gov. Bush.[189]

What is Senator Hillary Clinton's judicial philosophy? If Hillary becomes the 43rd US President, the Religious Right wouldn't want Senator Clinton to nominate a Ginsburg or a Souter.

Pat Robertson, a conservative evangelical and former presidential candidate, claimed in 2005 that a higher power told him the following: "I will remove judges from the Supreme Court quickly, and their successors will refuse to sanction the attacks on religious faith."

Supreme Court Justices are supposed to settle cases based upon the law. They are expected to ignore partisan politics, personal biases, and public opinion. Supreme Court Judges serve a lifetime in the highest Court of the land.

Walker Bush's appointee, Justice Souter, was a big blow for the Republican Party, but the biggest blow was President Ford's appointee, Justice Stevens. He became as liberal as Ginsburg.

Chief Justice John Roberts Jr. hasn't been as effective as past Chief Justices like John Jay, John Marshal, and Portland Chase.

A significant majority of regular voters consider Supreme Court appointees a key issue for presidential nominees. The nominees' stance on legal issues will be important for voters in deciding how they vote in the general election. The nominees' position on abortion would affect women voters.

Since the 1973 Supreme Court's landmark Roe v Wade ruling which guaranteed abortion right, changes have occurred in the Supreme Court that can now overthrow that controversial ruling.[190]

Greatest First Lady continues

Five year in the senate seat, Clinton's name has often been mooted as a possible candidate for president 44.

Clinton announced that she would seek a second term in the United States Senate. Meanwhile; her local opponent for the GOP nominee for senate from New York State was very popular. But just like Mayor Giuliani, former Westchester County District Attorney Jeannie Pirro dropped out of the senate race to challenge Clinton. The incumbent New York senator easily won the Democratic nomination in the primaries and overwhelmingly won over the Republican nominee in the general election. It was a cakewalk for Clinton, even though she spent $36 million towards her senate reelection campaign. She was lambasted by fellow Democrats for spending too much in a one sided race.

In her second term in the senate, a term which she may not complete as a seating senator, she called against the February 2007 troop surge in Iraq.

Clinton voted in favor of an Iraq war-spending bill that had a huge number of supports from lawmakers in Capitol Hill. A part of the bill required President Bush to begin withdrawing troops from Iraq within a certain deadline. President Bush vetoed the bill. [191]

The 2008 presidential election (February 07-December 07)

Rank and file Democrats have long known that Senator Clinton was going to run for president. Read a statement made by Senator Boxer: "I really think she should do it. She's one who thinks in large, visionary terms. She is a leader and we need leaders now. I very much want her to do it. She knows how I feel about it. I think she someday could be a great president" Sen. Boxer made this comment in 2000 when Clinton was contemplating running for the Senate. [192]

Probably Sen. Clinton was the reason why popular Democratic senator, Russ Feingold from Wisconsin, decided no on testing the water for president. After the midterm election, Senator Feingold said he was satisfied when the Democrats took over Congress.

"But how satisfied is he?" Toward the end of 07, his party has been labeled 'lame duck' with an approval rate of below 18 percent. The Democrats took over power in Congress in 2007, but overcoming a filibuster has been a level that eluded them. Clinton was said to have a fractured relationship with Russ Feingold. Reports ran out that Senator Clinton once yelled at Russ Feingold in the senate floor. The senator from Wisconsin was the only Democratic senator that voted against a motion to dismiss Bill Clinton's trial impeachment. Senator Joe Lieberman was the first senator to speak out against President Clinton's behavior. To the dismay of Feingold, Lieberman added insult to injury when he voted to dismiss the trial.

Senators Feingold, Biden, and Obama are the only potential candidates that will give Clinton a run for her money. She is definitely going to need more than the $36 million she spent in her senate campaign.

Hillary's 2006 reelection campaign was a curtain raiser for her presidential run.

Throughout 2007, Clinton led the field of candidates competing for the Democratic nomination in opinion polls; with both Sen. Obama and Sen. John Edwards trailing behind, probably tailgating too. [193]

Perfect role model continues

Regardless of what happened following the event of her husband's involvement in the Monica Lewinsky scandal, she held and tucked up her husband. The scandal was a subject of never-ending discussion, but she ignored all the criticism from the media.

Trouble will always come a politician's way.

As a consequence of the Whitewater scandal, she testified before a federal grand jury. The Whitewater scandal was a failed Arkansas real estate deal. The Clintons joined a partnership to buy acres of riverfront land and form the Whitewater Development Corp. The goal was to sell lots for vacation homes, but the partnership did poorly and it did dissolve, leaving the Clintons reporting a huge net loss of their investment. Hillary Clinton denied the involvement of her Whitewater partner's S&L, with her law firm's work. However, former senator Alfonso D'Amato called her statement "clearly misleading." Clinton has never been charged with any wrongdoing as long as she has occupied a government position. Independent Counsel Kenneth Starr was the chief investigator of the case. Toward the end of the nineties, Starr didn't called-off the Whitewater investigation, despite the lack of evidence. Kenneth Starr just wanted to make a name for himself in Washington; he succeeded, as he was the same attorney that was in charged of the Monica Lewinsky Scandal. [194]

The 2008 presidential election (February 07-December 07)

Way back in the seventies, Hillary was thought to have the potential to be a senator or president.

She has successfully become a senator. Will she be heading back to the White House as the commander –in-chief? And who will she choose to be her running mate? She might stick to her Democratic partners, like Barack Obama, the junior Senator from Illinois, or John Edwards, former senator from North Carolina. Or she might go more extreme with Democratic figures like Warner, Bayh, and Strickland.

Wesley Clarke and Dick Gephardt, Democratic heavyweights from the 90's, could be dusted off and brought to be a running mate for Hillary.[195]

Popular and polarizing

Clinton has been referred to as one of the most polarizing figures in American politics. Analysts and pundits described Clinton as someone with too much political baggage.

"Senator Clinton is popular but polarizing, and Democrats worry Clinton could hurt party." The polarizing factor by and large might be counterproductive on her presidential campaigned, but it won't hurt Hillary Clinton. [196]

Clinton's conservative ties had linked her with a Christian group. The group did include two of the most conservative Catholic lawmakers in Congress, former presidential candidate Sam Brownback (R-Kansas) and former number 3 Republican in the U.S. Senate Rick Santorum (R-Pennsylvania). Throughout all of her years in Capitol Hill, she participated in prayer and conservative bible study groups that were advocating for the teaching of Jesus Christ in Capitol Hill.

Clinton is said to have believed that it is likely that one could be a mind conservative and a heart liberal. Liberal critics said her faith is liberal, but her mind is conservative.

During the Monica Lewinsky scandal, her faith got her through: "People whom I knew were literally praying for me in prayer chains, who were prayer warriors for me."

Clinton's devotion to her religious beliefs was noticed despite the unacceptable comment made by conservative evangelical Christian, Rev. Jerry Falwell. The late Reverend said, "I certainly hope that Hillary is the candidate. I hope she's the candidate, because nothing will energize my (constituency) like Hillary Clinton. If Lucifer ran, he wouldn't." A Clinton spokesperson responded, "It seems like a new low has been reached in demonizing political opponents." [197]

The 2008 presidential election (February 07-December 07)

In October 07, after resigning from the White House, political strategist Karl Rove made several back-to- back media appearances during which he assailed Sen. Clinton. "She's got a record that's so spotty and poor on health care issues"... and "I think" her candidacy is "fatally flawed"... "She enters the general campaign with the highest negatives of any candidate in the history of the Gallup Poll." "She enters the presidential contest with higher negatives. The only person who comes close is- she–her's are at 49- the only other candidate to come close was Al Gore with 34, I believe... And there's nobody who has ever won the presidency who started out in that kind of position."

Pundits immediately claimed that Karl Rove 'Rovian' was using reverse psychology tactics against Clinton. The same tactic pundits claimed Rove used during the 2004 presidential election.

So who is Karl Rove really afraid of, Senator Obama or still the same Senator Edwards?

In the 2004 election, Rove was afraid that Edwards was a more electable candidate and would give President Bush more of a challenge than Senator Kerry. So instead of attacking Edwards, Rove attacked John Kerry. In reaction, the Democrats rallied around Sen. Kerry, but in the back of Rove's mind, he viewed Senator Kerry a weaker opponent.

So is that what is going to happen in the 2008 election? Rove will attack Mrs. Clinton instead of Sen. Obama in order for Clinton to win her party's nomination? [198]

President Bush said Clinton would definitely win the Democratic nomination, but Bush discounted Clinton as a future president. First Lady Laura Bush said she wouldn't vote for the person she succeeded, Hillary Clinton.

Madam Bush is adamant that Hillary Clinton is the first real serious female contender to be running for president. Madam Bush says Hillary is likely to be the first female president, but she will put party over gender.

Laura Bush, once a Democrat, indicated that "It doesn't matter to me. And I hope it doesn't matter to other people, I hope that people will choose the candidates that they think really has the views that they want." A poll in late 2007 found that about 11% of GOP women would vote for Hillary Clinton.

Clinton has been thrown under the bus by the two first tier conservative commentators in the nation. WABC's testicle lock box and the very impressive 'Stop Hillary Express,' were significant disadvantages against the junior senator from New York.

On the other hand, Air American's liberal commentators weren't defending Clinton from the smear campaign coming from the Rightwing Republicans. They pledged to remain neutral in endorsing only the Democratic presidential nominee. They ignored the fact that Hillary Clinton and few female Democratic senators were the people behind the foundation of Air America radio.

Should political degree majors, military veterans and political journalists only be allowed to run for Congress and for the Presidency? Not just the wealthy Americans? Well, even Shakespeare was involved in politics.

Clinton majored in and graduated with a political science degree. Clinton has the willpower to take the country to greater heights. Hillary Clinton is the epitome of success [199]

Chapter 10

21st Century: President George Bush vs. the War on Terrorism

The 2008 presidential election (February 07-December 07)

The United States President is George Bush and he is due to leave office at the very beginning of 2009. What if disaster strikes in America or anywhere in the world with America's interest?

Jep Bush hasn't made any headlines since his tenure as governor of Florida ended.

There is no time left for him to join the bandwagon of GOP presidential candidates. He is said to be a possible vice president candidate for whomsoever wins the GOP 2008 presidential nominee. If he gets the nod to be a vice president, he may follow in the footsteps of his father.

Walker Bush was the vice president in Reagan's presidency before becoming the United States president.

Walker Bush is rumored to be pushing for a Mitt Romney/Jep Bush 2008 Republican ticket.

Sources in Washington D.C. once speculated that Vice President Cheney would be replaced before the end of 2007. Senator Hagel, Senator Thompson, and Secretary Rice were mentioned as possible replacements for vice president.[200]

The John Warner Defense Authorization Act of 2007 was a bill overwhelmingly passed by the U.S. Congress and was signed into law on

October 17, 2007 by President Bush. Section 1076 of the John Warner Act was the Defense Appropriation Bill in which there were changes to the Insurrection Act.

The Insurrection act is a set of laws that limits and governs the president's power to deploy military troops within the domestic United States to suppress public order during a violent situation. The intent of this law is to use troops, with the consent of the state governor, to deal with insurrection from groups or individuals. Most especially if the violence is beyond the control of state or local authorities. The Insurrection Act and the Posse Comitatus Act limit the president's domestic law enforcement powers. Posse Comitatus is a law that prevents military troops from policing within the country. The text of the Posse Comitatus Act stated: "Whoever, except in cases and under circumstances expressly authorized by the Constitution or Act of Congress, willfully uses any part of the Army or the Air Force as a posse comitatus or otherwise to execute the laws shall be fined under this title or imprisoned not more than two years or both."

The original Insurrection Act is only specified basically for the rise of insurrection. However, the changes to the Insurrection Act found in the Warner Defense Act, Section 1076 stated:

> "The President may employ the armed forces, including the National Guard in Federal service, to restore public order and enforces the laws of the United States, as a result of a natural disaster, epidemic, or other serious public health emergency, terrorist attack or incident, or other condition in any State or possession of the United States, the President determines that domestic violence has occurred to such an extent that the constituted authorities of the State or possession are incapable of maintaining public order to suppress, in any State, any insurrection, domestic violence, unlawful combination, or conspiracy."

Martial Law is a "Law imposed in occupied territory by the military forces of the occupying power" {Webster's universal dictionary}.

The revived Insurrection Act enacted in 2006 is now designed under a new language to address public disturbance beyond an insurrection. It now includes natural disaster and terrorist attacks from outside the country. If the new Act is invoked by the President, Posse Comitatus is exempt, and federal troops are ordered to carry out law enforcement duties without the consent of a governor. The President can declare martial law and station federal military forces anywhere in the country. They can also take charge of the National

Guard without having to contact states authority, but the President must notify Congress. [201]

Project for the New American Century (PNAC) is an American neoconservative think tank founded in the late nineties by the editor of the Weekly Standard, Williams Kristol and Robert Kagan. Its major members and signatories include Donald Rumsfeld, Paul Wolfowitz, Richard Cheney, and Jeb Bush.

In January 98, senior members of PNAC compiled a letter to Bill Clinton calling for the ousting of Saddam Hussein from office, by any means necessary. They made reasonable claim that if Saddam Hussein succeeded in preserving what they maintained was a stockpile of weapons of mass destruction (WMD); Saddam would pose a significant threat to America, Western Europe, and Middle East oil resources regions. For those reasons, a conflict against Saddam would be justified. Iraqi officials were also unwilling to work with U.N. weapon inspectors. Other people associated with the PNAC included John Bolton, Richard Armitage, and Elliot Abrams. [202]

Cindy Sheehan, a Californian anti-war activist read

> "As a matter of fact, in interviews in 1999 with respected journalist, and long time Bush family friend, Micky Herskowitz, then governor George Bush stated: 'One of the keys to being seen as a great leader is to be seen as a commander -in-chief. My father had all this political capital built up when he drove the Iraqis out of Kuwait and he wasted it. If I have a chance to invade... if I had that much capital, I'm not going to waste it. I'm going to get everything passed that I want to get passed and I'm going to have a successful presidency."

The message implied that George Bush's militancy would have terrible consequences if Bush became president. [203]

Revisiting Iraq's alleged possession of weapons of mass destruction and the preemptive war against Iraq

Before the September 11th terrorists attack, the CIA and the FBI had been at odds with each other. This made it difficult for both parties to apprehend the attackers. Add to the fact that when Bush took office, he kept George Tenet as the CIA director. Tenet was appointed by President Clinton. The FBI had obtained evidence that terrorist Mohammed Atta was apparently in Florida at the time of the alleged meeting by the 9/11 plotters. However, Vice

President Dick Cheney said, "We just don't know" whether the allegations were true. And the CIA doubted the meetings took place.[204]

Time Line: Political rhetoric

After the September 11th terrorist attacks on America, President Bush had occasionally said, "Oceans no longer protect us." But the 9/11 attackers didn't fly planes over oceans outside of America into America. In August 2002, Vice President Dick Cheney claimed that "There is no doubt that Saddam Hussein now has WPD. There is no doubt that he is amassing them to use against our friends, against our allies, and against us." Bush backed his vice president: "On its present course, the Iraqi regime is a threat of unique urgency it has develops weapons of mass death."[205]

On September 18th, 2002, Defense Secretary Donald Rumsfeld told the Senate Armed Services committee: "There are a number of terrorist states pursuing weapons of mass destruction Iran, Libya, North Korea, Syria, just to name a few, but no terrorist state poses a greater or more immediate threat to the security of our people, and the stability of the world, than the regime of Saddam Hussein and Iraq."

President Bush further emphasized, "Saddam Hussein is a man who has told the world he wouldn't have WPD, and yet he deceived the world. He's got them. We know he's got chemical weapons, probably has biological weapons." The President highlighted just how important it was to disarm Saddam Hussein

> "Some people say, oh, we must leave Saddam alone; otherwise, if we did something against him, he might attack us. Well, if we don't do something he might attack us, and he might attack us with a more serious weapon. The man is a threat. He's a threat because he is dealing with al Qaeda. And we're going to deal with him." [206]

On CNN with Wolf Blitzer, Rice said "The problem here is that there will always be some uncertainly about how quickly he (Saddam Hussein) can acquire nuclear weapons. But we don't want the smoking gun to be mushroom cloud." Bush backed Rice's statement "Knowing these realities, America must not ignore the threat gathering against us. Facing clear evidence of peril, we cannot wait for the final proof- the smoking gun-that could come in the form of a mushroom cloud." The chief U.N. weapons inspector Hans Blix acknowledged that "The absence of smoking guns and the prompt access which we have had so far, and which is most welcome, is no guarantee that prohibited stocks or activities could not exist at other sites, whether above ground, underground or in mobile units." Ari Fleischer, White House press secretary, finally ended the concept of the smoking gun. He offered his assessment: "The problem with guns that are hidden is you can't see their smoke." [207]

In February 5th 2003, Secretary of State Colin Powell went before the United Nations Security Council. Powell provided substantive proofs that Iraqis have WMD sites. So it was now time for the next and direr stage. And on February 7, Donald Rumsfeld speculated how long the expected war would last. He hypothesized "It is unknowable how long that conflict will last. It could last six days, six weeks. I doubt six months" -Defense Secretary, on a trip to Italy. And again Rumsfeld foresaw a swift war in Iraq: "Any war with Iraq would be swift and not require a full US mobilization."

President Bush made the following statement during a radio address in February 8th 2003, "We know that Iraq is harboring a terrorist network headed by a senior al Qaeda terrorist planner." [208]

Secretary of Defense Donald Rumsfeld, a poet, made the following comment at a news briefing on February 12th 2003: "As we know, there are known knowns. There are things we know we know. We also know there are known unknowns; that is to say we know there are some things we do not know. But there are also unknown unknowns, the ones we don't know, we don't know." On February 13, 2003, Ken Adelman of the Defense Policy noted, "I believe demolishing Hussein's military power and liberating Iraq would be a cakewalk." [209]

According to the US Constitution, only Congress can declare war. And can provide funding for a possible war: "And money trumps peace, sometimes" Bush said.[210]

The U.S. Congress had to be convinced

In March 2003, Majority Leader Bill Frist (R-Tennessee) indicated, "Iraq is a grave threat to this nation. It desires to acquire and use weapons of mass terror and is run by despot with a proven record of willingness to use them. Iraq has had 12 years to comply with UN requirements for disarmament and has failed to do so. The President is right to say its time has run out." Whoa! Tom DeLay, Majority Leader in the House, has since weighed in "America must preempt threats before they damage our national interests." Tom DeLay also acknowledged that "Returning their government to the people of Iraq would signal Democratic reformers around the region that the United States is deeply committed to expanding freedom."[211]

The World Bank President, Paul Wolfowitz, the official mastermind of the preemptive Iraq invasion finally spoke out: "The Iraqi people understand what this crisis is about. Like the people of France in the 1940s, they view us as their hoped-for liberator." Sen. Bill Frist also stated, "Getting rid of Saddam Hussein's regime is our best inoculation. Destroying once and for all his weapons of disease and death is a vaccination for the world." Bill Frist was a medical doctor before he became a US senator. President Bush supported Powell's presentation during an address to the nation: "Intelligence gathered by this and other governments leave no doubt that Iraq regime continues to posses and conceal some of the most lethal weapons ever devised." [212]On NBC's Tim Russert's show, Vice President Cheney predicted that the United States army would be "greeted as liberators" in Iraq. United Kingdom Prime Minister Tony Blair finally joined the race. It kind of took a while; Blair had to be convinced by Richard Cheney. Tony Blair spoke to the House of Commons: "We are asked now seriously to accept that in the last few years, contrary to all history, contrary to all intelligence. Saddam decided unilaterally to destroy those weapons. I say that such a claim is palpably absurd."

The House of Commons is the elected lower house of the Great Britain Parliament. [213]

The War is on: March 20th 2003

Tony Blair was the first national figure to comment on the war: "I have always said to people throughout that our aim has not been regime change, our aim has been the elimination of WPD." On March 27th, when asked how long the already seven day war would last, President Bush said at a news conference with British Prime Minister Tony Blair: "However long it takes. That's the answer to your question and that's what you've got to know. It isn't a matter of timetable; it's a matter of victory." Ten days after the war began, Defense Secretary Rumsfeld on This Week with ABC's George Stephanopoulos, said "The area… that coalition forces control happens not to be the area where WPD were dispersed. We know where they are. They're in the area around Tikrit and Baghdad and east, west, south and north somewhat."[214] On the situation in Iraq, President Bush was ready to weigh in: "…We cannot live under the threat of blackmail. The terrorist threats to America and the world will be diminished the moment that Saddam Hussein is disarmed." Senator Bill Frist had to keep Congress motivated "We simply cannot live in fear of a ruthless dictator, aggressor and terrorist such as Saddam Hussein, who possesses the world's most deadly weapons"[215]

On April 3rd, 2003, President Bush gave his assertion in the ongoing war: "The goals of our coalition are clear and limited. We will end a brutal regime, whose aggression and WPD make it a unique threat to the world." In terms of American troops succeeding in Iraq, Cheney on 'Meet the Press' said, "We will have struck a major blow right at the heart of the base, if you will, the geographic base of the terrorists who had us under assault now for many years, but most especially 9/11." Bush was asked to address what he saw going on the horizon "We are learning more as we interrogate or have discussions with Iraqi scientists and people within the Iraqi structure, that perhaps he destroyed some, perhaps he dispersed some. And so we will find them."[216]

Aftermath of the Iraqi War

President Bush made an historical speech aboard warship. On May 1st, President Bush said: "My fellow Americans, major combat operations in Iraq has ended. In the battle of Iraq, the United States and our allies have prevailed." But no weapons of mass destruction (WMD) were found. Two days after Bush declared the end of combat operations, Bush opined "We'll find them (WMD). It'll be a matter of time to do so."[217] The next day Secretary Rumsfeld said "We never believed that we'd just tumble over WPD in that country. We're going to find what we find as a result of talking to people, I believe, not simply by going to some site and hoping to discover it." Next in line was Secretary Collin Powell: "I'm absolutely sure that there are WPD there and the evidence will be forthcoming. We're just getting it just now." Paul Wolfowitz, former Deputy Defense Secretary, boldly acknowledged, "For bureaucratic reasons, we settled on one issue. WMD because it was the one reason everyone could agree on." [218]

Former U.N. Ambassador John Bolton weighed in after Bush declared the end of combat operation. Weapons of mass destruction "Isn't really the issue" Bolton said. "The issue, I think, has been the capability that Iraq sought to have WPD programs." Defense Secretary Donald Rumsfeld corrected himself from previous statements: "I said, we know they're in that area. I should have said, I believe they're in that area. Our intelligence tells us they're in that area, and that was our best judgment." [219]

President Bush has Jokes

In March 2004, during the annual dinner for the Radio and Television News correspondents Association, Bush turned Hollywood actor. The President showed himself in an awkward poses searching behind White House Oval Office's furniture and he told an audience, "Those weapons of mass destruction have got to be somewhere... nope, no weapons over there... maybe under here?" as laughter erupted from the crowd of journalists. [220]

The Bush administration admitted that Iraq was not connected to the 9/11 attacks. And Saddam probably did not possess weapons of mass destruction

In a nationally televised appearance, Vice President Cheney asserted: "We don't know" whether Saddam Hussein was involved in the 9/11 attacks. President Bush told a group of reporters in the White House, "No, we've had no evidence that Saddam Hussein was involved with September the eleven." Sec. Donald Rumsfeld noted, "I've not seen any indication that would lead me to believe that I could say that" Hussein was connected to the September 11th attacks. In an interview, President Bush again acknowledged: "Now, look, I part of the reason we went into Iraq was…the main reason we went to Iraq at that time was we thought he had weapons of mass destruction. It turns out he didn't, but he had the capacity to make weapons of mass destruction."

Interviewer: What did Iraq have to do with that?

President Bush: What did Iraq have to do with what?

Interviewer: The attack on the World Trade Center.

President Bush: Nothing, except for its part of …and nobody's ever suggested in this administration that Saddam Hussein ordered the attack. Iraq was a …Iraq …the lesson of September the eleven is take threat before the fully materialize."[221]

In 2004 on CNN, televangelist Jerry Falwell begged for peace: "But you've got to kill the terrorists before the killing stops. And I'm for the president to chase them all over the world. If it takes 10 years, blow them all away in the name of the Lord."[222]

One year after the war ended, Secretary of State Collin Powell finally caved in when he was interviewed at Meet the Press

> "When I made that presentation in February 03, it was based on the best information that the central intelligence Agency (CIA) made available to me. We studied it carefully; we looked at the sourcing in the case of the mobile trucks and trains. There was multiple sourcing for that. Unfortunately, that multiply sourcing over time has turned out to be not accurate. And so I'm deeply disappointed. It turned out that the sourcing was inaccurate and wrong and in some cases, deliberately misleading. And for that, I am disappointed and I regret it."

At the Heritage Foundation, a conservative think tank, Defense Secretary Rumsfeld gave his take on the latest development:

"I can't guess how much longer it will take to get what we finally look and say was ground truth. I just don't know how long it will take. We certainly won't just discover anything. I mean, we did not just discover Saddam Hussein, and he was hiding in a hole that was big enough to put chemical weapons in it that would kill tens of thousands of people."[223]

In June 2004, President Bush summarized the problem with Saddam Hussein and the weapons of mass destruction:

"I always said that Saddam Hussein was a threat. He was a threat because he had used WMD against his own people. He was a threat because he was a sworn enemy to the United States of America, just like al Qaeda. He was a threat because he had terrorist connections- not only al Qaeda connections, but other connections to terrorist organizations; Abu Nidal was one. He was a threat because he provided safe-haven for a terrorist like Zarqawi, who is still killing innocent inside of Iraq. No, he was a threat, and the world is better off and America is more secure without Saddam Hussein in power."

British Prime Minister Tony Blair finally conceded, "I have to accept we haven't found them and we may never find them (WMD). We don't know what has happened to them. They could have been removed. They could have been hidden. They could have been destroyed."

Despite mounting problems in Iraq, Bush cut a relax figure when giving a press conference: "We are not leaving (Iraq) so long as I'm the president. That would be a huge mistake." [224]

Pundits had regarded PNAC's recommendation to President Clinton for the removal of Saddam Hussein from power and the significant number of PNAC royalties appointed to the Bush administration as clear evidence that the Iraqi war was definitely in the making. Pundits also asserted that if the war in Iraq did occur, the next step would be to use Iraq as a base to force a regime change in other Middle East countries. What happened next? The mini war in mid 2006 between Israel and Lebanon occurred in that region. Border tension between Hezbollah in Lebanon and Hamas in Gaza led to the capture of Israeli soldiers. PNAC members and signatories associated with the Bush Administration also included Richard Perle, Robert Zoellick, Zalmay Khalizad, and I. Lewis scooter Libby.[225]

Exit Iraq, Enter Iran

Central Intelligence Agency reports 2002 claimed: "Apart from Iraq, six other nations Cuba, Libya, Sudan, Syria, North Korea and Iran supports terrorism. Syria and Iran have biological or chemical weapons and are trying to get nukes, and the rest of the mention nations are trying to get all three." The reports came on the heels of Bush's 2002 State of the Union address in which Bush described Iraq, Iran, and North Korea as "Axis of Evil." Bush was referring to countries that pose a significant threat to United States' national security because of their alleged ties to terrorism and harboring mass destructive weapons. On January 19th, 2005, Sec Rice mentioned six terrorist States: "To be sure, in our world, there remain outposts of tyranny, and American stands with oppressed people on every continent, in Cuba, and Burma, and North Korea, and Iran, and Belarus, and Zimbabwe." Rice said America had to promote liberty around the globe.

In October 2005, Iran's president stated: "Israel must be wiped off the face of the map." Sec Rice immediately responded: "When the president of one country says that another country should be wiped off the map, in violation of all the norms of the UN, where they sit together as members, it has to be taken seriously." She concluded that: "We're working so hard to remind the world that Iran is probably the world's most important state sponsor of terrorism."[226]

Bush was asked to riff about the terrorists' effect on America: "If we do not defeat these enemies now, we will leave our children to face a Middle East overrun by terrorist states and radical dictators armed with nuclear weapons." President Bush admitted mistakes in the war in Iraq; however, he didn't concede: "Whatever mistakes have been made in Iraq, the worst mistake would be to think that if we pulled out, the terrorists would leave us alone."

Political analysts admitted the war in Iraq was over and the winner of the war was Iran. The US invasion of Iraq didn't go as plan; it led to a sectarian civil war with Shiite majority in total dominance.

The Shiite communities in Iraq are pro-Iranian. [227]

In the latter part of 2005, Rice was prompted to call on Russia, China, and India to join in threatening UN sanctions on Iran because of Iran's refusal to halt its nuclear program. Rice had to work with the President of the People's Republic of China, Hu Jintao, and the President of Russia, Vladimir *Putin.*

Russia and China are members of the Nuclear Non-Proliferation Treaty (NPT). NPT are countries that possess nuclear weapons. United Kingdom, France, and United States are the other Non- Proliferation's members.

In February 06, after Iran resumed its uranium enrichment program, Rice stressed: "There is simply no peaceful rationale for the Iranian regime to resume uranium enrichment. We're gravely concerned by Iran's long history of hiding sensitive nuclear activities from the international community." -Rice speaking on the behalf of American and the European Union. On May 2006, Madam Rice offered Iranians a direct negotiation with the United States and its allies. She requested a possible package of economic incentives for Iran in exchange for Iran to suspend its uranium enrichment program. The Iranian authority responded that they would "Never give up its legitimate rights, so the American preconditions are just unacceptable." Two months passed and Iran was still unwilling to suspend their uranium enrichment program. So in July 2006, Rice, NPT nations, and Germany came to agreements. And they sought a UN Security Council Resolution against Iran under Article 41 of Chapter seven of the UN Charter. After Rice and NPT countries finally delivered the coup de grace to Iran, the Iranians started a proxy war against the United States. [228]

In April 2006, Seymour Hersh, an Investigative reporter for the New Yorker Magazine, reported that ranking senior military officials were disturbed by the Bush administration's option of using 'bunker–busting tactical nuclear weapons' to destroy nuclear facilities buried underground in specific locations in Iran. Seymour Hersh also reported that the Bush administration was at odds with the Joint Chiefs of Staff (JCS) because of its refusal to take off the nuclear option. An intelligent official said, "Whenever anybody tries to get it out (the nuclear option), they're shouted down." The Joint Chiefs of Staff finally got the upper hand by convincing the White House to agree that using nuclear weapons to destroy Iran's uranium enrichment plants was unacceptable.[229]

Joint Chiefs of Staff are comprised of the five heads of the United States armed forces. Did the White House and the Joint Chiefs of Staff not being on the same page lead to changes in the JCS leadership position?

The leadership of the Joint Chiefs of Staff had been changed. General Peter Pace stepped down as the JCS chairman and Admiral Michael Mullen replaced Pace.

The Chairman of the JCS is the highest-ranking military officer in the United States. Traditionally, the JCS chairman position is held for four years.

General Peter Pace was in office for only two years. He stepped down in September 2007. General James Cartwright became the Vice Chairman of the JCS. He replaced Admiral Giambastiani, who resigned in July 2007 after only two years in office. The rest of the changes were in accordance with the traditional term limits in office.

The Chief of Staff of the United States Army is General George Casey, Jr. He replaced Gen. Schoomaker. Admiral Gary Roughed became the Chief of Naval Operation.

Roughed took over from Admiral Mullen, who outgeneraled other superior officers and was elevated to the chairmanship position. General Moseley and General Conway, the Chief of Staff of the United States Air Force and the commander of the Marine Corps respectively, also replaced Gen. Jumper and Gen. Hagee. [230]

Response to a possible declaration of Martial Law

Senator Edward Kennedy praised the revived Insurrection Act:

> "As I understand the amendment, it defines when the President can call on the Armed Forces if there is a major public emergency at home. The amended statute now lists specific situations in which the troops can be used to restore public order. This includes natural disasters, epidemics or other serious public health emergencies, and terrorist attacks or incidents that results in domestic violence to such an extent that State authorities are unable to maintain public order. These were not mentioned specifically before."

Kennedy said the slow response to Hurricane Katrina would not have happened if this Act had already been revived. However the Chairman of the Senate Judiciary Committee Patrick Leahy lamented,

> "We certainly do not need to make it easier for presidents to declare martial law. Invoking the Insurrection Act and using the military for law enforcement activities goes against some of the central tenets of our democracy. One can easily envision governors and mayors in charge of an emergency having to constantly look over their shoulders while someone who has never visited their community gives the orders."

Leahy further emphasized that by "Using the military for law enforcement, we will fail our Constitution, neglecting the rights of the States, when we make it easier for the President to declare martial law and trample on local and state sovereignty."

The state of Vermont is the only state which the President has not visited since becoming commander in chief.

Patrick Leahy was curious to know why: "Since hearing word a couple of weeks ago that this outcome was likely, I have wondered how Congress could have gotten to this point, It seems the changes to the Insurrection Act have survived the Conference because the Pentagon and the White House want it." [231]

Seymour Hersh, the veteran investigative journalist, reported that John Negroponte's removal as the director of National Intelligence (DNI) was because of the Bush administration's covert actions in Iraq. The administration had been allegedly funding radical Sunni groups in Iraq, which Negroponte strongly opposes because of its strong ties to al-Qaeda. The Administration' strategy for funding Sunni groups was to counter Shiite groups back by Iran. In April of 2006, when Negroponte was still in charge of DNI, he made the following statement when he was on NBC news: "Our assessment is that the prospects of an Iranian weapon are still a number of years off, and probably into the next decade." PNAC members, whom were advocating for a conflict with Iran on the case of Iran's uranium enrichment nuclear program, became enraged with Negroponte's statement. These same PNAC members advocated for a war with Iraq on the case of Iraq's possession of weapons of mass destruction. As a result of Negroponte's statement, a leading member of PNAC called for John Negroponte to be fired. The member claimed that John betrayed the President. However, Bush showed loyalty to Negroponte. Bush switched Negroponte from DNI chief to deputy secretary of state. [232]

After the Iraq Study Group's (ISG) final report was released in December 2006, Bush made it clear that he would not accept every recommendation on the reports. Lee Hamilton, a Democrat and former US congressman from Indiana, and former Secretary of State James Baker, a Republican, both chaired the Iraq Study group.

The independent study group was charged with assessing the situation on the ground in Iraq (The security and political development in Iraq).

However, Bush finally admitted that a new approach is needed in Iraq. Before Bush leaves office, Iraq will be a fait accompli. [233]

In 2007, the Bush administration asserted that Iran is intent on building nuclear weapons and is providing weaponry to insurgents in Afghanistan and Iraq. Vice President Dick Cheney has always advocated military action against Iran; however the next two top officials, the secretary of state and the defense secretary, are both against the wishes of the Vice President.

Towards the end of 2006, Cheney lost Rumsfeld. The former Defense Secretary was one of Cheney's major proponents for a conflict against Iran. Cheney was angered over Sec. Rumsfeld ouster. They worked hand-to-hand until the end of Ford's administration. And again they worked together on the Bush 43 administration. Cheney relished the chance to work with Rumsfeld again. As Secretary of Defense, Rumsfeld reverted to the post he held under President Ford. Their workmanship cumulated in the resignation of Rumsfeld.[234]

Infighting in the President's administration

Towards the end of 2006, the President stood by Sec. Rice in preferring diplomatic sanctions to slow down Iran's nuclear weapons program. Meanwhile, there was infighting going on between different flanks of the Bush's administration. The infighting was a typical example of the Ford's administration. Once again Cheney and Rumsfeld were involved as they were in the Ford's administration. US Diplomats were on one side and the Vice President and his national security team were on the other side. The two separate flanks engaged in infighting about their stance on the conflict with Iran.

Secretary Rice and Deputy Secretary of State John Negroponte led the diplomats. The Defense Department's Pentagon and top intelligence officials from the Justice Department were also standing by the diplomats. Most notable were the Director of National Intelligence Admiral Mike McConnell, the Director of the CIA Michael Hayden, and Defense Secretary Gates. [235]

In early 2007, Cheney was reported to have been frustrated with Bush because of the lack of diplomatic effort in Iran. After Donald Rumsfeld was given the marching orders, Cheney was no longer considered to be the boss of the Pentagon and the turf war between Cheney and Rice escalated. Cheney's top aides and some hawkish neoconservatives had the backing of neoconservative think tanks', PNAC, and the American Enterprise Institute.

Iran ranks high on Cheney's radar. He wants to be in charge of dealing with the Iranians. The Vice President believes Bush can't be relied on to deal decisively with Iran and Cheney needs to narrow the options before Bush. As a former Defense Secretary, Cheney is well versed in conflict resolution.

In mid 2007, one year makes a difference. The President flip-flops his position on dealing with Iran and now sides with the Vice President: "The balance has tilted. There is cause for concern" {Guardian.co.uk, July, 2007}.

After an internal review meeting comprised of the White House, the State Department, and the Defense Department, Intelligence officers maintained that the president and his acolytes are maneuvering a war with Iran before Bush and Cheney leave office in about 11 months time. "No one outside that tight circle knows what is going to happen. Many if not most officials believe that diplomacy is falling and top pentagon brass believes the same" an intelligence source reported. [236]   State Secretary Rice and Vice President Cheney are now set to resolve the disputes between them and work in sanctioning military actions against Iran instead of the diplomatic actions that Rice had long favored.

Their workmanship might finally end the bureaucratic infighting that had been looming since 2006.

> "When you go down there and see the body language, you can see that Cheney is still the Man. Condi pushed for diplomacy but she is no dove. If it becomes necessary she will be on board. Both of them are very close to the president, and where they differ they are working together to find a way to present a position they can both live with" {Telegraph reported, September, 2007}. [237]

In August 2007, the proxy war that Iran is engaging with United States troops in Iraq has been extended to Afghanistan.

The Secretary of Defense Robert Gates concretely accused Tehran, the capital of Iran, of supplying weaponry to the Taliban in Afghanistan.

Before the United States invaded Afghanistan in 2001, Northern Afghans were in serious conflict with the Taliban in Afghanistan. And the Iranians supported the Northern Afghanis with weaponry to use against the Taliban.

Now, the Iranians supplying weapons to Taliban is not about arming and supporting the Taliban, it is about arming the Taliban with weaponry to use against the United States military in Afghanistan. 'The enemy of my enemy is my friend.' After September 2001, Iran's former enemy, the Taliban, is now the enemy of the United States.

Iranians are avenging the Americans because of what America did during Reagan's presidency.

In the time of the Persian Gulf War, the United States helped Iraq outgunned Iran. [238]

Washington D.C. again accused Iran of exporting improvised bombs to Iraq that the Iraqi militants use to kill United States troops in Iraq. And in September 2007, U.S. officials began crafting a plan to bomb Iran.

How long with the Proxy war against America continues? Richard Cheney is said to have urged the use of earth-penetrating nuclear weapons to attack Iran's nuclear sites. Secretary Rice's last word is that the White House must win an approval from Congress before going to war with Iran.

Intelligence sources reported that the Pentagon has released contingency plans for a possible strike on various sites in Iran. "One is to bomb only the nuclear facilities" and another "Is for a much bigger strike that would- over two or three days- hit all of the significant military sites as well. This plan involves more than 2,000 targets."

US's 277 warships are stationed close to Iran, including two aircrafts carrier groups. [239]

Bush's humorous segment

Bush had no appetite for political issues, but he had an appetite for pig.

This dialogue took place in 2006 after the Israeli's bombing of the Beirut airport in Lebanese and Iran's refusal to meet a U.N. deadline to stop enriching uranium.

Interviewer: "Does it concern you that the Beirut airport has been bombed? And do you see a risk of triggering a wider war? And on Iran, they've, so far, refused to respond. Is it now past deadline, or do they still have more time to respond?

President Bush's replied: I thought you were going to ask me about the pig.

Interviewer: I'm curious about that, too (laugh)

President Bush: The pig? I'll tell you tomorrow after I eat it."

Earlier that day on his way to the G-8 summit in Russia, Bush made it clear "I'm looking forward to that pig tonight."

On June 14, 2006, another exchange occurred during a news conference in the Rose Garden. Bush called on a reporter who raised his hand. But when the reporter stood up to utter a question, the reporter had sunglasses on.

Bush: "Are you going to ask that question with shades on?

Reporter: I can take them off

Bush: I'm interested in the shade look, seriously

Reporter: All right, I'll keep it, then.

President Bush: For the viewers, there's no sun.

{Laughter came out pouring from the press corp.}

Reporter: I guess it depends on your perspective.

Bush often teases members of the White House press corps.

Bush later apologized to the reporter because he wasn't informed that the reporter had Stargardt's Disease, a type of muscular degeneration. The reporter wore the sunglasses to protect his eyes from bright lights.[240]

Fait accompli

In conclusion, Senator Patrick Leahy and Senator Bond (R-Missouri) have been pushing legislation to repeal changes to the Insurrection Act. But as it stands, the Insurrection Act gives Bush the legal authority to declare martial law, and that's an accomplished fact.

Thom Hartmann, an experienced liberal commentator, said an economic disaster has been pushed by Alan Greenspan's successor Ben Bernanke, the Chairman of the Federal Reserve, until after the election of 08 which could lead to the President declaring martial law.

Late in 2007, an overwhelming majority of Americans want a strike in Iran, largely due the mass hysteria of Iran's 'proxy war.' So will Bush heed to the poll reading?

Bush once told America "I hear the voices, and I read the front page and I know the speculation. But I'm the decider, and I decide what's best. And what is best is for..." as a response to imposed military actions on Iran? [241]

Sources in D.C. said Bush and Cheney don't trust the next President to make the right decision on Iran. The Bush administration's "inner circle" has concluded that the President won't leave office without ensuring that Iran is incapable of developing nuclear weapons: "Bush is not going to leave office with Iran still in limbo" {Guardian 2007}.

As for Iraq, the past few years have heralded remarkable improvement. Bush's commented stating "I thought an interesting comment was made when somebody said to me, I heard somebody say, "Now, where's Mandela?" Well, Mandela is dead, because Saddam Hussein killed all the Mandelas," was taken out of context by some anti Bush bloggers. What the President meant in part was that the former Iraqi brutal dictator had killed all the brave men in that country.

Richard Cheney is clearly in favor of war with Iran. Bush's only concern is Secretary Rice. The Telegraph reported that Bush has wholeheartedly promised Rice that he will consult with Congress before he orders an attack on Iran; on the agreement that Rice will resign if Bush doesn't stand by his word. No military action against Iran is expected until after April of 2008. In the meantime, the State Department may again try to make a last ditch attempt to pursue the diplomatic route. [242]

Iranian President Mahmound Ahmadinejad had admitted that Iran wanted to negotiate with the United States: "I think that if the U.S. administration, if the U.S. government, puts aside some of its old behavior, it can actually be a good friend for the Iranian people, for the Iranian nation." Bush, however, will stick to Cheney's words, "We don't negotiate with evil; we defeat it." [243]

Bush started the war in Iraq and he finished the war in Iraq.

Bush started the occupation in Iraq and the occupation will come to an end before or after the end of 08. If the bloody occupation is not over, it will be wise for Bush to stay in office and bring an end to the occupation. "If you break it, you own it," Colin Powell said. Bush broke it, so he has to repair it. Bryon McCane, an Ohio activist, said: "And don't you start and not finish, you are with it or you against it... On the hit list, couldn't resist it, you risk it, here to stick with it." Saddam Hussein was on the hit list, and the Bush administration couldn't resist it. President Bush risked it and the American people are stuck with it. Finally, Dick Cheney eloquently said "Make no mistake, the President is acting to protect us against further attacks, even when that means moving aggressively against would-be attackers."[244]

After Bush completes his term as the 43rd United States President, he might stay below the radar for a short period of time. And he might opt to work internationally, like ex British's Prime Minister Tony Blair. Bush has set the standard for a successful 21st century president.

Bush fought for all the right objectives and he never faltered in his mission.

The Democratic Party has reprimanded President Bush for seven years but he has never personally trashed any Democratic leaders. But he has killed them by appointing Supreme Court judges against their wishes.

The two Justices Bush appointed, Alito and Roberts, would interpret the Constitution, rather than to legislate from the bench.

Throughout Bush presidency, Bush has never run away from the American peoples' problems, he has never run away from any tar baby. Bush, unlike other politicians, is willing to hug the tar baby.

Bush has never kept Cheney out of the loop in any White House activities. Bush has shared the office of the presidency with Cheney unlike other past presidents. President John Adams, the nation's first vice president, called the vice president's office "The most insignificant office that ever the invention of man contrived," and Vice President Nelson Rockefeller called it "standby equipment."

President G. Bush loves to read. Karl Rove, the man behind Bush's successful presidential elections, confessed to Rush Limbaugh that he read more books than Bush. In 2006, Rove said that Bush read 94 books while he read 110 books. A German tabloid asked Bush to name the most wonderful moments of his presidency. The President answered that it was while on vacation, fishing on my private lake. God in Heaven will always bless the United States President, God bless George Bush. [245]

Chapter 11

Bill O' Reilly: Most Influential Person in the American Media

Bill gets all the respect and the best ratings. There is absolutely no question that the most influential political anchorman in America is Bill O'Reilly. What would cable news be without his trademark in American news media? Even in the future when he is gone, no anchorperson will be able to fill his shoes.

Most Democratic senators and House members are reluctant to appear on his show. If Bill runs for a senate seat it will be a cakewalk.

Christopher Dodd, the senior senator from Connecticut, was the respectful scapegoat for the Democratic Party that went on to challenge Bill O'Reilly. The Democratic presidential candidate swallowed his pride and appeared on the Factor. While listening to their dialogue, it seemed more like Bill was the respectful senator. The Senator attacked O'Reilly's anti terrorism rhetoric and accused O'Reilly of recommending al-Qaeda to blow up San Francisco. Bill yelled, "You are wrong. I didn't say it here. You don't know what the hell I said with all due respect. You got it from Media Matter." Senator Dodd said, "Focus on your legitimate criticism." His statement provoked O'Reilly to respond: "You are a propagandist. I used to respect you. I don't have any respect for you. Because this is vile and you're legitimizing it." The senator ended by saying Bill "Makes derogatory comments about individuals and groups once every 6.8 seconds. That's nine times a minute. That's your history." [246]

The controversial excerpt reads:

> "Listen, citizens of San Francisco, if you vote against military recruiting, you're not going to get another nickel in federal funds. Fine, you want to be your own country? Go right ahead. And if al-Qaeda comes in here and blows you up, we're going to say, look, every other place in America is off limits to you, except San Francisco."

> O'Reilly's comment about San Francisco might have elicited cries of bigotry, if taken out of context.[247]

The executive branch has its enforcer, the FBI. The legislative branch has it enforcer, the sergeant of arms. The judicial branch has it enforcer, the US Marshals. And in the media, the News branch has its enforcer too, Fox Security, courtesy of Bill O' Reilly. Committed leftists Richard Bey, Keith Olbermann, Janeane Garofalo, David Brock, an endless list…can't stop putting his name in their mouth. [248]

Bill O'Reilly is an American political commentator, and he is the host of the Fox cable news program 'The O'Reilly Factor.' Bill has achieved the highest educational degree. He is a Master degree holder in Broadcast Journalism from Boston College. He also holds another Master degree of Public Administration in Harvard's John Kennedy school of Government. That is one of the reasons why O'Reilly is the best in the business.

O'Reilly had previously worked for WCBS-TV, ABC News and King World Production.

For many years now, 'The O'Reilly Factor' has been the highest rated show in the nation. Bill O'Reilly's television program is full of scintillating segments. As you already know, "I am not the smartest guy in the world," Bill intoned. [249]

Mr. O'Reilly helped cause the Red Cross to significantly increase payments to affected people after the World Trade Center disaster. After months of stonewalling, the Red Cross finally saw the writing on the wall and did the right thing. Mr. O'Reilly claimed: "It was pressure by my TV program 'The O'Reilly Factor' that put the Red Cross on the hot seat. Night after night, I pounded away at the injustice of asking Americans for specific donations and then not living up to the pitch. Finally, The New York Times stepped up as well, challenging the Red Cross in an editorial." A spokesperson for the Red Cross apologized: "We deeply regret that our actions over the last eight weeks have not been as sharply focused as the American public wants or the victims of the tragedy deserve."[250]

Ultimatum to the White House

What was Bill O'Reilly's position on the preemptive war in Iraq and the notion of Iraq harboring weapons of mass destruction? In Early 2003, right before we invaded Iraq, Bill famously said on Good Morning America, "If the Americans go in and overthrow Saddam Hussein and it's clean, he has nothing, I will apologize to the nation, and I will not trust the Bush administration again." Bill believed that the Iraqis had WMD and was certain that liberating Iraq and overthrowing Saddam was the right thing for the Bush administration to undertake. However, Bill was furious when on May 1st, 2003, the President declared the end of combat, but didn't declare the discovery of weapons of mass destruction. O'Reilly challenged the White House and he threatened to censure the Bush administration if no weapons of mass destruction were found. In the next few weeks, Bill risked incurring the wrath of the White House by saying

> "It is possible the President did lie, but most of the credible evidence points to wishful thinking on WMDs, rather than outright deception. By the way, the President must tell us his feelings on the guerrilla action in Iraq and the WMDs, or risk losing popularity. We the people deserve an extensive update from the President before he goes on summer vacation. This is not a partisan issue. This is a people issue. There are things we have the right to know about, and the president must tell us."

But a year went by and no WMDs were found. Bill was patient with the Bush administration, but it wasn't for long. [251]

After the long wait, Mr. O'Reilly hesitantly apologized to the American people on Good morning America, the same program on which he said he would denounce the Bush administration if no weapons were found. On NPR, Bill O'Reilly said, "America will accept mistakes if mistakes were made honestly, but it need to be defined by the Bush administration why the intelligence was faulty. And, uh, you know, there is no spin on that. They have to do it." After Bill O'Reilly denounced the President's administration, he found himself on the fringes of the Republican Party. [252]

O'Reilly had interviewed President Bush and made favorable remarks about Bush "Even though most Americans believe the country is not in good shape right now, most Americans do not hate President Bush. But the 'Take Back American' crowd is full of Bush haters and people who routinely reject all but far-left thought." Even though Bill O'Reilly's Republican credentials had dramatically improved, he wasn't able to interview Dick Cheney. The Vice President has turned down offers to appear on his show. [253]

Caution: you are about to enter the no spin zone with Kenny Miller. Bill O'Reilly also has a radio berth; he hosts the Radio Factor, a program syndicated by Westwood One.

In 2006, Bill dropped a caller's call from his live Radio Factor program for mentioning the name of MSNBC's anchorman, Keith Olberman. Bill accused the caller of being part of a large mass of individuals that had been purposely calling his show just to mention Mr. Olbermann, which is very disrespectful for a caller to do. The caller said "I like to listen to you during the day. I think Keith Olbermann show..." The caller was cut off and Bill responded by stating that

> "Mike is he's a gone guy. You know, we have your phone number, by the way. So if you're listening, Mike, we have your phone number, and we're going to turn it over to Fox Security, and you will be getting a little visit. When you call us, ladies and gentlemen, just so you know, we do have your number, and if you say anything untoward, obscene or anything like that, Fox Security then will contact your local authorities, and you will be held accountable. Fair."

This experience stated the whole Fox Security story and it had American talking about it. [254]

Leftwing attack machines

Bill has drawn criticisms from many notable figures including Al Franken, David Letterman, George Clooney, and Bill Moyer among others. Almost all the leaning Left wing figures have excoriated Mr. O'Reilly on many fronts.

The host of PBS's Bill Moyer Journal news program has gone on the record severely bashing Bill O'Reilly and Fox News. Moyer charged that "The Fox News have not only mongered for war along with the administration, not only embraced the administration's policies because they were conservatives, including going to war, but also mounted a smile machine to discredit any journalist who dared to stand against the official view of reality." Moyer then attacked Mr. O'Reilly "If a journalist tried to tell the truth about the intelligence the O'Reillys would come down on them and you know slander them, discredit them. So that good reporting lost it power to break through because of this, this avalanche of opposition and venom directed at them." Bill Moyer, an advocate for far Left causes on his show, concluded that: "Bill

O'Reilly does not have the courage to come on my show and answer the questions I wanted to ask him."[255]

A Media watchdog group published a book 'The Oh Really? Factor.' The author smeared the title of O'Reilly show. The book author accused Bill of inaccuracies.

Media Matters for America, a liberal organization, often criticizes Bill O'Reilly. And they observe him like a watchdog. He is one of their main targets.

O'Reilly retaliated against Media Matter: "The most vile, despicable human beings in the country who listen to every word of the program. And then they try to feed stuff out to the mainstream media to discredit me. I mean that's what they do every single day of the year, they do this."[256]

Critics said O'Reilly made lots of money from the Passion of Christ movie, but he turned around and trashed the film on his show. What Bill O'Reilly said about the film was: "The movie is ultra-intense and violent. To me, the violence became numbing. Gibson's movie is not for everybody. But if you see it, you may wonder why Gibson himself has been so brutally attacked." David Letterman, host of Late Show with David Letterman, acknowledged: "I'm not smart enough to debate you point to point, but I have the feeling that about 60 percent of what you say is crap." Janeane Garofalo, a liberal talk show host, used obscene language against O'Reilly on Bill Moyer's show.

Regardless of all the public service Mr. O'Reilly has done for the country, it is not enough to douse the firestorm of criticisms coming from the Left, i.e. Democrats and liberals.

O'Reilly uttered, "Every corrupt media out there, if this continues, I will hunt you down. The smear stops here" (a paraphrase.) But the smear from the left continued and O'Reilly made the following request: "So all those clowns over at the liberal radio network, we could incarcerate them immediately. Will you have that done, please? Send over the FBI and just put them in chains."[257]

United Nations deeds

Right after September 11th, 2001, Bill O'Reilly had been thrashing United Nations Secretary General Kofi Annan and the U.N. as an international organization. O'Reilly acknowledged that the Secretary General was against America expanding the war on terror to Iraq because there was a possibility that it would result in destabilizing the region "Annan gets the Nobel Peace Prize" O'Reilly noted: "But he is unable to come up with solutions to lasting peace. Milosevic, America got him out. Terrorism, the UN has done nothing to combat the rise of Muslim fundamentalism. The Middle East, Annan is clueless." The Secretary General pleaded, "Any attempts or any decision to attack Iraq will be unwise. It can lead to major escalation in the region, and I would hope that would not be the case." About the Noble Peace Prize awarded to the Secretary General, Bill O'Reilly felt that instead, it "Should be given to the armed forces of the United States. Those brave men and women are risking their lives so the world can have a lasting peace." Throughout his tenure, Kofi Annan wasn't able to effectively prevent mass atrocities in Africa. [258]

In May 2003, Bill O'Reilly exposed an alleged corruption in the United Nations' oil-for-food program. The executive director of the U.N. oil-for–food program admitted on ABC News that the U.N. "looked the other way" while Iraq's president Saddam was stealing billions of dollars from the oil-for-food budget. But when he made his first appearance on the 'Factor,' he denied the alleged corruption. After the interview, Bill O'Reilly had this to say: "We told you the U.N. was not honest, was not looking out for Americans, and did not care about right and wrong. It is good to be right, but it's frustrating as well. The U.N. will continue to be a corrupt institution."

The oil-for-food program was started by the United Nations in 1995 and was terminated in late 2003 after Saddam Hussein was removed from power. The Iraqis, through the program, sold oil on the world market in exchange for commodities.[259]

In 2004, Bill O'Reilly continued his attacks on U.N. Secretary General Kofi Annan. Bill accused him of being incompetent. O'Reilly said "When you look at Rwanda, 800,000 people were slaughtered under his watch. That tells me something is wrong." A supporter of Secretary Annan claimed that "The secretary general has been one of the most successful ever." But the supporter couldn't defend what went wrong in Rwanda. O'Reilly said the bottom line was that Kofi Annan could not prevent genocide in the poor African country, and the U.N. was swimming in corruption. [260]

Incompetence in the United Nations

In July of 2006, the most unlikely politician in America to defend the U.N. actually stood by the organization. John Bolton, the former ambassador to the United Nations, made headlines when he threw U.N. under the bus "There is no such thing as the United Nations. If the U.N. secretary building in New York lost 10 stories, it wouldn't make a bit of difference" Bolton's comment came over a decade ago. Bill O'Reilly called the U.N.'s Security Council a joke: "I just think the whole place is a rat's nest. They can't stop the slaughter in Darfur; they couldn't do anything in Iraq. We're almost going it alone,

British and the United States." O'Reilly lamented: "The United Nations doesn't even understand there's a worldwide war on terror. Even though India gets bombed; even though Somalia, now, is making trouble with Ethiopia, and country after country. They still don't get it. What's it gonna take for them to get it?" However, Ambassador Bolton partially defended the organization: "Well I think what we're trying to do is advance American interests."

O'Reilly recalled that in "Rwanda, 750,000 people died because the U.N. took their own time." Bill asked the Ambassador, "You must have the most frustrating job in the world?" He continued, "Because you can't reason with people who won't band together to stop worldwide war on terror, to stop the terrorists, I mean, how frustrating is that?" Bolton had the last word: "Well I think the thing to keep your eye on is making sure that American interests are protected and interests of our allies. And, that makes it worthwhile because if we weren't there protecting them, it would be trouble."[261]

Bill O'Reilly has previously hinted at a possible run for the White House. Americans want Bill O'Reilly to run for president. He may run for the US Congress. His versatility has been an asset to the Republicans. O'Reilly has written six books, and certainly books have been written about him. The majority of all Bill O'Reilly books reached #1 on the New York Times Best Seller List. Two of his books are titled 'The O'Reilly Factor: The Good, the Bad, and the completely ridiculous in America life.' and the 'The No Spin Zone.' Bill O'Reilly is certainly the most influential person in the American media. [262]

Chapter 12

Sean Hannity: One of the most Influential People in America

"From coast to coast, from border to border, and from sea to shining sea," Sean is a definite force to be reckoned with in the American news media network. Mr. Hannity is a man of principle, a 'Reagan conservative.' Sean is very capable of attracting an enormous number of top government officials on his show. Imagine having the likes of Oliver North, Gov. Romney, Sen. Kay Bailey Hutchison, and Speaker Gingrich on his show in just less than three hours?

Sean Hannity has hosted all the senior members of the president's administration.

The 2008 presidential election (February 07-December 07)

All through the second half of 2007, both GOP presidential hopeful Mayor Giuliani and Governor Mitt Romney had frequently been a guest on Sean Hannity's show.

Sean is like a magnet, he attracts all the big names and he draws enormous praises from conservative, Republican, and Independent politicians. They have so much respect for Sean Hannity. In the 2008 presidential election, whom is Sean endorsing? Because of the former Mayor of New York's frequent invitation to Sean's program, liberal commentators like Richard Bey and Rachel Maddow have penciled down Sean for an indirect endorsement to Giuliani. Sean would be making a mistake endorsing any first tier GOP candidates at this early stage for president. [263]

Except for Senator John McCain, all the GOP candidates have pled to be on Hannity's show. They surely know where their conservative supports will come from. Sean tells his listeners that he personally likes Senator McCain, but he has fundamental policy disagreements with the senator from Arizona.

Talking about the presidential election, President Bush revealed to Hannity that his biggest challenge was the actual campaigning for a year to become the party's nominee. And Bush also said campaigning to be the commander- in- chief is a heck of a fight. [264]

Democratic leaders cut and run

On September 12, 2007, Bush endorsed General Petraeus' withdrawal plan of 30,000 US troops from Iraq by mid 2008. The military commander in Iraq and the ambassador to Iraq outlined the achievement of the 'troop surge.' They pleaded to Congress to allow the troops to complete their mission. Sean called Senator Clinton a fatally fraud candidate. The reason for this was that Clinton told General Petraeus in a congressional hearing that the progress reports on the war in Iraq were a "Willing suspension of disbelief." Hannity perceived this statement as Senator Hillary Clinton attacking a four star general: "Clinton is a liar and a propagandist; smearing a war hero just to get ahead. General Petraeus, putting his life everyday is nothing but propaganda for Clinton. And the general is taking a failure for Bush?" (a paraphrase) Hannity went on to say that the September 07 ads, from MoveOn.org, referring to General Petraeus as "General Betray US" were unacceptable. The General Betray US's smeared phrase was actually started by an Air American hostess.

Moveon.org is a liberal advocacy group.[265]

The Democrats were beside themselves with anger over the Petraeus plan. They said it is unacceptable to pull out only 30,000 troops and keep 130,000 troops. And they also called for all the US troops in Iraq to be withdrawn by the end of April 08. They don't care about the ramifications of pulling out of Iraq. Democrats didn't agree with Petraeus' assessment that the security situation in Iraq had really improved and it's no longer a quagmire.

Sean Hannity lambasted the Democrats when they intensified their outrage on the strategy outlined by the general. They complained that the administration plan was simply a return to the force level that existed before the 'troop surge.' The troop surge took place on February 7th, 2007. That was when the president increased the number of United States troops deployed in the Iraqi region. The Democrats were reluctant in accepting the troop surge plan by Bush; they would rather have accepted the status quo or a complete withdrawal of our troops from Iraq.

Over the course of the war in Iraq, the Democrats have been reluctant to fund for the war, they have repeatedly tried to cut off funding on combat for our troops: "I think the American people are getting tired of sending the money with no end in sight," Schumer, senior senator from New York, hypothesized. Democrats still want our troops home even though there have been changes that have reduced the necessity of American military involvement.

The American military role has been shifted more to training and counterterrorism. [266]

After his ups and downs at New York University, Hannity had been living on a knife-edge until he moved to Atlanta. Sean worked at WGST-AM in Atlanta. His ABC Radio Network show began airing in the early 2000's.

Over the years, Sean has been one of the most popular commentators in America. His radio program is titled 'The Sean Hannity Show,' and the show is syndicated in many stations in all of America. His show can also be heard on the Armed Forces Radio Network. He uses his show to resurrect and promote Reagan's conservative agendas. He is well equipped for the long haul. Because according to Talker magazine, Hannity is safely ranked No. 2 in the Top 100 Talk Show Hosts in America. He calls his radio callers 'Hannitized Americas.' [267]

The 2008 presidential election (February 07-December 07)

Sean Hannity has been chastising the Democratic 08 candidates for President.

Whether it is Hillary Clinton or Sen. Obama, Sean goes for broke. "The Stop Hillary Express' will be up and running and it is topic A," Sean admits.

Hedge Fund mogul George Soros, had contributed a lot to Sen. Clinton: "He is the man behind the curtain, the man with the check book, a philanthropic" Sean said. Soros, in 2004, swore to stop the reelection of George Bush "It is the central focus of my life, a matter of life and death," Soros declared. He donated millions of dollars to the Kerry- Edwards presidential ticket to make sure his wishes come true: "America, under Bush, is a danger to the world. And I'm willing to put my money where my month is," Soros concluded. Apart from George Soros' contributions, the other big sources of Clinton's cash are an unlikely address: "Sleepovers in the Lincoln bedroom," Hannity said. "Democratic donors and all their payments to Clinton; which she forced them to donate." This brings back memories of the 1990's White House sleepovers in Lincoln Bedroom. [268]

Sean Hannity is a great American and he is the last beacon of truth in a troubled time. Americans are guessing the troubled time Sean is talking about. Hillary Rodham Clinton is about to become our next president, or the re-reviving of the Fair Doctrine act, catapulted by Senator Dublin and co. Regardless, Sean intoned: "Let your heart not be troubled." Mr. Hannity has been stressing that his radio program "Is not a Right vs. Left show, it is a Right vs. Wrong show."

Mr. Hannity reprimanded the anti-military remarks of extremist leftwing orthodox liberals like Rep. Murtha, Senator Obama, Senator Kerry, Senator Reid, and Senator Dublin. John Kerry said: "There is no reason that young American soldiers need to be going into the homes of Iraqis in the dead of night, terrorizing kids and children, you know, women." Barrack Obama said: "We've got to get the job done there and that requires us to have enough troops so that we're not just air- raiding villages and killing civilians, which is causing enormous pressure over there." Senator Reid claimed the war in Iraq is lost and Obama's senate partner, Senator Dublin, compared our troops to the Nazis.

The last anti-military remark comes from Rep. John Murtha: "There was no firefight. There was no IED that killed these innocent people. Our troops overreacted because of the pressure on them, and they killed innocent civilians in cold blood."[269]

Hannity, a handsome conservative activist, attacked the Democratic Senate and House leaders: Senators Reid, Senator Schumer, Senator Dublin, Speaker Pelosi, and Rep. Clyburn.

The style of the 2007 Democratic leadership can be compared to the 1972 McGovern style of liberalism. "Non- binding legislation upon non-binding legislation is an ideological struggle, a resolution to condemn. The Democrats are invested in defeat in the war in Iraq, they keep on moving the goal post and the bar keeps getting raised," said Hannity. It really speaks volumes about the Democratic leadership. By cutting funding for the war, the Democrats are looking to take money back from the troops and then go on the record to say that they support the troops. They are undermining our troops. The Democratic Party is scared that they will lose their support from the American people. They are afraid that the public would see them as not supporting the troops.

In the 2006 midterm elections, the Democratic Party turned their back on a senior member, Joe Lieberman and voted for someone else. Sean admitted "Joe Lieberman is the only real Democrat left,-Lieberman belongs to the class of real traditional Democrats like FDR, Truman and JFK not McGovern, Carter and Mondale" (a paraphrase). [270]

In 2004, Sean stock rose further, as he was largely responsible for the last presidential election that witnessed Bush defeating his Democratic opponent. Sean had a big influence in the coverage of the election.

Sean and Rush Limbaugh are the two first tier commentators in the country. Sean's show claims that "five days, three hours a day is all we asked for," though that is not really the case because Hannity is also on cable television.

Sean Hannity joined the Fox News Channel in the mid nineties, as a co-host of Hannity and Colmes. Hannity anchored as the program's conservative television talk host.

Sean's Fox News show is the second highest-rated program in cable news television. Between Sean's radio and television program, he has hosted thousands of government dignities. He hosted former Mexican President, Vicente Fox and ex-Israeli Prime Minister Netanyahu. Hannity has had a dialogue with the entire GOP rank and file and who is who in the Republican Party. [271]

Middle East threats

Should we take out Iran's nuclear facilities? And make the decision for the United States to engage Iran before they have nuclear weapons? From the 'Hate Hannity Hotline,' "Hannity has been salivating for war against Iran with other people doing the fighting and dying." Sean always gets verbally attacked by anti-war protesters.

Iran's President wants Israel to be wiped off the map and he acknowledged the world would be better without America.

In September 2007, red flags were raised when Ahmadinejad, during his conference at the United Nations, requested to lay a wreath at the World Trade Center site. The Iranian's president had the guts to request a tour of Ground Zero. The United States Constitution guaranteed Americans, not Iranians, freedom of speech. Questions were raised as to whether US authorities should permit Ahmandinejad to enter Ground Zero and lay a wreath to pay condolences to the victims of 9-11. But the larger question was whom does Ahmadinejad wanted to pay condolence to? The innocent American victims who died? Or the terrorists responsible for crashing the two planes in the WTC tower, killing three thousand Americans?

The Iranian president has a track record of being anti-American and anti-Semitic. Americans can't envision Ahmadinejad touring the World Trade Center's site. [272]

Before his initial request to tour Ground Zero, the Iranian president had doubted the death of the 3,000 Americans that died after the WTC attacks. Hannity was 105% against it, "A modern day Nazi, a holocaust denier, who is anti Semitic, who threatened to wipe Israel out of the map; and the 'proxy war,' arming the Iraqis with guns thereby providing the Iraqis weaponry to kill the Americans for the Iranians." Ahmadinejad also called the Holocaust a myth: "If the holocaust is reality of our time, a history that occurred, why is there no sufficient research that can approach the topic from different perspectives?" The NYPD and the Secret Service turned down his request. [273]

Ahmadinejad wasn't allowed to go to Ground Zero, but he was allowed to give a speech at Columbia University. Mr. Hannity asked, "He denies the Holocaust, he's providing weaponry killing American troops, here's a guy that, you know, why would you provide a prestigious forum for such a maniacal, evil dictator, and a guy that wants to wipe Israel off the map?" Hannity stressed on, "Where in the Constitution says we can allow a terrorist to speak at a University in America." Ahmadinejad, the Iranian president, did damage his credibility when he said, "In Iran, we don't have homosexuals, like in your country." Ahmadinejad was also asked why Iranian women are harshly treated. He answered, "Women in Iran enjoy the highest levels of freedom."[274]

"Sean Hannity straight ahead" on Iraq Speaker Gingrich, a Fox News contributor, said that "To stay the course I think in the long run is not a very sound strategy." And we should work effectively to stop Iran's 'proxy war' against U.S. forces in Iraq.

When the liberal media labeled Hannity as a rubberstamp for President Bush, Mr. Hannity replied, "I have disagreements with Bush that we chronicle on my program…I was against prescription drugs, the nomination of Harriet Miers as a Supreme Court judge and the Dubai Ports take over." [275]

In 2006 Dubai Ports World, a firm owned by United Arab Emirates, had made arrangements to take over management of US's ports in New York, Florida, Pennsylvania, New Jersey, Maryland, and Louisiana. However, the deal was postponed and then canceled because Congress and the media strongly criticized the proposal. Dubai Ports World had the backing of the executive branch. Gordon England, the Deputy Defense Secretary, appeared before Congress and gave a substantial review on the proposal. He tried to convince the Senate not to derail the transaction. The Dubai Port deal faced criticism because their government had been linked to terrorism. For instance, two of the September 11th hijackers came from UAE, and part of the money used to fund the terrorist attacks were funneled through Dubai. The bipartisan opposition by Congress over the Dubai ports led the deal to be terminated. A spokesperson from UAE elaborated, "…Like if it was an African or European country, it would not have been subjected to this kind of scrutiny. But since this is just purely an Arab country, I think it just stopped some of the lawmakers who are making a big deal out of a purely legitimate business transaction." Bush backed the takeover proposal and previously threatened to veto any legislation that would interfere with the deal. UAE is one of America's most important allies in the Middle East and has cut ties to terrorists after 9/11. They have joined America in fighting the war on terror.

Bush said there was no outcry about a British company managing the ports. He called on lawmakers to "Step up and explain why all of a sudden a Middle Eastern company is held to a different standard. It's really important that we not send mixed messages to allies." [276]

Let freedom reign

Sean Hannity, one of the most aggressive proponents of conservative beliefs, lauded Habitat for Humanity in rebuilding the Golf Coast. In 2004, Sean received the Marconi Radio Award for Network syndicated personal of the year. In 2007, Hannity was awarded another Marconi accolade for his scintillating efforts in advancing the conservative agenda. He successfully hosted his freedom concert. Sean Hannity also hosted solution day with Newt Gingrich.

Sean's goal for the country is a free market solution to health care, energy independence, border control, improvement in education, fighting terrorism and earmark control. Sean said a change is imminent, "American needs a change of coursed. Change is good, but not change for change," Hannity said.

Sean has two interesting books to his credit, 'Deliver us from Evil. Defeating Terrorism, Despotism and Liberalism' and 'Let Freedom Ring: Winning the War of Liberty against Liberalism.'[277]

President Jimmy Carter

Sean has severely criticized former President Jimmy Carter on the anti-Semitic things Carter said that have been chronicled. Carter was responsible for the rise of the Islamic faction's movement in Iraq. The birth of Islamic terrorism in the Middle East started during the Carter's presidency.

In the 21ˢᵗ century, Americans have to deal with what President Carter started. Sean points at the way Carter was beaten by President Reagan during the 1980 presidential election. "Can you imagine a 44 states landslide Reagan victory over a sitting president?" Hannity said, "For crying out loud, President

Carter is a Nazi appeaser, who attacked Vice President Dick Cheney." Sean often paid tribute to Reagan and other true conservative politicians. [278]

Liberal media bias

Sean said the liberals carry the mainstream news media's water. He called Keith Olbermann the "left wing Media Matters guy." Sean wondered why he was not being asked to moderate a Democratic presidential debate. He trashed MSNBC for picking "leftwing hawk" Chris Matthew to moderate a Republican presidential debate. Sean Hannity reacted to a comment made by presidential candidate John Edwards. The former Democratic senator's comment was in regards to African Americans either ending up in jail or dead. Sean said it is a double standard because the media didn't criticize John Edwards. But if a Republican had made the exact statement, it would be an issue to discuss. The whole mainstream media would echo it and the individual would be excoriated by the Democrats. [279]

On 'Hannity and Colmes', Sean hosted Neil Boortz, a radio talk show host on the topic "Will Media Matters force media outlets to correct Air America false mugging story?" First of all, Mr. Boortz owed Habitat for Humanity a decent amount of money. Sean was unfair for inviting a debtor to talk about Ms. Rhodes, a partner with Habitat for America. Boortz didn't trash Rhodes but he made his presence known: "Oh I mean she's gone on the air and just told unbelievable blatant lies about me." Rhodes was reportedly mugged and beaten in New York City. A liberal talk show host immediately blamed Rhodes' brutal beating on a possible right wing supporter. However, sources revealed that Rhodes wasn't beaten, and no mugging activities occurred. She was believed to have fallen while walking her dog. Boortz then went on to wish her a speedy recovery. [280]

On Fox Cable television, Hannity also hosts the one-hour weekend program called 'Hannity's America.' Bringing back the Fairness doctrine may be scaring the life out of Sean; well, at least it won't affect Hannity's cable television programs.

Sean claimed that "Conservatives want equal opportunity but not equal result."

Sean Hannity's lessons are from the heart: "Freedom, if you live life in fear, you are not going to live life. Don't let fear come into your life; the minute you do, you will stop living. Don't do it if your heart tells you not to do it. You will never lose when you stand on your principles and values." The depth of Sean Hannity's reverence is understood in his fundamental beliefs. [281]

Sean's theme song:

Martina McBride, Independence Day
"Let freedom ring...
Let the white dove sing...
Let the whole world know that today is a day of reckoning
Let the weak be strong...
Let the right be wrong...
Roll the stone away, let the guilty pay
It's Independence Day." [282]

Chapter 13

AIR AMERICA RADIO, one of the most Influential Bodies of Media

Finally, the rise of progressive liberal radio

Air America is a counterweight to conservative talk radio.

On March 21, 2004, Air America radio started its programming. The radio network was first pioneered by Randi Rhodes. Popular figures Al Franken and Jerry Springer also joined the network. Air America took a fall in 2006, but they never went out of business. However on March 6, 2007, a Democratic New York politician Mark Green, along with Stephen Green, invested in Air America Radio.

Mark Green launched the newly reformed station with the likes of Sen. Clinton, Sen. Obama, and Ralph Nader. They were all in support for the station. Some of the old staffers were considered surplus to requirements by the new management. They were either axed or given lesser time on air.

In the beginning, the fact of the matter was that without Randi Rhodes and Al Franken, Air America would not be in existence. They both had good ratings. [283]

Time Line: Randi invaded the President's administration: Probing White House activities

President Bush said, "And if somebody committed a crime, they will no longer work in my administration." Gonzalez, Mier, Taylor, Griffen, Rove, Bolten, and Goodling, did they all commit a crime?

In early 2007, the Bush administration quietly fired and replaced nine U.S. attorneys.

By law the Bush administration is allow to fire and replace the federal prosecutors.

However, some of the attorneys that were given marching orders were said to have been investigating GOP and White House members. Meanwhile, a Patriot Act provision allowed the fired attorneys' replacements to circumvent Senate confirmation. Brett Tolman, who worked in the office of Senator Specter, was the staffer who slipped into the Patriot Act renewal, the provision on the appointment of interim U.S. Attorney. Most notable was the appointment of Timothy Griffin as the new U.S. Attorney in Arkansas. Because of Brett Tolman's action, Griffin, a Karl Rove prodigy, didn't have to be confirmed by Congress.[284]

In July 2007, Harriet Mier, a former White House Counsel, twice rejected orders from the House to honor a subpoena for her testimony on the firing of the US Attorneys. Because Harriet Miers refused to show up after being subpoenaed, the House's Judiciary Committee voted out contempt charges for Ms. Miers. White House Chief of Staff Josh Bolten was also summoned. Ms. Miers, who withdrew her nomination for US Supreme Court judge, claimed immunity so as not to appear before the House. However, the House subcommittee overruled her claims. Rep. Conyers, the Chairman of the Committee, said: "Her failure to comply with our subpoena is a serious affront to this committee and our constitutional system of checks and balances. We are carefully planning our next steps." Refusal to show up before lawmakers could subject Miers to inherent contempt power.

> "Under the inherent contempt power, the individual is brought before Congress by the Sergeant-at-Arms, tried at the bar of the body, and can be imprisoned. The purpose of the imprisonment or other sanction may be either punitive or coercive. The inherent contempt power has been recognized by the Supreme Court as inextricably related to Congress's constitutionally-based power to investigate." [285]

White House Counsel Fred Fielding said, "Ms. Miers has absolute immunity from compelled congressional testimony as to matters occurring while she was a senior adviser to the president." Finally in July 2007, Speaker of the House Nancy Pelosi moved forward the case against Miers. Pelosi promised a full House's congressional contempt charge for Mrs. Miers. However, Miers immediately claimed executive privilege. "Some type of over privileged executive" a congressional staffer acknowledged. Randi Rhodes said "Even the privilege are privilege; the executive privilege should not imply because it is not in the U.S Constitution."

Executive privilege is a claim by the president that certain communications with members of the executive branch may be withheld from the legislative and the judicial branches of government. [286]

The purge of the prosecutor's probe continued when the Acting Associate Attorney General William Mercer asked the President to withdraw his nomination to be the official no. 3 man in the Justice Department. Mercer was scared to testify under oath on what he knew about the smeared Republican's U.S. Attorney. But not scared to testify under oath was Sara Taylor, a former White House's adviser. She appeared before the Senate Judiciary Committee to testify about the axed U.S. attorneys. But she also invoked executive privilege. Sara Taylor only agreed to respond to particular questioning. She didn't damage the credibility of White House's top aides. [287]

Caging List

In the caging list case, emails from architect Karl Rove's office ended up in the hands of a BBC journalist. Caging list was a technique of using mails to prevent people from voting. It was crafted to disenfranchise thousands of minority voters; largely homeless people and soldiers sent abroad. Again Tim Griffin, the interim U.S. attorney of Arkansas, was singled out.

In the caging list, if you don't reply to the mail, the assumption will be that you are not illegible to vote. The instructions on the face of the mail read 'Do Not Forward, Return to Sender'

Mr. Palast received emails from the 2004 Bush's presidential reelection campaign. Tim Griffin allegedly sent lists of voters (mainly minority voters) to state Republican Party leaders for their (minority voters' ballots) not to be counted. If affected voters demand to appeal, party organizers will challenge their votes. Since Griffin was an aide to Karl Rove, it is conventional wisdom that Rove was involved too. However, assistant to the Attorney General Monica Goodling and Deputy Attorney General Paul McNulty were called upon to testify before Congress. Griffin tried to defend the whole operation:

> "The real story is this. There were thousands of reported illegal/fake voter registrations around the country, so some of the Republican State Parties mailed letters welcoming new voters to the newly registered voters. The Republican State Parties ultimately wanted to show that thousands of fraudulent registrations had been completed."

Goodling testified against McNulty in the House Judiciary Committee. She claimed that Paul McNulty "Failed to disclose that he had some knowledge of allegations that Mr. Griffin had been involved in vote 'caging' during his work on the President's 2004 campaign." Liberal critics said, "Sending soldiers to Iraq, then turning around and ensuring that their votes will not be counted, as they take bullets on behalf of the administration that sent them there, ranks among the most traitorous acts imaginable in the United States of America." [288]

Infighting in the Justice Determent

Investigations into the Bush's administration continued when Congress discovered an illegal warrantless wiretapping program. The program had been conducted against the American people in secret. Since early 2000's, Congress had been asking for information about the warrantless wiretapping order. Congress was investigating whether an early 2004 infighting within the Bush administration had to do with the NSA warrantless domestic wiretapping program or whether it was other national security programs. James Comey, the former Acting Attorney General/ Deputy Attorney General, muddied the waters when he went before Congress and revealed that the Bush administration tried to take advantage of former Attorney General John Ashcroft while he was in the process of recovering from a surgery operation in his Intensive Care Unit. James Comey prevented this bizarre effort by the White House. The Bush administration had high expectations that Ashcroft, a man who was gravely ill and under the influence of painkillers, would sign off on a criminal order to wiretap Americans. [289]

In mid 2007, Attorney General Gonzales testified before the Senate Judiciary committee and he admitted that the 2004 hospital meeting was not about a National Security Agency (NSA) domestic surveillance program. However, while testifying before a House Committee, FBI Director Robert Mueller totally contradicted Gonzales's under oath testimony. Mueller acknowledged that John Ashcroft had informed him that the 2004 hospital meeting with Andy Card and Alberto Gonzalez was about the NSA's warrantless wiretapping program.

Terrorist Surveillance Program (TSP) is the White House term for National Security Agency (NSA).

FBI Director Mueller's conversation with Rep. Jackson Lee (D-Texas)

Congresswoman Lee: Did you have an understanding that the discussion was on TSP?

Mueller: I had an understanding that the discussion was on a NSA program, yes.

Congresswoman Lee: I guess we use 'TSP' we use warrantless wiretapping, so would I be comfortable in saying that those were the items that were part of the discussion?

Mueller: I- it was- the discussion was on a national- a NSA program that has been discussed, yes. [290]

The White House sent Gonzalez, then White House legal counsel and Andy Card, then White House Chief of Staff to persuade Ashcroft to overrule James Comey and reauthorize the wiretap program. While testifying before Congress, Gonzalez told lawmakers that a meeting with the 'Gang of Eight' on March 10th 2003 was in regard to former Acting Attorney General Comey's concerns. He said the meeting wasn't about the Terrorist Surveillance Program (TSP) that the President had confirmed. To make matters worst, John Ashcroft, once a United States senator, testified in secret to the senate about the NSA domestic spying program. He also contradicted Gonzalez's sworn senate testimony. CIA Director Gen. Michael Hayden, who was then the Director of National Security Agency (NSA) and Deputy Secretary of State John Negroponte, who then was the director of national intelligent (DNI), both contradicted Gonzales's statement. This brought the tally to five contradictions against Mr. Gonzalez. [291] Although Gonzalez faced allegations that he perjured himself before Congress, he still stood by his statement. Gonzalez's sworn testimony is in print: "The disagreement that occurred, and the reason for the visit to the hospital, Senator, was about other intelligence activities. It was not about the terrorist surveillance program (TSP) that the president announced to the American people," [292]

The members of the 'Gang of Eight' representing the Republican Party included Bill Frist, Dennis Hastert, Pat Roberts, and former CIA boss, Porter Goss. And the Democratic Party members of the 'gang of eight' were Daschle, Pelosi, Rockefeller and Harman. The 'Gang of Eight' was comprised of the congressional leaders in both houses. The 'gang of eight' meetings usually took place either in Cheney's office or the White House Situation Room. James Comey told lawmakers that he was outraged that the White House sent Card and Gonzalez to go behind his back to see Ashcroft. Comey was refusing to reauthorize what was believed to be the NSA warrantless eavesdropping program. Members of the Gang of Eight were worried about Comey's refusal to reauthorize the NSA program. After the failed attempt to evade Comey's presence at the hospital, Gonzales, allegedly lying through his teeth, claimed, "We went there because we thought it was important for him to know where the congressional leadership was on this." After one of the 'gang of eight' meetings, Senator Tom Daschle obviously said "Cheney talked like it was something routine. We really had no idea what it was about whether the process is legal and should continue." Rep. Nancy Pelosi, who was then the minority leader, was reluctant to comment on the meetings. She said "I made clear my disagreement with what the White House was asking." Senator Rockefeller complained that the congressional 'Gang of Eight' leaders were unclear about the White House agenda. [293]

Randi said that Bush was actually listening to our conversations; on April 20th 2004, President Bush made the following statement:

> "Now, by the way, any time you hear the United States government talking about wiretap, a wiretap requires a court order. Nothing has changed. When we're talking about chasing down terrorists, we're talking about getting a court order before we do so. Its important for our fellow citizens to understand, when you think Patriot act, constitutional guarantees are in place when it comes to doing what is necessary to protect our homeland, because we value the Constitution."

Ms. Rhodes said that the President was caught lying, that was why Bush made the next public statement: "The FISA law was written in 1978. We're having this discussion in 2006. It's a different world."

Bush is not using Jimmy Carter's FISA Law of 1978 as a benchmark for domestic spying by the NSA. [294]

Gonzales was involved in the firing of the attorneys, the caging list, and the illegal wiretapping program. On April 19th, when Gonzalez appeared before the Senate Judiciary Committee, he claimed 72 times that he did not recall to events in question regarding the nine fired attorneys. Dana Milbank of the Washington Post said "Gonzales uttered the phrase 'I don't recall' or 'I have no recollection or I have no memory.' That along the way, his answer became so routine that a Marine in the crowd put down his poster protesting the Iraq war and replaced it with a running 'I don't recall' tally."

The Attorney General frustrated many senators on the committee. Charles Schumer told the committee "If the attorney general cannot answer a straightforward, factual question from a senator about recent events, how can he possibly run the department?" Gonzales again came under fire when Senator John Rockefeller called his statement inaccurate and misleading. However, Dick Cheney, who was said to be responsible for sending Gonzales and Card to the hospital, came to the defense of Gonzales: "Alberto is a good man, good friend, on a difficult assignment." Cheney was then asked if he was disturbed by the appearance of Gonzalez perjuring himself: "Well, I don't want to get into the specifics with respect to his testimony and the questions that were asked. I know Alberto on a personal and professional basis and I hold him in high regards." [295]

Senator Specter was disappointed that Gonzalez wasn't more forthcoming in his under oath testimony. Specter (R-Pennsylvania) said a special prosecutor might be needed to confirm whether or not Gonzalez committed perjury. And Gonzales was reminded that the maximum penalty for lying to congressional lawmakers was five years in prison.

A jail is station in the Capitol complex.

Randi called Gonzalez a "World heavyweight perjurer champion... 72 times I don't recall?" And in the latter part of 2007, the Bush's administration sent former Defense Secretary Donald Rumsfeld to testify before Congress about the killing investigation of Pat Tillman in Iraq. Randi joked that the White House sent Rumsfeld to teach and show Gonzalez how to lie before Congress.[296]

Senator Clinton also weighed-in; she called on Gonzales to resign for his role in the dismissal of several U.S. attorneys. Clinton told ABC News: "The buck should stop somewhere. The attorney general who still seems to confuse his prior role as the president's personal attorney with his duty to the system of justice and to the entire country, he should resign." Clinton further added: "There is a great difference when a new president comes in, a new president gets to clean house. It is not done on a case-by-case basis where you didn't do what some senators or members of Congress told you to do in terms of investigations into your opponents. It is let's start afresh and every president has done that." At a news conference, Senator Chuck Schumer made headlines when he said "The attorney general took an oath to tell the truth, the whole truth and nothing but the truth. Instead he tells the half truth, the partial truth and everything but the truth – and he does it not once, not twice, but over and over and over again." The New York Times also weighed in: "In the United States attorneys scandal- the controversy over the political purge of nine top prosecutors- Mr. Gonzalez and his aides have twisted and mutilated the truth beyond recognition." [297]

Gonzalez did finally resign. After the resignation of Attorney General Gonzalez, Fox news star anchorman Brit Hume acknowledged that "Gonzales was a man almost without fans in Washington at the end, because he was never much appreciated or accepted by the conservative base of the Republican Party and the conservative activists in Washington. And he certainly wasn't popular among the Democrats. He was simply a crony."[298]

Gonzalez replaced John Ashcroft as the attorney general in 2005. Because Gonzalez was an aide to Bush in Texas and in D.C., his selection as attorney general was a foregone conclusion. Gonzalez was chosen for the post by Bush in preference to Comey because he was guaranteed to be a rubberstamp for the President. After Alberto Gonzalez finally resigned, Randi stated the fact that the justice department was in disarray and eight ways to Sunday because there was no attorney general, no deputy attorney general, and no associate attorney general. So Solicitor General (the government lawyer) Paul Clement, the 4th in line off the Justice Department, was the acting attorney general, the acting deputy attorney general, and the acting associate attorney general.

Meanwhile, Americans are looking for jobs.

Gonzalez's resignation also prompted Air America hostess Rachel Maddow to say "Don't let the crimes against humanity hit you on your way out." [299]

Effectiveness of liberal talk radio

The Information Security Oversight Office, an office that oversees the government security system, is required to officially examine the office of the president and the vice president to ensure they safeguard classified national security documents in a proper manner.

The Vice President's office refused inspection from the information security oversight office and also made an effort to temporarily shut down the office. For the first two years as vice president, Cheney allowed inspectors. But from 2003, Cheney's office began refusing to let in inspectors. And in 2004, Cheney's office blocked an onsite inspection by the oversight office.

Cheney claimed executive privileges regarding his early 2000's top-secret energy meetings. The Vice President balked at GAO's request for files of his energy task force. In a long run, the White House finally admitted to six meetings between the Vice President's energy task force and Enron representatives. But the White House continued to block efforts by the General accounting Office to find out the names of the representatives who met with Cheney.

The General Accounting Office (GAO) is the investigating arm of the legislative branch.

And in mid 2007, Vice President Cheney claimed that he was not part of the executive branch. He decided that he was a member of the legislative branch. Cheney then went on to claim that he was a member of both the executive and legislative branches of government. And finally, Cheney claimed he was back in the executive branch but not an entity within it. [300]Cheney alternated between the legislative and executive branches simply because he was looking for a way to avoid oversight and accountability. Rep. Waxman (D-California) said: "It is absurd, reflecting his view from the first day he got into office that laws don't apply to him. The irony is that he is taking the position that he is not part of the executive branch." Dana Perino, a White House press spokeswoman gave her take: "This is an interesting constitutional question that legal scholars can debate." A critic said: "It is quite a leap to go from hiding in a secure, undisclosed location in the capital to hiding in a secure, undisclosed location in the Constitution." [301]

In 2005, Randi was a guest on the Al Franken show; a wish that came true for their listeners. Imagine Al and Randi co hosting a show together. Randi has trashed almost every politically involved person; as long as they've made deceptive rhetoric. For example, conservative pundit Ann Coulter said that Sen. Max Cleland, a disabled former army veteran, dropped a grenade on himself. Randi has also trashed fellow liberal/moderate media anchorpeople Blitzer, King, Carlson, and Matthews. She said about Keith Olberman: "The only progressive voice that I can find in the mainstream media."

Some of the 'Randi Rhodes show's skits "Randi Rhodes, the woman that Karl Rove wishes he could be… The Randi Rhodes show, transcript available at Karl Rove's office… The Randi Rhodes show supports the troops by telling the truth… The Randi Rhodes show number 1 on the NSA most listened to list."[302]

Al Franken Show

Al Franken's show was strictly on the political news stories on the issues of the day. On March 31, 2004, his show debuted as the 'O' Franken Factor,' imitating the name from Bill O'Reilly's 'The O'Reilly Factor.' The name of his show was later changed to 'The Al Franken Show'. He started his show with co-host Katherine Lanpher. One of their program features was called 'The Oy Yoy Yoy Show.' Lanpher left the show after about a year and six months. Al wrote a book titled 'Lies and the living Liars who tell them.' Franken said that the book was in reference to Bill O'Reilly. His intention was to provoke Bill to sue him again, thus generating the media fuse between conservative commentators and uprising liberal commentators. Fox News and Bill O'Reilly had sued Al Franken for using Fox's trademark 'Fair and Balance.' Right from the premiere of his show, Al ridicules right-wingers, mainly Bill O'Reilly, Glenn Beck, and Michael Savage. Franken surprisingly hosted conservative frontrunner commentator Sean Hannity. "Senior Moment," "Wait Wait... Don't lie to me" and the "Hate Mail of the Day" were some regular interesting features on 'The Al' Franken Show.' [303]

Nationally, Franken is known for his books and his performances on Saturday Night Live. Franken is also known as a comedian and a pundit.

He might soon be known as a senator from Minnesota. His chief opponent is Norm Coleman, the incumbent senior senator.

Al's stated his main reason for becoming a talk radio host in the following manner: "I'm doing this because I want to use my energies to get Bush unelected. I'd be happy if the election of a Democrat ended the show" [304]

Some of the Al Franken show's sound bites on Bush's eagerness to catch Osama bin Laden

Right after 9/11, President Bush said "I want justice." And Cheney said he would gladly accept bin Laden's "head on a platter." President Bush also declared "And there is an old poster out West, I recall, that says, 'Wanted: Dead or alive.'" Bush went further: "All I want and America wants is to see them brought to justice. That is what we want." How important was it to Bush to capture bin Laden? "The most important thing is for us to find Osama bin Laden. It is our number one priority and we will not rest until we find him." Years later, Bush changed his rhetoric: "So I don't know where he is. You know, I just don't spend that much time on him." And Bush continued: "I'll repeat what I said. I truly am not that concerned about him. I know he is on the run."[305]

Although Bush won the election of 04 against the wishes of Al Franken, in the 2006 midterm election the Democratic Party won both houses of Congress. Randi Rhodes and Al Franken ensured that the Democratic Party was victorious.

Al's regular guests were professional pundits and conversationalists; they included Tom Oliphant, veteran American columnist, Norman Ornstein, resident scholar at the American Enterprise Institute, and Lawrence O'Donnell, a widely known political analyst. They were the listeners' favorite guests throughout Franken's three years on the radio. Al Franken never took calls from his listeners, yet his ratings were good. Other important regular guests were: Al's favorite Christy Harvey, from the Center of America Progress, Melanie Sloan, the Director of Citizens for Responsibility and Ethnics in D.C., David Brock, the founder of Media Matters, Paul Krugman, a columnist for New York Times, Joe Conason, a national correspondent for The New York Observer newspaper, Michael Isikoff, a Newsweek reporter, Jonathan Alter, a Newsweek columnist, and David Scrota, a political journalist. They were all specialized experts. Bill Kimball and Andy Barr, his working mates, contributed to his show. Franken also occasionally hosted other high profile political figures.

Al Franken announced his retirement from radio; none of his listeners ever imagined that that day would come. It came on Valentine's Day of 2007. All of a sudden all of his listeners were left in the cold; they all felt the impact left by Franken. In only about three years, he touched many liberals and Democrats. Al quickly evened the score with his listeners by announcing at the end of his final show that he was in the race for a senate seat come 2008. [306]

Exit Franken, Enter Hartmann
Talk Radio for the Rest of Us

Thom Hartmann is an American internationally known commentator.

His radio program was chosen to replace Al Franken's largely because of his ratings. Thom Hartmann normally chastised Rush Limbaugh's political views. Thom Hartmann's favorite sound bites "Roosevelt is dead. His policies may live on, but we're in the process of doing something about that as well" That was a statement by Rush Limbaugh. However, Thom Hartmann defended the former President "No Roosevelt was a good guy and what he did was right and did save capitalism from itself and he did bring greatness to this country."[307]

Hartmann is down to earth, a true voice for the American people. He stands up to the bad guys and he fights for what is right. So who are the bad guys Hartmann is referring to? Thom trashes conservative commentators and government officials, but only if he feels their comments is misleading. He debates members of the Ayn Rand institute and other conservative think tanks. Since 2004, his weekly guest has been Bennie Sanders, the independent junior senator from the state of Vermont.

Thom wrote an article titled 'Talking Back to Talk Radio.' The article laid a solid foundation for Air America Radio. Randi Rhodes and Thom Hartmann ranked as the number one and number two progressive talk show hosts in America in terms of total listeners nationwide. Hartmann was a strong supporter for Republican presidential nominee Sen. Barry Goldwater. Thom campaigned for the senator's presidential election in the 1960's. Thom Hartmann attended Michigan State University. [308]

Founding Fathers and the commons

"We the People," are the first three words in the US Constitution.

"What are we doing about the commons? Who is in charge of the commons? Who is looking out for all of us Americans?" Thom asked. "The most important of the commons is our government and the government is here to protect our commons. We own our government and our commons, and the government must not be a stepping stone to private profiteering," Hartmann stated. Another one of Hartmann's favorite sound bites: "And if the government has nothing to hide, then why is it hiding everything." Ask Thom what the Government is hiding?

Mr. Hartmann said Dick Cheney was hiding everything in his executive branch office or his legislative branch office. Thom uttered "God help us; if Dick Cheney was the president of the country and was in charge of the war in Iraq, we would all be living in parking lots" (a paraphrase.) "Heads up to Richard Cheney's Halliburton Co; its stock has tripled since the war in Iraq began" Thom said. There were alleged reports that Halliburton was bankrupt before the war in Iraq began.[309]

Its 360 days, 6 hours, 6 minutes, and 6 seconds "before the constitution mandates that George W. Bush must leave office," Thom said. He continued, "If you look at the high crimes and misdemeanors and treasonous acts he has committed in office, I'd say he should leave now, but that would require impeachment in the House and Senate." Mr. Hartmann further added, "They are willing to subvert the Constitution. They are willing to convert the public commons into private gain. They are willing to proactively take steps that cause the death of people in order to gain political advantage." Hartmann confirmed that impeachment was mentioned six times in the constitution.

And can President Nixon's comment be added to this content?

President Nixon said, "Well, when the president does it that means that it is not illegal." Mr. Hartmann said even Julius Caesar, the Roman military and political leader, who manipulated elections and had the masses, did not have more power than President Bush.

The US Constitution is the decision maker, not George Bush; the president is seeking to undo the Constitution by engaging in egregious behavior. [310]

In 2007, Michael Ratner, from the Center for constitutional rights, admitted that he tried to have Donald Rumsfeld arrested on charges of crimes against humanity. He said that after Rumsfeld finished giving a speech in France, the former Defense Secretary used the backdoor to avoid being arrested. [311]

President Ronald Reagan

President Reagan was asked what "the nine most terrifying words in the English language are?" And President Ronald Reagan said, "I'm from the government and I'm here to help." Thom Hartmann agreed and said to tell that to Katrina people. Mr. Hartmann often emphasized that President Reagan declared war on the middle-class people. Reagan raised taxes twice. And the largest tax increase in the history of America happened on his watch. In the Reagan regime, the hopes of middle class- ness gradually disappeared.

And Reagan supported immigrants by granting them amnesty. Reagan's administration allowed European and African exodus to America.

The Democrats have been attacking Bush's high budget deficit and they claimed that Bill Clinton had to come and clean up the budget deficit left by both the Reagan's and Walker Bush's administrations. However, it did not sound so promising when Cheney indicated that "Reagan proved deficits don't matter." [312]

Thom Hartmann goes back in time to visit the 18th and 19th century's Hamilton, Jefferson, and Karl Marx. Out of all the Founding Fathers in the 18th century, he only talks about Hamilton, Madison, and Jefferson. He rarely mentions George Washington, Samuel Chase, John Adams, or Benjamin Franklin.

Alexander Hamilton, the former treasury secretary, wanted the United States to be a super power. On the other hand, Thomas Jefferson wanted the United States to be small local communities. Jefferson didn't want the United States to be like London, Hartmann concluded, "but we have fulfilled Alexander Hamilton's agenda." Hartmann wrote a book on the separation of Church and State. 'The Founding Father warned against the notion of America becoming a Christian nation. What Would Jefferson Do?' 2004. [313]

From time to time, Thom also goes back to the early/mid 21st century. He talks about the impact left by FDR and JFK. Thom revisits President John F Kennedy's 1961 inauguration speech that started the idea of the Peace Corps: "Ask not what your country can do for you, ask what you can do for your country." The Peace Corps is an organization designed to help third world countries by American's volunteers.

During the Great Depression era, American listened to a 1933 first inaugural address by President Franklin D Roosevelt: "This great nation will endure as it has endured, will revive and will prosper. So, first of all, let me assert my firm belief that the only thing we have to fear is fear itself -nameless, unreasoning, unjustified terror which paralyzes needed efforts to convert retreat into advance." [314]After the September 11th disaster, Bush told Americans to go shopping. President Bush said "It's my job to worry about it. It's your job to go about your business." But in the late 1930's when America was just coming out of the Great Depression and when there was no military, President Roosevelt called for all Americans to kick in and contribute to the redevelopment of the country. The Great Depression was an era of economic crisis. The country was suffering in the throes of depression. It started from the crash of the stock market of 1929. Thom Hartmann told his audience that a day after the destruction of the World Trade Center, a French Newspaper prints: 'We're all Americans Now.' And the "The Taliban offered Osama bin Laden, so long as he would be sent to a third country where he would get a fair trial and Bush said no. He needed his anti-hero. He wanted war popularity" [315]

Road to the Presidency

Paul Weyrich is the Republican strategist who was responsible for President Reagan's election. He is also the founder of the Christian coalition, and made the following statement while speaking in church:

> "Now many of our Christians have what I call the goo-goo syndrome. Good government. They want everybody to vote. I don't want everybody to vote. Elections are not won by a majority of people. They never have been from the beginning of our country and they are not now. As a matter of fact, our leverage in the elections quite candidly goes up as the voting populace goes down." [316]

On December 13, 2000, the day after an important Supreme Court ruled, Vice President Gore announced that he was ending his presidential campaign "I accept the finality of this outcome, and tonight, for the sake of our unity as a people and the strength of our democracy, I offer my concession." Florida officials immediately certified the state's twenty-five electoral votes for Governor George Bush and Secretary Cheney. And this gave Bush a total of 271 Electoral College votes, just one more than needed to become the 43rd president of USA.

Although Bush won the Electoral College in 2000, he became only the 4th president in US history to win office while losing the popular votes to his main rival. Bush followed the same road to victory as that of past presidents Adams, Hayes, and Harrison. Bush captured 47.88% of the popular vote right behind Al Gore, who captured 48.39% of the popular votes.

Bush found momentum in 2004; he led in both the popular and the Electoral College vote count over Senator Kerry. Big thanks to Republican running mate, Cheney. In the only vice president (running mate) debate, Cheney assailed Kerry and Edwards' records. They both voted to authorize a war with Iraq and later voted against funding for the war. Cheney said they're unsteady in their position on Iraq: "Whatever the political pressures the moment requires, that's where you're at. You've not been consistent and there's no indication at all that John Kerry has the conviction to successfully carry through on the war on terror." Senator Edwards accused Cheney of misleading the United States into a war with Iraq. Cheney claimed that Edwards was politically inexperienced, and if we elect a Democrat, by and large terrorists will hit us again. Cheney's performances gave the Bush reelection ticket a huge momentum going into the next presidential debates. The first debate witnessed a poor showing by Bush. [317]

Ever since Gore lost the 2000 election, the liberals have been trying to get rid of the Electoral College. Thom Hartmann concluded that Gore, unlike Kerry, is the only president that never served.

Rep. Katherine Harris and Gov. Jep Bush had a prominent role in the vote recount of the 2000 presidential election. But Tom DeLay was said to be the lawmaker that was responsible for the election of Bush. DeLay was believed to have ordered some of his acolytes from D.C. to fly to Florida and stop the vote recount in that State. Their actions led to the Supreme Court deciding the final verdict.

The people of Florida said Bush was appointed to the presidency by a partisan Supreme Court. When John Roberts pushed to stop the vote recount of the 2000 election in Florida, Gore was pressured to step down because there were protesters 24/7 shouting: "Get out of Dick Cheney's house, get out of the Vice President house." The first modern day judicial branch's alleged Coup d'état took place after the Supreme Court rendered its verdict. [318]

In the general election, Americans always choose their president with their direct (popular votes) ballots. Elected members of the Electoral College will then cast their vote for the President. While Americans vote for a presidential candidate whose name appears on the ballots, they are actually voting for a slate of electors in their states. The number of electors is equal to the number of their various states' House and Senate members in Congress. [319]

The 2008 presidential election (February 07-December 07)

Whom will Thom endorse for the 08 election? He seems to want to endorse Ms. Rhodes' Gore draft.

Back in 2000 Thom voted for an Independent candidate, Ralph Nader, instead of Al Gore for president – even though Hartmann knew that Nader had no chance to be president. Well, Hartmann confessed that he didn't vote for Nader because he was against Gore. It had to do with the state of Vermont supporting the Green Party by raising federal majority funds for the next election cycle. However, Gore won the state of Vermont in the general election. Hartmann said Gore had made some mistakes, for example choosing Joe Lieberman as his vice president running mate.

He said since 2000, Gore has improved and he is willing to cut Gore some slack. And if Gore decides to run, Thom will rally for him. Albert Gore, the Nobel peace prize winner, can provide a strong counterweight to the crimes of the Republicans in Congress. This is particularly true since Speaker Nancy Pelosi's motto is still 'All options are off the table.'[320]

In 1996, Bill Clinton was elected by plurality with less than 50% of the popular votes. But he won a landslide in the Electoral College votes with 379. Thom labeled Bill Clinton as the best modern Republican President since Dwight Eisenhower.

Thom said if any of the first tier Democratic presidential candidates win the presidency in 2008, his inclination is to believe that Hillary Clinton will be the next FDR, Barrack Obama will be the next JFK, and John Edwards is somewhere in between.

Pope John Paul 11 noticed Thom Hartmann for his 2004 book on spirituality, 'The Prophet's Way.' Thom said in his program that "Jesus Christ was the first liberal." He released his 2006 book, 'Screwed: The Undeclared War against the Middle Class and What We Can Do about It.' Thom was interviewed on the Al Franken show about the book. He emphasized the erosion of the American middle class. [321]

Hartmann has been to many European countries promoting his political ideology. He went to Croatia and Germany. Darfur, Sudan was on his schedule too. "The Thom Hartmann show, defending America from the weapon of mass deception." White House correspondent Ellen Ratner and Talk Radio News Service Victoria Jones contribute to the Thom Hartmann Show. The Hartmann show motto is, 'Where the spear is not an option.'

Thom's 2007 book is called 'cracking the code,' and it explains how to win hearts and change minds in order to restore American's vision.

He hosted Valerie Plame, the C.I.A covert operative who was smeared by her own country. In her book, 'Fair Game: My Life as a Spy, My Betrayal by the White House,' Ms. Plame said that she was accused by the Bush administration of nepotism. Thom Hartmann amazingly hosted former US ambassador John Bolton. Ambassador Bolton parted company with the Bush administration largely because of mistake in policies. In his new book, 'Surrender Is Not an Option: Defending America at the United Nations.'

The ambassador said that if Iran gets nuclear weapons other nations will follow Iran's footsteps. Hartmann also hosted Pat Buchanan on 'Day of Reckoning' and Lou Dobbs on 'Independents Day.' "Democracy begins with you, activisms begin with you, tag, and you're it!" Hartmann exits. [322]

Chapter 14

MSNBC, one of the Most Influential Media Bodies in America: 'The filibuster show' Hardball with Chris Matthews and Countdown with Keith Olbermann

Chris Matthews is the hottest political anchorman in the American media. Chris Matthews has been running and playing hardball with his guests on his show. He will stop the filibuster from among his guests often to disagree and force them to answer his questions. He has been the heartbeat of MSNBC for a decade.

Keith Olbermann is a news anchorman and political commentator. He is the host of his own show titled 'Countdown' with Keith Olbermann. Countdown is the highest-rated program on MSNBC – it has been referred as the 'flagship MSNBC franchise.' [323]

Conservative and liberal views

One question MSNBC viewers want to know is: is Chris a Democrat or Republican? Liberal media watch dog organizations have accused Matthews of inviting panel of guests with a conservative viewpoint. On the other hand, conservative watchdog organizations have accused Chris of always embracing Left-wing positions.

For the Republicans, Chris voted for George Bush for president, and he supported Barry Goldwater for president. And for the Democrats, he worked for Jimmy Carter's presidency. And he also worked for Tip O' Neil, a former long serving Democratic Speaker of the House. However Chris once said, "I'm more conservative than people think I am." [324]

The Media Research Center, a conservative think tank, has accused Olbermann of having a liberal bias because of his criticisms against the president's administration, his alleged support for Bush's impeachment, and his calls for the President to resign. They have accused him of attacking Bill O'Reilly and Fox News. Olbermann has defended allegations of liberal bias by stating that he would also be critical of a Democratic President's administration if they were incompetent. Keith Olbermann addressed the issue in the following manner:

> "I've been accused of being a liberal, which is interesting because the last time I was on doing the news in the 90's I did 218 conservative shows about Bill Clinton and Monica Lewinsky. I mean, no one in 1998, no one accused me of being a liberal in 1998 because I was covering the Lewinsky scandal. It's very interesting the way you can be soft of pigeonholed. I like to think of myself politically as correct." [325]

MSNBC v Fox News

Can it be because of Bill O'Reilly that Keith and Countdown are getting all the ratings?

Over the years Mr. Olbermann's show has generated media controversy because of its criticism against Murdoch's Fox News Channels and Olbermann's long lasting feud with O'Reilly. Keith frequently lampooned Bill O'Reilly. He referred to Bill as Ted Baxter's Evil Twin. In 2005, their state of media enmity began after Olbermann publicly celebrated a sexual harassment suit involving Mr. O'Reilly. A former Fox News employee brought a sexual harassment lawsuit against Bill O'Reilly. [326]

Their feud escalated after Bill O'Reilly dropped a caller's call on his radio program. The caller deliberately mentioned Keith's name with the intent of provoking Mr. O'Reilly. Bill felt disrespected and immediately said he was going to send Fox News securities to the caller's home. Olbermann reacted to O'Reilly's outcry and poked fun at Bill's sexual harassment lawsuit: "Bill thinks he has his own police. So, now I'm expecting that soon I will be getting a visit from the Bill O'Reilly police, armed with loofahs." Pundits like Al Franken defended the caller. And he asserted that Bill had no right to send Fox securities to the caller's home. Thanks to their rhetoric, the months of rancor between Bill and Keith ceased. The buck stops here! On his show, Keith said "I m sorry, Bill. I can't play with you right now. I have bigger fish to fry" Olbermann was handing responsibilities to other anti O'Reillians. Keith Olbermann's juvenile statement was a step to finally end their feud. Bill said that Olbermann's MSNBC "Is a true ratings disaster."[327]

Conservative/Liberal views continues

During one of the 08 presidential debates, former Speaker Gingrich trashed Chris Matthews. The Speaker described Matthews in the following manner: "You're watching an utterly irrelevant, shallow television celebrity dominate everybody who claimed they want to lead the most powerful nation in the world." Gingrich added, "These are not debates, these are auditions. By definition, the psychology of an audition reduces the person auditioning and raises the status, for example, of Chris Matthews."

Politics can really get personal.

In 2006, Chris Matthews was a guest on Jay Leno's Tonight Show. The host asked Mr. Matthews what he thought of the former Speaker's claim that the Israel-Lebanon conflict going on in the Middle East was World War 3. Matthews answered, "I think Newt is World War 3." [328]

Howard Dean, former governor of Vermont, is rumored to have lost his 04 presidential campaigns because he appeared on Chris Matthews show. Everybody knows Chris Matthews asks tough questions to his guests. That is why top 2008 presidential contenders like Sen. Clinton turned down invitations to appear on Hardball. Read the conversation between Dean and Mathews during Dean's 2004 presidential campaign.

Hardball: There are so many things that have been deregulated. Is that a wrong trend and would you reverse it?

Dean: I would reverse it in some areas. First of all, eleven companies in this country control ninety percent of what ordinary people are able to read and watch on their television. That's wrong. We need to have a wide variety of opinions in every community. We don't have that because of Michael Powell and what George Bush has tried to do the FCC.

Hardball: Are you going to break up the giant media enterprises in this country?

Dean: Yes we're going to break up giant media enterprises. That doesn't mean we're going to break up all of General Electric. What we're going to say is that media enterprises can't be as big as they are today. To the extent of even having two or three or four outlets in a single community, that kind of information control is not compatible with democracy. [329]

General Electric is a major military contributor and manufacturer of military equipment. The ownership of MSNBC belongs to General Electric. Are they against the war in Iraq? Because of the war going on in Iraq, General Electric has a contract in Iraq.

Chris once favored the war in Iraq: "We are all neo-cons now." But in 2006-07 he was against the war. He called on George Will and Bill Buckley to take back the Republican Party from the neo-conservatives. Political observers notice that Chris is someone that changes his view depending on how the political issue is polling. MSNBC can't do without Chris since he has the ratings, but he is speaking out against the war in Iraq.

Phil Donahue was released by MSNBC. Donahue was against the war in Iraq, but he also had great ratings. [330]

Nazis in the 21st century

Keith Olbermann attacked the Bush administration about comments they had made regarding Adolf Hitler and the Nazis. Olbermann said: "Then Defense Secretary Donald Rumsfeld thought that he could equate those who doubted him with Nazi appeasers, without reminding anyone that the actual, historical Nazi appeasers in this country in the 1930s were the Republicans." In 2006, Keith Olbermann responded to a Bush Press Conference and claimed that Bush was "Following his former Secretary of Defense down the path of trying to tie those loyal Americans who disagree with his policies or even question their effectiveness or execution to the Nazi of the past, and the al Qaeda of the present." The President stated that there was "A media campaign to create a wedge between the American people and their government." Bush continued, "The world ignored Hitler's words, and paid a terrible price." Olbermann lashed out at Bush's speech: "Whatever the true nature of al Qaeda and other international terrorist threats, to ceaselessly compare them to the Nazi State of Germany serves only to embolden them." [331]

Keith also harshly singled out former Majority Leader Tom DeLay, because DeLay compared his critics to Hitler. Keith noted, "Mr. DeLay believes that accusation that he violated Texas campaign finance laws was a lie. He is equating anybody, charging him- just him- with anything, even if it were a lie, with the Nazis." Keith continued, "Just by going after Tom DeLay, you are like that old scoundrel Hitler."

Olbermann also took offense at Sec. Rice's comment. The Secretary of State on 'Fox News Sunday' discussed what would happen if Congress were to revise the 2002 authorization of the war in Iraq. In so doing, she compared World War II with the state of Iraq. Condoleezza Rice's statement was as follows: "It would be like saying that Adolf Hitler was overthrown, we needed to change, then, the resolution that allowed the United States to do that, so that we could deal with creating a stable environment in Europe after he was overthrown." On Countdown, Olbermann responded,

> "Here we go again. From springs spent trying to link Saddam Hussein to 9/11, to summers of cynically manipulated intelligence, through autumns of false patriotism, to winter of wars, we have had more than four years of every cheap trick and every degree of calculated cynicism from this administration, filled with Three-Card Monte players." [332]

Imperial presidency in 21ˢᵗ century

Government officials were lobbying MSNBC to change the policy of their show. The White House scrutinized Matthews' show, telling him what particular stories to cover and what issues not to cover: "They will not silence me! They have finally been caught in their criminality," a comment Matthews made referring to Bush and Cheney. Chris Matthews probably wondered who died and made government officials the boss to tell him what particular story to cover on his show.

The 1974 Nixon resignation in the Watergate scandal thwarted a president's intent for an unchecked imperial presidency. In 2006, Chris Matthews compared the Bush administration to the imperial presidency of Richard Nixon. [333]

In August of 07, Chris severely questioned the 1994 www.youtube.com video on Cheney making a case against going into Baghdad in the wake of the first Gulf War. Cheney acknowledged:

> "If we'd gone on Baghdad we would have been all alone. There wouldn't have been any body else with us. It would have been a US occupation of Iraq. Once you got to Iraq and took it over, took out Saddam Hussein's government, then what are you going to put into its place? It's a quagmire if you go that far..."

The story echoed so loudly that the whole mainstream media blasted the Vice President. Various news media outlets headlines' read: 'Dick Cheney knew Iraq a quagmire in 1994,' 'Dick Cheney two-faced with Iraq,' and 'Cheney does 180 degree turnaround.'[334]

On September 14, 2007, in an address to the nation, President Bush outlined a beginning for troop withdrawals from Iraq. Chris and Olbermann hosted the MSNBC coverage of Bush's address to the nation. The address came on the heels of congressional testimony given earlier by Gen. David Petraeus, the top U.S. commander in Iraq, and Ryan Crocker, the Ambassador to Iraq. After the president's prime time speech, in his attempt to sell the Petraeus plan, Chris hosted Senator Joe Biden. Chris asked the Democratic presidential candidate about Bush's mention of the 36 allies we have over in Iraq. The honorable senator replied, "It is a beauty to me."- the 36 allies may be secretaries somewhere" (a paraphrase.) In other words they were not combat troops; they were just secretaries working with the military.

Chris Matthews stated that the "United Kingdom and South Korea have over 1,000 troops, Turkey and Japan have two soldiers, and the rest of the remaining so-called 36 allies have only one representative" (a paraphrase). Bush invoking the help of 36 other countries fighting the war against the insurgents in Iraq "Is an insult to the American troops," said Biden, the Chairman of Senate's Committee on Foreign Relations. [335]

CIA leak case

After the revelation that Richard Armitage, a former deputy secretary of state, was the source of the CIA leak case, the mainstream media refused to cover the story. However, Countdown continued and thoroughly covered the Valerie Plame story. Pundits believed the case could end the career of White House political adviser Karl Rove. Valerie Plame was an undercover agent for the Central Intelligence Agency. Her name appeared in a syndicated newspaper column by veteran journalist Robert Novak. The CIA assumed that White House officials might have conspired to leak Ms. Plame's identity as political payback against Ambassador Joe Wilson. The Ambassador accused the Bush administration of twisting information on Saddam Hussein's effort to develop nuclear weapons. [336]

Karl Rove had been suspected to be the staffer that leaked Valerie Plame name to journalists. Lewis Libby, the Chief of Staff to the Vice President, was reported to have had several conversations with journalists concerning Valerie Plame.

In June 2005, reporters from the New York Times and Time magazine were held in contempt of court for refusing to testify before a federal grand jury investigating the leak naming Valerie Plame as a covert CIA operative. They were threatened with jail time if they did not cooperate. Matthew Cooper from Time magazine agreed to testify unlike New York Times' Judith Miller, who was jailed for refusing to testify. After spending 85 days in prison, Miller was released. Cooper told the authorities that he had learned the identity of Valerie Plame from Karl Rove. The CIA demanded an investigation by a special prosecutor. [337]

The events that led to the CIA leak case can be track back to Italy.

In 2001, La Repubblica, an Italian newspaper reported that Italian military intelligence provided alleged false documents to Britain and United States' intelligence. Silvio Berlusconi, the Prime Minister of Italy, was believed to be aware of the alleged forged Niger yellowcake documents. Counterfeit Niger's letterhead was allegedly smuggled from the Niger embassy in Rome.

The uranium documents specified that Saddam had purchased yellowcake uranium from Niger. This led to the Iraqi war and the CIA leak case. In order to ascertain the truth of the matter, the CIA sponsored Joe Wilson's trip to Niger to investigate if Niger sold yellowcake uranium to Saddam Hussein.

Joe Wilson is the husband of Valerie Plame.

Other journalists like NBC's Tim Russert and Washington Post's Bob Woodward were called on as witnesses. Special prosecutor Fitzgerald suspected that the White House deliberately revealed Ms Plame's CIA identity as a covert agent. Patrick Fitzgerald was keen to hear Miller's version of her conversations with Libby. Judith Miller finally took the witness stand for the prosecution of Libby. Judith Miller disclosed to the court that she had met with Libby on three occasions between June and July of 2003. Libby's defense lawyers maintained their client was too busy to recall the details of those meetings. Miller's meeting with Libby on July 03 was two days after Joe Wilson's op-ed piece in the New York Times entitled 'What I Didn't Find in Africa.' And six days later, conservative Robert Novak revealed Valerie Plame's identity in a column. [338]

The President was asked if he knew who leaked the name of the CIA operative. Bush responded,

> "You tell me, how many sources have you had that's leaked information that you've exposed or have been exposed? Probably none; I mean this town is a -- is a town full of people who like to leak information. And I don't know if we're going to find out the senior administration official. Now, this is a large administration, and there's a lot of senior officials. I don't have any idea. I'd like to. I want to know the truth. That's why I've instructed this staff of mine to cooperate fully with the investigators – full disclosure, everything we know the investigators will find out. I have

no idea whether we'll find out who the leaker is – partially because, in all due respect to your profession, you do a very good job of protecting the leakers. But we'll find out."

Richard Armitage and Karl Rove were not charged with leaking Valerie Plame's name to the media. Only Lewis Libby was charged. In March 2007, Libby was convicted of lying to the FBI and to a grand jury. Libby was also convicted of obstructing the investigation. Libby was the most senior White House official ordered to prison since Oliver North's Iran contra. [339]

According to Joe Wilson, when his wife's cover was blown, she scrambled to protect her operation and her colleagues. "There have been specific threats," Joe Wilson said. The leak case had been looming since 2003, when Joseph Wilson publicly chastised the White House for twisting intelligence thereby accomplishing a war with Iraq. Patrick Fitzgerald complained that the case was too complicated and that he could not figure out who was really behind the leaking of the identity of a CIA operative.

Robert Novak said he was confident that Bush knew who leaked the information. In response Bush said, "I appreciate his bold assertion." Paul Wolfowitz made Lewis Libby known to Cheney. The origin of neoconservatives emerged from them. [340]After Bush commuted the Vice President's Chief of staff, Olbermann called for the resignation of the Vice President himself.

Which liberal conversationalists haven't yet called for the resignation of Bush and Cheney? On what grounds should they resign?

Keith Olbermann is responsible for MSNBC being the second most-watched cable news network. FOX News, of course, is the number one most-watched cable network. MSNBC maintains it leads over CNN both in demographics and in total viewers. [341]

Chapter 15

CNN, One of the Most Influential Media Bodies in America: Spearheaded by Wolf Blitzer, 'the favorite name in media,' and seasoned anchorman, Larry King

Who doesn't know Larry King? Or at least who hasn't heard his name? Larry King is a household name, and a legendary anchorman. King is a CNN broadcaster. His show is CNN's most-watched program. The show can be seen all over the world on CNN international. King has interviewed many prominent individuals, politicians, and average Americans. Among those King interviewed are: President Clinton, President W. Bush, President Jimmy Carter, President Ronald Reagan, and Prime Minister Margaret Thatcher. Larry King Live has also conducted interviews with other foreign presidents and prime ministers, several foreign political figures, past and present prominent members of the US government, notable dignitaries and many more – the list is endless.[342]

Wolf Blitzer is an American Broadcasting network journalist.

Blitzer hosts the Situation Room, previously called Wolf Blitzer Reports.

He started anchoring the show in 2005. As a journalist Wolf wrote a book called "Territory of Lies," relating to an Israeli spy in the American naval intelligence. Wolf Blitzer had a big role in the Israel –Egypt Peace Treaty.

Wolf is also the host of 'CNN Sunday talk show Late Edition.' Jack Cafferty and Carol Costello are a few CNN journalists that contributed substantively to the 'Situation Room.' The difference between CNN's 'Situation Room' and other politically oriented shows is its international coverage of worldwide events. There is a fair and balance coverage between CNN's national coverage and CNN's international coverage. [343]

CNN's ratings have declined over the years, debatably because of King's sensational news story. MSNBC has overtaken CNN in the ratings race for the number two most-watched cable news station in America.

Mr. King is known for asking soft questions. His softball questioning gives him an advantage over other TV programs. It allows him to attract guests who would be reluctant to be featured on other provocative shows. Political satire/comedian Bill Maher and Nancy Grace have guest hosted for Larry King. [344]

CNN in the White House

King sometimes goes to his guests. For example, he interviewed Dick Cheney in the White House. King has also conducted interviews in people's homes, the prison cells of inmates, and other stunning places.

Larry King always brings out the best in Cheney anytime he hosts the Veep.

In June 05, King interviewed Cheney about the ongoing war in Iraq. Cheney then made headlines: "I think we may well have some kind of presence there over a period of time. The level of activity that we see today from a military standpoint, I think, will clearly decline. I think they're in the last throes, if you will, of the insurgency." The Wyoming statesman predicted that the fighting would end before the Bush administration leaves office. The Vice President said he was "Absolutely convinced we did the right thing in Iraq." The United States has gained ground and changes have begun to take place in Iraq. For instance; a transitional government has been installed in Iraq. And parts of the country were undergoing a sea change in improved security. Cheney claimed that "America will be safer in the long run when Iraq and Afghanistan as well, are no longer safe havens for terrorist or places where people can gather and plan and organize attacks against the United States." [345]

CNN and Wolf Blitzer got nailed down by three big hammers. Michael Moore, Dick Cheney, and John McCain had an encounter with Wolf in the 'Situation Room.' What was their situation with Wolf?

After Bush's 2007 State of the Union speech, CNN's Situation Room hosted the Vice President. Wolf started by asking Cheney about bin Laden and why they can't find him and his number two man. Talking about the so called number two man, Blitzer said: "His number two, Ayman al- Zawahiri, is

Cheney: Zawahiri's much more visible. Yes.

Blitzer: I mean he's on television almost as much as I am

Cheney: Well, I don't know if anybody's on as much as you are, Wolf, but-no, he's more of a public figure than Osama is."

That was the first sign of a bad day for Wolf, and toward the middle of their conversation, Wolf angered the Vice President. Wolf wanted to pick and choose Cheney's friends.

Blitzer continued: Here's what Jim Webb, senator from Virginia said in the Democratic response last night 'the President took us into this war recklessly. We are now, as a nation, held hostage to the predictable and predicted disarray that has followed.'

Blitzer continued: And it's not just Jim Webb, it's some of your good Republican friends in the Senate and the House are now seriously questioning your credibility, because of the blunders and the failures. Gordon Smith…

Cheney: Wolf, Wolf, I simply don't accept the premise of your question. I just think its hogwash.

Wolf immediately switched topics and got personal with Cheney. He asked Cheney about his lesbian pregnant daughter.

Blitzer continued: All of us are happy she's going to have a baby. You're going to have another grandchild. Some critics are suggesting- for example, a statement from someone representing 'Focus on the Family,' "Mary Cheney's pregnancy raises the question of what's best for children. Just because it's possible to conceive a child outside of the relationship of a married mother and father doesn't mean that it's best for the child." Do you want to respond to that?

Cheney: No

Blitzer: She's, obviously, a good daughter.

Cheney: I'm delighted I'm about to have a sixth grandchild, Wolf. And obviously I think the world of both my daughters and all of my grandchildren. And I think, frankly, you're out of line with that question.

Blitzer: I think all of us appreciate.

Cheney: I think you're out of line.

Blitzer: We like your daughters. Believe me; I'm very sympathetic to Liz and
     Mary. I like them both. That was a question that's come up, and it's
     a responsible, fair question.

Cheney: I just fundamentally disagree with you. [346]

In July 07, Cheney again appeared on Larry King's show. King asked
about Cheney's take on Congress's investigation into the firing of the nine
U.S. attorneys. "A bit of a witch hunt," Cheney said briefly. "First of all, there's
no charge. What's the allegation of wrongdoing here? Frankly, there isn't any.
They keep rolling over rocks hoping they can find something, but there really
hasn't been anything come up that would suggest there was any wrongdoing
of any kind," Cheney concluded. Larry King then asked Cheney if former
Deputy White House Chief of Staff Karl Rove needed to testify before the
Senate on the firing of the attorneys. Cheney defended the President's adviser
despite the alleged rumors that Rove disliked Mr. Cheney and was against
Cheney becoming the vice president. [347]

Situation Room in Iraq

In March 2007, John McCain claimed that General Petraeus went out in
Baghdad almost every day in an unarmed humvee. The senator said, "There
are neighborhoods in Baghdad where you and I could walk through those
neighborhoods; today the US is beginning to succeed in Iraq." After CNN
investigated Senator McCain's assessment, they revealed their results: "I
checked with General Petraeus's people overnight and they said he never
goes out in anything less than an up-armored humvee. No Iraqi government
official, coalition soldier, diplomat reporter could walk the streets of Baghdad
without heavily armed protection" -CNN Barry McCafffrey issued the report.
However, the next day, McCain visited a Baghdad market and acknowledged
that "Things are better and there are encouraging signs." But he was wearing
a bulletproof vest, was accompanied by over a hundred troops, and was
escorted by US attack helicopters. [348]

During an interview on CNN's 'Situation Room' John McCain told
Wolf that he needs to "get up to speed" and stop reporting three-month-old
talking points from Iraq.

According to the senator, the surge of American troops in Iraq is working
and there are substantive developments in that part of the region.

Wolf asked McCain, "Why Americans still aren't able to safely leave the
Green Zone in Iraq." McCain replied, "You know, that's why you ought to
catch up on things, Wolf, General Petraeus goes out there almost every day
in an unarmed humvee. I think you ought to catch up. You are giving the old
line of three months ago. I understand it. We certainly don't get it through the

filter of some of the media." Wolf then turned to his correspondent in Iraq Michael Ware, a CNN reporter: "You have been there for four years. You're walking around Baghdad on a daily basis. Has there been this improvement that Sen. McCain is speaking about?" Ware responded: "McCain is way off base to suggest that there's any neighborhood in this city where an American can walk freely is beyond ludicrous. I'd love Sen. McCain to tell me where the neighborhood is and he and I can go for a stroll." Michael Ware continued, "Honestly, Wolf, you will barely last twenty minutes out there. I don't know what part of Neverland Senator McCain is talking about." CNN's Ware laughed off McCain's assertion that Petraeus traveled in an unarmed humvee and he also provided evidence that discredited McCain's assertion when Ware spoke to military sources in Iraq. "There was laughter down the line. I mean certainly the general travels in a humvee. There is multiplehumvees around it, heavily armed," Ware stated when ending his dialogue with Wolf. [349]

Wall of Separation: Politics and Hollywood

Michael Moore also slammed Wolf Blitzer on live TV. However, it wasn't because of Wolf's incompetence, rather the incompetence of his fellow CNN colleague. Before hearing Moore's take on the situation, CNN aired a segment on Michael Moore's film called 'Sicko Reality Check.' Its contents concluded that Mr. Moore "did fudge the facts." The CNN segment implied that Moore's documentary film was deceptive by portraying better health care systems in Canada and some European countries. When given the chance to speak, Moore immediately assailed Wolf and CNN. "First of all, Wolf, yeah, well I would like about 10 minutes to respond to what was said." Wolf responded, "Give us a couple of headlines, what you'd like to say." Moore replied,

> "I don't talk in sound bites. So that report was so biased. I can't imagine what pharmaceutical company's ads are coming up right after our break here. Why don't you tell the truth to the American people? I wish that CNN and the other mainstream media would just for once tell the truth about what's going on in this country."

Moore continued,

> "You're the ones who are fudging the facts. You've fudged the facts to the American people now for I don't know how long about this issue, about the war, and I'm just curious, when are you going to just stand there and apologize to the

American people for not bringing the truth to them that isn't sponsored by some major corporation?"

Blitzer said he would stand behind CNN's record on the medical issues. After the interview, fellow CNN hosts Lou Dobbs and Jack Cafferty consoled Mr. Blitzer. [350]

Any person with a little bit of name recognition has a free ticket to be a guest on CNN Larry king Live. King is busy interviewing Kid Rock and Britney Spears, etc. Meanwhile his main audiences are the 65 years old and above, how absurd is that? King should be talking about social security for the elders instead of Hollywood. Regardless of how ancient Larry's show is, King is a well-respected individual.

King marked 50 years in broadcasting with over 40, 000 interviews to his credit. [351]

Cronyism

Friends, the ones you can depend on, the ones that will betray you, and the Almighty one that will come to get you at the very end.

Stage one: How many of us have them?

We are growing up and playing a role of a kid, like gathering your peers on the block. And we are calling everyone our friends. We can't blame ourselves because that was all we knew at the time. We all passed through that phase. Now we are playing the role of a teenager, still having so many friends surrounding us and still figuring out who is who. You are receiving them just the way you are seeing them, and you're counting your eggs before they hatch. We are all in a rush. As each of us *readies ourselves to be adults* but still keeping a lot of so-called friends, so-called dudes, so-called lads, and so-called folks around us at all times.

Your friends can be your lecturer, your spiritual guidance, your mentor, your business partner, your emotional partner, your leader, your bodyguard, your entourage, your family friend. Like Jesus Christ, his friends were his disciples. On the threshold of Jesus Christ's mission, Jesus started with twelve friends. How many are you going to start with? Will you start with twelve, twenty-something or an enormous number? "Better watch your back for the people you think are you friends, all up in my face." *-Stanley Howse* [352]

Money is the most substantive issue in this stage. If you happen to be blessed with riches, wait, see, and experience how many friendly faces will be smiling at you once that money is all gone. That is human nature and it can't be solved. In this stage, you didn't get burned so you will never learn. But eventually, you will have a little idea of what friendship is all about.

Stage Two: It is not a matter of how many friends you have

They are the ones you love. You are oblivious to their traitorous activities. But take note, not all are meant to be betrayers. Judas betrayed Jesus Christ, yet Jesus still loved him. The original wicked wind will definitely come, and that is an important way of figuring out who your real friends are. The ones that were meant to be your friends are the ones God prepared for you. Don't get too excited or uptight and lament, "Oh I thought they were your friends." Some of them can survive wicked wild winds and still be lurking. Waiting and scheming for the day they will catch you slipping. Your mother should have told you to "Watch your friends; they can be enemies within quick to pretend like they fit in, get in, and they bring it all to an end." *-Anthony Henderson[353]*

He betrayed you and that was the last thing you thought would ever happen. And it might have an impact on you like I can't live anymore; I'm going to commit suicide. No! As long as you are alive, Jesus Christ will always be your friend. Christ will send you better friends.

After that experience, you thought you had learned. But you didn't learn because you didn't get burned. Even though you were too close to the fire, that same fire that Prophet Elijah sent from heaven to destroy the false prophets of Baal, Christ protected you. Epitomes of your false friends that will make you want to commit suicide, thereby serving your own homicide.

Don't worry about people pretending to be your friends. "When you pray prophetically you will get enlighten by the Holy Spirit." *-Reverend Bassey Ekpenyong[354]*

Jesus will liberate us and set us free from spiritual bondage. And they "Thought that the coast was clear. But they couldn't see or hear me slowly creeping in silence." *-Stanley Howse[355]*

The only way you can advance from this stage is to constantly be suspicious of your friends. And still expect them to backstab you. The act of backstabbing is just a lesson. Nobody living in the flesh is beyond becoming a victim of backstabbing. It is a lesson that you will use against any intruder to decipher between right and wrong. Unless you elevate yourself from this stage, it will always be a never-ending process.

Space/time and money issues are the two factors that lead to parting of friends in this stage. Only death of friends can be carried over to the next stage; depending on how truly devoted you were to the deceased. But space/time and money issues can't be carried over to the next stage. Money issues start at the first stage but will meet their fate at this second stage. You should be able to tell who needs you because of your riches. We all need space and time, but that doesn't mean you should abandon your cronies. Jesus Christ needed space and time so he indirectly abandoned his disciples when he slept in the ship, and the ship almost sank. But Jesus woke up and saved his disciples, saying "Peace, be still!" to the storm. Jesus just wanted to test the faith of his disciples. We all can't "peace be still," so we backstab our friends. Jesus had space and time for his disciples; we should always have the time and space for our friends.

Stage three and beyond: Friends till the very end of time

There is no more turning back. You can only reach this stage if you have finally selected you real friends, the "Chosen Ones." The ones you don't have to worry if "They cannot choose survival, pinch you." -***Anthony Henderson*** [356]

The depth of this stage goes as far as giving your life for them if the time comes. And if it's real, it will not be so hard to swallow. In this stage, once you have finally made up your mind, you can't include anymore people to your short list of best friends. Only death can set apart you from your true friends: "Let death be the only separation." -***Bryon McCane*** [357]

When the veil of the temple was rent in two, from top to bottom, Jesus Christ was physically separated from his disciples. It culminated when Christ died in the cross of Calvary.

No matter how caring anybody that comes your way is, they are not your final friends. Don't judge a book by its cover. They are there to confuse, mislead, and separate you from your original friends. Don't be deceived by their hospitality. They are there to put envy into your chosen friends' hearts in regard to you. Where were they when you were going through all the ups and downs with your chosen friends? Some of them might be good, and some of them might be sent by God. But it is reproved because they weren't around through the tribulation days of your life. They're not lifers. They're just there to guide you or misguide you over a short period of time.

Right from the significant beginning of Christ's mission, Peter was Jesus Christ's closest disciple/friend to the very end. But Peter denied Jesus Christ three times, and this was during the height of a difficult period Christ was going through. Yet Jesus still saved him. No matter what your chosen friends do to you, it should be ignored. Ignorance is bliss; happiness is what you should feel in your heart for your cronies. There has to be that feeling of togetherness, saving the best for last, and cherishing your friends.

"I won't need no more friends, I don't want no more friends, and I can't take no more friends because they always end up backstabbing in the end." -***Steven Howse*** [358]

In this stage, you don't have to worry about backstabbing anymore. Backstabbing will seldom occur, but you should know that it is Satan, the evil one's, doing. Emotionally you have to take heart and spiritually you have to pray to God for the deliverance of your friends. But don't part with any of your chosen friends because you will be making a mistake. And if you render an adverse verdict, it can totally destroy your friendship. And don't appease yourself and still hold a grudge against them. In backstabbing, the real is going to feel, it is really going to be a test. If you can survive the test, you ought to be able to overcome any difficulties in life. It is no longer a lesson;

it's the devil's work, temptation onto the next one. Finally you have learned what friendship is all about and you have gotten burned. Even though you have learned at the expense of your true friends, don't use it against them. Instead, use what you have learned against the challenges of life, and against the phony friends which will always be a part of life.

Because we are still in the flesh, we won't be able to "Seek and destroy any persons that throw the decoy." -**Steven Howse** [359]

Don't let evil tear you apart from your friends. Jesus Christ was tempted by the devil three times, but of course, Jesus overcame Satan. But what was "Jesus greatest temptation? It was when Satan used Peter to tempt Jesus Christ." -Apostle *Mark Excell* [360]

That is what this stage is about. It is a quagmire of its own. Satan used the closest of Jesus' disciples to tempt Jesus. Satan knew that Jesus will not fall into his trap, so he went deeper. Thank God for Jesus, he overcame Satan. We will not be able to overcome ours because we are all sinners: "Let the one without sin cast the first stone." Satan, the greatest decoyer in the world and the master and inventor of sin, will always cast the first stone; just to mislead us and make us think we are righteous. Satan's doing can never boomerang against the evil one because Satan is a spirit and his place is already in hell. The depth of this stage is no longer in the flesh; it's now in the spirit. By and large we should be able to forgive our cronies because they let the devil in, not you.

Realities v actualities

Even though in all reality the 'chosen ones' are your friends up till the very end, the "Son of a chicken there are no friends when it comes to the end." -*Bryon McCane* [361]

But in all actuality, there are no friends when it comes to the end. When you take your last breath, "I know it isn't no more time, it's almost time. Let us get ready for Armageddon; it is going to get us, are you ready? What about your friends? Friends till the very end through the breeze and wicked winds." -*Anthony Henderson* [362]

When it is time for judgment day, will you be able to save your friends? Will you be able to tell God what they did while on earth? Will you be able to beg God to forgive them, if they didn't repent? No! Judgment day is every man for himself. That is why you should keep all of your last surviving friends, all your below zero degree freeze together friends, up to the very end. Most importantly, you have to lecture them with the gospel of God. Let them know that the only way they can get to God in heaven is through Jesus Christ. They have passed through all the obstacles, all the stages, and through all the final wicked wild winds. Now they have to pass the last test, which will be the kingdom of God. Unfortunately, they have to pass away and be in another life, in order to be in the 4ᵗʰ stage.

We humans have come so far. You're a true friend to a fellow human being; you should also be a true friend to God. The Almighty God in heaven, which is the whole nine yards that we should be searching for. God sent his only begotten son to die for us in the cross. We should be able to forsake all our earthly friends for Jesus Christ.

God in heaven made us and gave us life. Let's fight for forever eternal life in the spirit; otherwise our flesh and our soul will be destroyed in hell. And there is no if's, and's, or but's or maybe's about that fact. "And I will meet you in hell if all else fail, oh well." -*Steven Howse* [363]

Yes, we will meet Satan in hell if we don't repent and easily follow Christ. Let your first love be your religion, which is God in heaven: "Since we can't be like God at least let us be like the stars in the sky." -*Anthony Henderson*[364]

In conclusion, let death, the threshold to eternal life, be eternal life rather than to abide in the abyss, which is hellfire.

End

(Endnotes)

ALL Sources are available Online

CHAPTER 1

[1] "(Keith) Rupert Murdoch Biography," Biography.com www.biography.com/search/article.do?id=9418489; "K Rupert Murdoch Profile,"Forbes.comforbes.com/finance/mktguideapps/personinfo; "Fox Television Stations, Inc. (K. Rupert Murdoch) - Delaware 1986"www.collectstocks.com/foxtestinde1.html; dictionary.reference.com/browse/sedition

[2]Michiko Kakutani, "Books of The Times; Thatcher Deciphers Her Indelible Mark on Britain ..."New York Times, November 17, 1993; Mail online, "Blair hires Clinton's man for multi-million pound memoirs deal," August 16, 2007; www.biography.com/search/article.do?id=9418489; www.collectstocks.com/foxtestinde1.html

[3]www.biography.com/search/article.do?id=9418489; www.collectstocks.com/foxtestinde1.html

[4]Russ Baker, "Murdoch's Mean Machine," Colombia Journalism Review, May/ June 1998; Dante Chinni and Jessica Goldings, Media Channel –Home mediachannel.org/wordpress/2007/.../publisher-murdochs-us-track-record

[5]Jack Shafer, "The filth and the fury of Rupert Murdoch," Slate Magazine, June 22, 2007; www.biography.com/search/article.do?id=9418489; www.collectstocks.com/foxtestinde1.html

[6]Charles P. Pierce, "Fox populi," Salon.com, August 22, 2002

[7]*Paul Farhi, "Loopholes Boost Murdoch's Profits,"* WashingtonPost.com, December 7, 1997; Page A01; Russ Baker, "Murdoch's Mean Machine," Colombia Journalism Review, May/ June 1998

[8]"Federal Communications Commission (FCC)," Home Page www.fcc.gov

[9]Interview with the Financial Times, October 2006 www.internet-library.net/Fox News.htm

[10]William Shawcross, "Rupert Murdoch," Time.com, November 03, 1999

[11]Eric Boehlert, "Strange alliance," Salon.com, July 9, 2004; Page 2; www.biography.com/search/article.do?id=9418489; www.collectstocks.com/foxtestinde1.html

[12]Eric Boehlert, "Trent Lott, populist hero,"Salon.com, September 22, 2003; Stephen Labaton, "F.C.C. Media Rule Blocked in House in a 400-to-21 Vote," NYTimes.com, July 24, 2003

[13]FMQB, "NAB Files Against New Owenership Rules," August 20, 2004; David Hatch, "Pressure from Congress on FCC spurs changes at agency," Government Executive.com, December 6, 2007; Randi Rhodes, "The Randi Rhodes Show," Air America Radio, n.d

[14] David Streitfeld, "Papers Web firms need 'a new deal,' Zell says," Los Angeles Times, April 6, 2007

[15]Jane Schulze, "Rupert Murdoch celebrates market milestone, "News.com.au, October 20, 2007; The Australian; "FT 500 The world's largest companies," FT.com www.ft.com/reports/ft5002007 ; "The Big Six," Free Press, www.freepress.net/ownership/chart/main ; Los Angeles Times, "Viacom, the New One, Pays $5.4 Billion to CBS," September 06, 2006

[16]Journalism.org, "The State of the News Media 2007" stateofthenewsmedia.org/2007/narrative_cabletv_audience.asp?cat=2& ; www.biography.com/search/article.do?id=9418489; www.collectstocks.com/foxtestinde1.html

[17]WashingtonPost.com, "Edwards Urges Fellow Democrats to Reject Murdoch's Money," August 3, 2007; Page A04; Nedra Pickler, "Edwards Assails Rivals Over News Corp," ABC News, August 2, 2007; Anne Davies, "Murdoch backs old adversary Clinton," Sydney Morning Herald, December 1, 2007; www.biography.com/search/article.do?id=9418489; www.collectstocks.com/foxtestinde1.html

[18]Mark Landler, "Time Warner-Murdoch Feud Entangles MCI Satellite Plan," New York Times, November 16, 1996; Mark Landler, "Giuliani Pressures Time Warner to Transmit a Fox Channel," New York Times, October 4, 1996; Kevin Maney, "Silicon Valley CEOs don't pull verbal punches," USA TODAY, January 15, 2002; Russ Baker, "Murdoch's Mean Machine," Colombia Journalism Review, May/June 1998

[19] Seth Sutel, "Dow Jones Takes Over News Corp. Talks,"FOXNews.com, **June 20, 2007;** Sarah Ellison and Dennis K. Berman "Murdoch May Make Concessions, Up to a Limit, in Dow Jones Talks," World Street Journal, June 4, 2007; 'The Rush Limbaugh Show' "Murdoch Will Take on the Times," August 1, 2007

[20]Roy Greenslade, "Their Master's Voice," The Guardian, February 17, 2003 www. dmiblog.com/archives/2006/05/hillary_clintons_mating_ritual.html

[21]The Thom Hartmann Show, Air America Radio, n.d. Forbes.com www.forbes. com/lists

CHAPTER 2

[22] The Randi Rhodes show on Air America Radio http:// www.therandirhodesshow. com/live; "Left-leaning radio hostess carves out an audience, a living," Tribune News Service, September 9, 2004; http://www.accessmylibrary.com/coms2/ summary_0286-8562076_ITM; airamerica.com/shows/randirhodes/bio.asp; Randi Rhodes, "The Randi Rhodes Show Live Commentary," Air America Radio, July-December 2007

[23]Randi Rhodes, "The Randi Rhodes Show Live Commentary," Air America Radio, July-December 2007

[24]WJNOCITY of license West Palm Beach, Miami Herald, June 29, 1994 www. kerala.com/wiki-WJNO Shortstop, "Talk Radio's Other Voice (Randi Rhodes)," Free Republic, March 29, 2004, www.freerepublic.com/focus/fr/1107085/posts; NewsMax.com, America's News Page, "NewsMax's Top 25 Radio Talk Show Hosts," Randi Rhodes; Randi Rhodes, "The Randi Rhodes Show Live Commentary," Air America Radio, July-December 2007

[25]GreatOne, "The Coming Rise of Liberal Talk Radio," Free Republic February 10, 2004

[26]Randi Rhodes, "The Randi Rhodes Show Live Commentary," Air America Radio, July-December 2007

[27]Think Progress, "House Resolution Supporting Limbaugh," October 1, 2007; Matthew Balan, "After Imus, CNN Now Targets Rush Limbaugh," NewsBuster. com, April 12, 2007

[28]CNN.com, "Student Tasered at campus forum for Kerry," September 18, 2007; Randi Rhodes, "The Randi Rhodes Show Live Commentary," Air America Radio, July-December 2007

[29]Joe Kovacs, "Air America radio host: punish me if I broke law," WorldNetDaily, April 28, 2005

[30]Catherine Moy, "Peace Mom" (Cindy Sheehan) leads Freedom Fig," The San Diego Independent Media Center, Monday, July 09, 2007; Randi Rhodes, "The Randi Rhodes Show Live Commentary," Air America Radio, July-December 2007

[31]mississippireview.com/2005/Vol11No4-Oct05/1104-100105-goldhammer. html;Bill O'Reilly "A Message for the Democratic Party," FoxNews.com, June 16, 2006; thinkprogress.org/2007/05/02/oreilly-derogatory; www.amazon.com/Big-Encyclopedia-Republican-Hypocrites/dp/1401352480; Randi Rhodes, "The Randi Rhodes Show Live Commentary," Air America Radio, July-December 2007

[32]www.commondreams.org/views07/0125-21.htm; White House, "President Bush Announces Combat Operations in Iraq Have Ended," May 1, 2003 www.state. gov/p/nea/rls/rm/20203.htm; BBC News "Rumsfeld foresees Iraq war, February 7 2003; USATODAY.com, "Confronting Iraq," April 1, 2003; CBS News, "Bush: No Saddam Links to 9/11," September 17, 2003; Dana Milbank, "Bush Disavows hussein-Sept. 11 Link," Washinton post.com, September 18, 2003, Page A18; White House, "President Bush Holds Press Conference," March 13, 2002 www. whitehouse.gov/news/releases/2002/03/20020313-8.html; Randi Rhodes, "The Randi Rhodes Show Live Commentary," Air America Radio, July-December 2007

[33]White House, "Remarks by the President on Teaching American History and Civic Education," September 17, 2002; White House, "President Bush, President Arroyo Hold Joint Press Conference," May 19, 2003

[34]New York Times, "Iraq insists on withdrawal timetable for US troops, September 17, 2007; Sabrina Tavernise, "US Contractor Banned by Iraq over shooting," New York Times, September 18, 2007; Boston.com, "Court Allows Suit Against Air America," January 2, 2007; Air America Radio "The Rachel Maddow Show," www.airamerica.com/maddow; Randi Rhodes, "The Randi Rhodes Show Live Commentary," Air America Radio, July-December 2007

[35]CNN.com, "Transcripts CNN Sunday Morning, June 5, 2005 transcripts.cnn. com/TRANSCRIPTS/0506/05/sm.01.html; Randi Rhodes, "The Randi Rhodes Show Live Commentary," Air America Radio, July-December 2007

[36]www.scottclifton.com/katrina.htm; *Timothy Dwyer and Michael A. Fletcher,* "Along Gulf, Aiding the Living and Counting the Dead," Washingtonpost.com, September 6, 2005; Page A01; www.thinkprogress.org/katrina-timeline; Scott Gold, Lianne Hart and Stephen Braun, "New Orleans Death Toll May Soar," Los Angles Times, September 1, 2005; Seth Borenstein, "Federal Government Wasn't Ready for Katrina, Disaster Experts Say," Knight Ridder Newspapers, September 2, 2005; Randi Rhodes, "The Randi Rhodes Show Live Commentary," Air America Radio, July-December 2007

[37]White House, "President Arrives in Alabama, Briefed on Hurricane Katrina," September 2, 2005 www.whitehouse.gov/news/releases/2005/09/20050902-

2.html; Randi Rhodes, "The Randi Rhodes Show Live Commentary," Air America Radio, July-December 2007

[38]ADL "Offensive Holocaust Remarks on Air America," September 26, 2005 http://www.adl.org/media_watch/radio/20050926-Air+America.htm; Editor& Publisher, "Barbara Bush: Things working out," September 05, 2005

[39]http://newsbusters.org/people/television/chris-matthews?page=8; Tim Graham, "BBC: Katrina Shows U.S. Still Has Too Many Blacks 'At The Bottom Of The Pile,'" Newsbusters, August 28, 2006; Randi Rhodes, "The Randi Rhodes Show Live Commentary," Air America Radio, July-December 2007; www.whitehouse. gov/news/releases/2005/09/20050902-2.html; MSNBC.com, "Bush takes blame for Katrina flaws - Katrina, The Long Road Back," September 13, 2005

[40]Air America Place Message Boards "The Randi Rhodes Alaska Cruise," August 19, 2007 www.airamericaplace.com/index.php?act=findpost&pid=210007; Andrea Koppel, Ted Barrett and Abbi Tatton, Sen. Stevens is 'the secret senator,' CNN.com, August 30, 2006; Randi Rhodes, "The Randi Rhodes Show Live Commentary," Air America Radio, July-December 2007

[41]Nicholas Lemann, "The Southern Strategist," New York Times, March 7, 1993; Thom Hartman, "The Thom Hartman Show,"Air America Radio, n.d.; Randi Rhodes, "The Randi Rhodes Show Live Commentary," Air America Radio, July-December 2007

[42]Jane Burns, October 16, 2007 www.madison.com/tct/entertainment/burns/251332; Journalism.org, "Talk Hosts Turn Into "Live Earth" Reviewers," July 8 - 13, 2007; www.journalism.org/node/6597; Randi Rhodes, "The Randi Rhodes Show Live Commentary," Air America Radio, July-December 2007; TALKERS magazine, "2007 New Media Seminar,"_66.227.50.219/main/index.php?option=com_con tent&task=view&id=%0A%20%20%20%20%20%20%20%20%20%20; Greg Palest, "Randi Rhodes and Greg Palast HuntA Giuliani's Favorite vulture," Smirking chimp, June 21, 2007

CHAPTER 3

[43]"Tom DeLay, biography," Encyclopedia.com, www.encyclopedia.com/doc/1E1-DeLayT.html; "Tom DeLay" World biography www.worldbiography.net/delay_tom.html

[44]Leadership Positions: Roles and Responsibilities www.ncsl.org/programs/leaders/LRDRoles.htm

[45]washingtonpost.com/wp-srv/.../special/clinton/stories/delay121698.htm;   Eric Pianin, and Kevin Merida, "Hammer' Time / Tenacious GOP leader revives once-faltering movement," San Francisco Chronicle, December 16, 1998

[46]Ari Berman, "Hammer Time on the Hill," The Nation, November 22, 2004; Ann Curley, "DeLay, Gingrich support Hastert for House speaker," CNN.com, December 19, 1998

[47]May 13, 2003, edition of CBS Evening News by Dan Rather; Media Researched Center "Texas Democrats Walk Out but DeLay...", May 16, 2003 www.mrc.org/cyberalerts/2003/cyb20030516.asp; CNN.com, "Texas House paralyzed by Democratic walkout, May 19, 2003; Philip Shenon, "Texas Legislative Dispute National," New York Times, May 15, 2003

[48]Candy Crowley, "Election 2002," CNN.com, November 7, 2002 www.cnn.com/ELECTION/2002

[49]William M. Welch, "Reid eyes top Senate post after Daschle's loss," USA TODAY, November 3, 2004

[50]Jonathan Weisman and Chris Cillizza, "DeLay to Resign From Congress," WashingtonPost.com, April 4, 2006; Page A01

[51]Julie Hollar, "The DeLay Chronicles," The Texas Observer, February 4, 2000

[52]MSNBC.com, "DeLay assails GOP colleagues in new book," March 21, 2007; Tom Delay and Stephen Mansfield, "No Retreat, No Surrender: One American's Fight," (New York; Sentinel HC, 2007), Page 112 and Page 115; Robert Novak, "The Wrath of Tom DeLay," Washingtonpost.com, March 15, 2007; A19; Robert Dreyfuss, "DeLay Incorporated," The Texas Observer, February 4, 2000

[53]Walter Roche Jr and Sam Verhovek, "DeLay's Own Tragic Crossroads," Los Angeles Times, March 27, 2005;Good Morning America, "DeLay Says He's Not Giving Up Schiavo Fight," ABC News, March 19, 2005; www.cnn.com/interactive/us/0503/gallery.schiavo.reax/content.7.html Bill Nichols, "Politicians might feel repercussion of Schiavo case," USATODAY.com, March, 2005; Atheism.com, "Tom DeLay on the Terri Schiavo's death," March 31, 2005 http://atheism.about.com/b/2005/03/31tom-delay-on-the-terri-schiavo

[54]Ben Pershing, "DeLay's Departure a Relief for GOP,"CREW, April 4, 2006; Online NewsHour "House Majority Leader DeLay Criticized," PBS, March 15, 2005

[55]Robin Toner, "A Partisan Leaves; Will an Era Follow?" New York Times, April 5, 2006; Boston.com, "DeLay leaves Congress with defense of partisanship," June 8, 2006

[56]Barbara Ferguson, "Congress Defies Bush, Snubs Palestinians on Aid Issue," Arab News, March 26, 2005; The Washington Times, "Lott urges Bush to give DeLay 'aggressive support," April 18, 2005; American Arab Anti Discrimination Committee www.adc.org/action/1999/27jan99.htm; David Firestone, "DeLay Is to Carry Dissenting Message on a Mideast Tour," New York Times, July 25, 2003

[57]Tom Delay and Stephen Mansfield, "No Retreat, No Surrender: One American's Fight," (New York; Sentinel HC, 2007), Page 156; huffingtonpost. com/2007/03/24/delay-book-likens-democra_n_44163.htm

[58]WashingtonPost.com, "Election 2006" www.washingtonpost.com/wp-srv/politics/ interactives/campaign06; Charles Babington, "Lott Rejoins Senate Leadership," Washingtonpost.com, November 16, 2006; Page A04

[59]December 11, 2006 Edition of Fox News 'Hannity and Colmes'; News Hounds, "Tom DeLay Blames Iraq war problem on liberals," December 12, 2006

[60]USATODAY.com, "A look at the Abramoff scandal and where it goes next," WashingtonPost.com, "Key Players in the Investigation of Lobbyist Jack Abramoff," June 26, 2007; E.J. Kessler, "Senate Probe of Lobbying Puts Heat on DeLay Ally," Forward.com, November 26, 2004

[61]www.ask.com/reference/dictionary/ahdict/13599/pardon   United   States Constitution, Article II, Section 2: www.constitution.org/constit_.htm; Jim VandeHei, "Lobbyist Told Reporter of Nearly a Dozen Contacts with Bush, Washington post.com, February 10, 2006; Page A08; Deborah Charles, "Ex-Bush official linked to Abramoff convicted,"Boston.com, June 20, 2006; Randi Rhodes Show, Air America Radio, n.d

[62]CNN.com, "Crooked congressman going to prison," March 3, 2006; CBS News, "Disgraced Rep. Gets 8 years in Prison," March 3, 2006; WashingtonPost.com, "Key Players in the Investigation of Lobbyist Jack Abramoff," June 26, 2007

[63]Shaheen Pasha, "Skilling gets 24 years," CNNMoney.com, October 24, 2006; Carrie Johnson, "Skilling Gets 24 Years for Fraud at Enron," Washington Post, October 24, 2006; A01; Peter Overby, "Rep. Jefferson Indicted on Fraud, Bribery Counts," NPR All Things Considered, June 4, 2007; CNN.com, "Affidavit: $90,000 found in congressman's freezer," May 22, 2006

[64]Robert Novak, "The Wrath of Tom DeLay," Washingtonpost.com, March 15, 2007; A19

CHAPTER 4

[65]"Richard B. (Dick) Cheney Biography," Biography.com www.biography.com/search/article.do?id=9246063; "Vice President of the United States - Richard B. Cheney" www.whitehouse.gov/vicepresident/vpbio.html

[66]FOXNews.com, "Richard Cheney, Interview on FOX News Sunday," February 6, 2005

[67]New York Times, "Timeline of the C.I.A.'s 'Family Jewels,'" June 26, 2007

[68]CNN.com, "Election 2000-The Republican National Convention," July 30, 2000 archives.cnn.com/2000/ALLPOLITICS/ stories/07/30/talk.wrap/index.html; Sue Pleming, "Cheney defends voting record in Congress,"CNN.com July 27, 2000

[69]Robert Parry, "Covering Up Iran-Contra," Consortium News, November 5, 2000

[70]Jeffrey Steinberg, "A New 'Halloween Massacre' Will Sink Cheney-Rumsfeld," Executive Intelligence Review, October 28, 2005

[71]January 27, 1993 edition of "Larry King Live," CNN; OILEMPIRE.US, "Vice President Richard Cheney: the man behind the throne," January 17, 2007; Allen Myerson, "Halliburton Picks Cheney to be Chief," New York Times, August 11, 1995; www.biography.com/search/article.do?id=9246063; www.whitehouse.gov/vicepresident/vpbio.html

[72]www.usconstitution.net/const.html NewsMax.com, "Cheney Residency Dispute to Be Appealed," November 23, 2000; Media Research Center, "Cheney a "Reasonable Conservative," CyberAlert, July 24, 2000, www.mrc.org/cyberalerts/2000/cyb20000724.asp; CNN.com, "Capital Gang: Sen. Pete Domenici Discusses Bush's ...," July 22, 2000

[73]usinfo.state.gov/products/pubs/outusgov/ch1.htm

[74]September 16, 2001 edition of "Meet the Press" with Tim Russert, NBC, **whitehouse.gov**/vicepresident/news- speeches/speeches/vp20010916.html; BBC NEWS, "Americas Profile: Dick Cheney," July 11, 2002

[75]Telephonic interview of the Vice President by Rush Limbaugh March 22, 2004 http://www.whitehouse.gov/news/releases/2004/03/20040322-5.html

[76]CNN.com, "Iraq insurgency in 'last throes,' Cheney says," 'Larry King Live,' May 31, 2005

[77] MSNBC.com, "Bush has 5 polyps removed," July 21, 2007 The Constitution of the United States www.constitution.org/usconsti.htm; White House, "Text of a Letter from the President…,"July 21, 2007; Deb Riechmann, "Doctors remove polyps from Bush's colon," The Boston Globe, July 22, 2007

[78] White House, "Vice President's Remarks to the Traveling Press," February 27, 2007; Fox News.com, "Cheney, Safe after Homicide Bombing at U.S. Base," February 27, 2007; Jonathan Karl, "'I heard a Loud boom' Cheney Discusses Assassinating," ABC News, February 27, 2007; 13abc.com, "Suicide bombing in Afghanistan during Cheney visit," February 27, 2007

[79] "Line of Succession," Time.com, July 2, 1945 www.time.com/time/magazine/article/0,9171,775967,00.html

[80] NPR, "Full Transcript, NPR Interview with President Bush, January 29, 2007 *www.npr.org/templates/story/ story.php?storyId=7065633;* Mark Silva, "Waxman questions legality of Cheney's secrecy," The Swamp, June 21, 2007; Online NewsHour "Vote 2004 Candidates Dick Cheney Vice President,"; Glenn Kessler, "With Vice President, He Shaped Iraq Policy," Washington Post, October 29, 2005; Page A01; John Nichols, "Cheney Vs. Journalism," CBS News, July 13, 2005; *Martin Frost, "Replacing Cheney Gives White House," FoxNews.com, February 14, 2007*

[81] Richard Cheney, Interview by Larry King, Larry King Live, CNN.com, July 31, 2007 www.whitehouse.gov/news/releases/2007/07/20070731-2.html; USATODAY.com, "Cheney: Al-Qaeda must not find home in Mideast,"

[82] U.S. Constitution www.house.gov/house/Constitution/ Constitution.html PREAMBLE, www.leg.state.or.us/orcons/usconst.html

[83] OIC Report: Introduction, New York Times on the Web, www.nytimes.com/specials/starr/ 5intro.html; PBS, "Impeachment: A NewsHour Special-The Censure Option," December 19, 1998; TIME, "The President On Trial: Impeachment Articles," December 19, 1998; www.senate.gov/~rpc/archive/impeach/THEMEMO.htm; Eric Pianin and Kevin Merda, "How GOP's Enforcer Propelled the Process," Washingtonpost.com, December 16, 1998, Page A1; CNN.com, "Transcript: President Clinton comments on end of Senate trial," February 12, 1999; Washingtonpost.com "The Watergate Story," www.washingtonpost.com/wp-srv/politics/special/watergate/index.html; CharlesS, "Dennis Kucinich Files Articles of Impeachment Against Cheney," Free Republic, April 25, 2007; CNN.com, "Democrats bucks party line to vote with GOP in Clinton hearing," January 28, 1999; CNN.com "House Impeaches Clinton," December 19, 1998

[84] "Resolution 333," November 6, 2007 thehollytree.blogspot.com/2007_04_01_archive.html

[85] Richard Cheney, Interview with Dick Cheney by Neil Cavuto, FOXNews. com, June 25, 2004; Transcript, CNN.com, June 25, 2004 edition.cnn.com/ TRANSCRIPTS/0406/25/lad.03.html; Dana Milbank and Helen Dewar, "Cheney Defends Use of four-Letter Word," Washingtonpost.com, June 26, 2004; Page A04; CNN.com, "Cheney says he felt better after cursing at Leahy," June 26, 2004

[86] eMediaMilWorks, "Text: Bush meets with Congressional Leadership," December 18, 2000; CBS News," Cheney: The Fourth Branch?, Special Contributor Lloyd Garver Wonders," July 4 2007

[87] Huffingonpost.com, "Cheney Gets Funding For Executive Branch He Says He's Not Part Of," June 23, 2007; CNN.com, "Cheney: Congressional Probe of attorneys' firings ' a witch hunt'," July 31, 2007; Richard Cheney, Interview of the Vice President by Mike Allen, Jim Vandehei and John Harris, the Politico, December 6, 2007 www.whitehouse.gov/news/releases/2007/12/20071206.html; Interview of the Vice President by Larry King, CNN, July 31, 2007 www.whitehouse.gov/ news/releases/2007/07/20070731-2.html USATODAY.com, "Cheney stance on information challenged," June 24, 2007
CNN.com, "Cheney makes Capitol Hill rounds," January 5, 2001; www.whitehouse. gov/news/releases/2007/07/20070731-2.html

[88] "Biography of Vice President Richard B. Cheney," Embassy of the United States Stockholm, Sweden, August 9, 2002; stockholm.usembassy.gov/cabbio/cheney. html; CNN.com, "Cheney's history of heart problems," November 13, 2004

CHAPTER 5

[89] "Rush Limbaugh: Biography and Much More," Answers.com www.answers.com/ topic/rush-limbaugh; www.merriam-webster.com/dictionary/fairness+doctrine; Robin Toner, "Politics: On The Air; Radio Talk Show Host Fears For True Conservatism's Fate," New York Times, February 23, 1996; Seattlepi.com, "Rush Limbaugh moves to new radio station," July 15, 2003; Rush Limbaugh, "The Rush Limbaugh Show Live Commentary," WABC, July-December 2007; John 1. 1 (King James Version).

[90] Rusty Shackleford, "Jon Stewart: Democratic Majority Kingmaker," Townhall.com, November10, 2006; "Rush Limbaugh," TV.com www.tv.com/rush-limbaugh/ person/2903/summary.html; Rush Limbaugh, "The Rush Limbaugh Show Live Commentary," WABC, July-December 2007

[91] December 20, 2007 Edition of The 'Rush Limbaugh Show'; Rush Limbaugh, "The Rush Limbaugh Show Live Commentary," WABC, July- December 2007

[92]Interview with Vice President Richard B. Cheney, 'The Rush Limbaugh Show,' April 5, 2007; Rush Limbaugh, "The Rush Limbaugh Show Live Commentary," WABC, July-December 2007

[93]CNN.com, "Limbaugh lawyer denies any talk of plea deal," January 26, 2004; CNN.com "Random drug test, no guns for Limbaugh," May 1, 2006; John Pacenti, Palm Beach Post, January 3, 2004; palmbeachpost.com/localnews/content/news/limbaugh/010304_limbaugh.html; Jeff Leeds, "In Legal Deal, Limbaugh Surrenders in Drug Case," New York Times, April 19, 2006; Peter Whoriskey, "Rush Limbaugh Turns Himself In On Fraud Charge In Rx Drug Probe," Washington post, April 29, 2006, Page C01; CNN.com, "Charge in Limbaugh drug case rarely used," January 4, 2004; Susan Spencer –Wendel, "Limbaugh turns himself in for Doctor shopping," Palm Beach Post.com, April 29, 2006

[94]Rush Limbaugh, "The Rush Limbaugh Show Live Commentary," WABC, July-December 2007

[95]MSNBC.com, "Senators grid for battle over judges," May 13, 2005; Shailagh Murray and Paul Kane, "Senators Pull All-Nighter For Debate On Iraq War," Washingtonpost.com, July 18, 2007; Page A01; Laurie Kellman, "Democrats running the Senate _ all night long,"Washingtonpost.com, July 18, 2007; FoxNews.com, "After All-Night Debate, Senate rejects measure…," July 18, 2007; Laurie Kellman "Democrats running the Senate," Sfg.com, July 18, 2007; Rush Limbaugh, "The Rush Limbaugh Show Live Commentary," WABC, July-December 2007; www.senate.gov/artandhistory/history/minute/Compulsory_Attendance.htm

[96]Rush Limbaugh, "The Rush Limbaugh Show Live Commentary," WABC, July-December 2007

[97]Chip McLean "In Defense of Rush Limbaugh," The Conservativevoice.com, October 07, 2007; www.amazon.com/Rush-Limbaugh-Big-Fat-Idiot/dp/0440508649

[98]The Rush Limbaugh Show, "Elite, Effete Media Snobs Up in Arms over Rush-Rove Interview," WABC, August 16, 2007; Rush Limbaugh, "The Rush Limbaugh Show Live Commentary," WABC, July-December 2007

[99]September 26, 2007 edition of the "Rush Limbaugh Show"; Carrie Budoff, "Rush To Judgment," CBS News, October 1, 2007; CNN.com, "Clear Channel defends Limbaugh after 'phony soldiers' remark," October 3, 2007; The Rush Limbaugh Show, "The Anatomy of a Smear: "Phony Soldiers,'" September 28, 2007; The Rush Limbaugh Show, "Rush's Approval Rating Higher Than Dingy Harry Reid's in Nevada," WABC, October 15, 2007

[100]Rush Limbaugh, "The Rush Limbaugh Show Live Commentary," WABC, July-December 2007

[101]Anne Flaherty, "GOP support for Iraq war slips," USATODAY.com, June 25, 2007; ABC News, "Republican Revolution: Another GOP Senator Breaks with Bush," June 25, 2007; MSNBC.com, "GOP shows Fissures on Iraq, , June 27, 2007; Edward Epstein, "Lugar shakes capitol," San Francisco Chronicle, June 27, 2007; Columbiatribune.com, "Voinovich adds his voice to growing GOP dissent," June 27, 2007

[102]Nico, "Specter: 'We Have To Face The Fact' That Iraq Is A Civil War," Think Progress.org, October 23, 2006, rhinkprogress.org/2006/10/23/specter-civil-war-iraq; Rush Limbaugh, "The Rush Limbaugh Show Live Commentary," WABC, July-December 2007

[103]Rush Limbaugh, "The Rush Limbaugh Show Live Commentary," WABC, July-December 2007

[104]Landmark Legal Foundation, "Landmark Legal Foundation Nominates Rush Limbaugh For 2007 Nobel Peace Prize," February 1, 2007 www.landmarklegal.org/DesktopDefault.aspx?tabid=167

[105]Rush Limbaugh, "The Rush Limbaugh Show Live Commentary," WABC, July-December 2007

[106]E.J. Dionne, "Dukakais is Termed Extreme Liberal," New York Times, May 20, 1988; E.J. Dionne, "Poll shows Dukakis Leads Bush; Many Reagan Backers Shift Sides," New York Times, May 17, 1988

[107]American Experience, George H.W. Bush, PBS   www.pbs.org/wgbh/amex/bush41/more/bush.html; CNN.com, "Transcript, CNN.com," January 6, 2002 archives.cnn.com/TRANSCRIPTS/0201/06/le.00.html; R.W. Apple Jr, "The 1992 Campaign: Ross Perot; Noncandidate still, Perot could still be a spoiler" New York Times, September 13, 1992

[108]The Rush Limabaugh show, "Obama's Dangerous Ignorance," WABC, n.d CNN.com, "Alma Was Alarmed," April 11, 1996

[109]The Nation, "Indecision 2000," November 27, 2000; James Gerstenzang and Edwin Chen, "Gore: Man of Too Many Details?" Los Angeles Times, December 14, 2000; New York Times, "Lieberman became the first prominent Democrat to chastise Clinton for the Lewinsky," August 8, 2000

[110]CNN.com – "Poll: Kerry tops Bush in debate," October 1, 2004

111November 8 2006, Edition of the Rush Limbaugh show, WABC; Michael Levenson, "Romney's shift on abortion, gay rights sincere, Weyrich says,"The Boston Globe, November 7, 2007...; Brian C. Mooney, "Giuliani continues his conservative shift," The Boston Globe, August 13, 2007

112James Bowman, "The leader of the opposition - political commentator Rush Limbaugh," National Review, September 6, 1993; Graham Hunter "Larsson to stay on for Sweden,"UEfA.com n.d Rush Limbaugh, "The Rush Limbaugh Show Live Commentary," WABC, July-December 2007

CHAPTER 6

113"Condoleezza Rice Notable Biography, "Encyclopedia of World Biography http://www.notablebiographies.com/news/Ow-Sh/Rice-Condoleezza.html; Secretary of State Condoleezza Rice Biography www.state.gov/r/pa/ei/biog/41252.htm

114CongressLink: "Congress: The Basics Lawmaking Civil Rights: Major," www.congresslink.org/print_basics_histmats_civilrights64text.htm

115Scott Johnson, "Birmingham's New Legacy," Weeklystandard.com, January 31, 2005 weeklystandard.com/Content/Public/Articles/000/000/005/...?pg=2; U.S. Department of Labor, "Title VII, Civil Rights Act of 1964, As Amended," www.dol.gov/oasam/regs/statutes/2000e-16.htm; U.S Department of Justice, "The Voting Rights Act of 1965," www.usdoj.gov/crt/voting/intro/intro_b.htm; United States Environmental Protection Agency (EPA), "Title VIII of the Civil Rights Act of 1968 (Fair Housing Act) 2http://www.epa.gov/civilrights/titl8.htm

116http://www.notablebiographies.com/news/Ow-Sh/Rice-Condoleezza.html; www.state.gov/r/pa/ei/biog/41252.htm

117"Condoleezza Rice - Early Career," www.indepthinfo.com/condoleezza-rice/early-career.shtml

118Dan Eggen and Robin Wright, "Tenet Recalled Warning Rice," Washingtonpost.com, October 3, 2006; A03; CNN.com, "Spokesman: Rice didn't 'brush off' terror warnings," October 3, 2006; Washingtonpost.com, "Two Months Before 9/11, an Urgent Warning to Rice," October 1, 2006; Page A17; Anne Gearan, "Rice: I don't recall alert about attack," Boston.com, October 2, 2006; http://www.notablebiographies.com/news/Ow-Sh/Rice-Condoleezza.html; www.state.gov/r/pa/ei/biog/41252.htm

119CNN.com, "Rice: 'Nothing to hide' from 9/11 commission," March 29, 2004; The New York Times, "Transcript: Testimony of Condoleezza ..." August 8, 2004

120Foreign Affairs magazine, "Campaign 2000 -- Promoting the National Interest," January/February 2000; Late Edition with Wolf Blitzer,"CNN.com, September

8, 2002; New York Times, "Why We Know Iraq is Lying," A Column by Dr. Condoleezza Rice

[121]**Pittsburgh Post-Gazette,** "Rice defends war while Dems condemn appearance here," October 21, 2004; Global Policy Forum, "Bush Officials Change Tune on Iraqi Weapons," May 14 2003

[122]CBS News, "Rice Confirmed By Senate, New Sec. Of State Approved Despite Criticism ..." June 26, 2005

[123]US State Department, "Country Reports on Terrorism," April 28, 2006 www.state.gov/s/ct/rls/crt/2005/66236.htm; US State Department, "Transformation Diplomacy," January 18, 2006 www.state.gov/secretary/rm/2006/59306.htm; VOA.com, "Rice on Palestinian Elections," January 18, 2006; Philip Shenon, "Rice urges 2 Palestinian Groups to Halt Violence," New York Times, October 4, 2006

[124]US State Department, "Special Briefing on Travel to the Middle East and Europe," July 21, 2006; Tony Karon, "Condi in Diplomatic Disneyland," TIME, July 26, 2006; WashingtonPost.com, "Dr. Vitali Silitski, Outposts of Tyranny: Belarus," April 12, 2005

[125]US State Department, "Remarks with Senator Lugar…," July 29, 2005; Condoleezza Rice, Interview by Bill O'Reilly, The O'Reilly Factor, U.S. Department of State, August 1, 2006 http://www.state.gov/secretary/rm/2006/69838.htm; Guardian.co.uk, "UN delays peacekeeping action," July 31 2006

[126]NewsMax.com "Cheney, Rice at Odds over Iran," June 3, 2007

[127]US State Department, "Remarks with Senator Lugar…," July 29, 2005

[128]Elizabeth MacDonald and Chana R. Schoenberger, "The World's Most Powerful Women,"Forbes.com, September 1, 2006; "Condoleezza Rice, The Most Powerful Women," Forbes.com www.forbes.com/lists/2005/11/MTNG.html; The Australian, "Time Magazine's Most Influential," May 4, 2007 www.theaustralian.news.com.au/story/0,25197,21669892-2,00.html; www.time.com/time/specials/2007/time100/0,28757,1595326,00.html; Stanford News Service, "Provost challenges managers to work hard, adapt to change," November 30, 1993; James Robinson, "Velvet-glove forcefulness," Stanford News Service, June 9, 1999

[129]Condoleezza Rice, Interview by Bill O'Reilly, The O'Reilly Factor, U.S. Department of State, September 14, 2005 www.state.gov/secretary/rm/2005/53155.htm; Eugene Robinson, "What Rice Can't See," Washington Post, October 25, 2005;

Page A21; Carletta Skinner, "Castigation of Condi Betrays Black Tradition," African-American Political Opinion, July, 22, 2006

[130]CNN.com, "Rice spars with Democrats in hearing," January 19, 2005; Glenn Kessler, "Rice stays close to Bush policies in hearing," Washingtonpost.com, January 19, 2005; Page A01; Condoleezza Rice, Interview by David Sanger, Thom Shanher and Helene Cooper of the News, US State Department, January12, 2007 www.state.gov/secretary/rm/2007/78682.htm; Helene Cooper and Thom Shanker, New York Times, "Exchange turns into political flashpoint," January 12, 2007; Washington Times, "White House rips Boxer over Rice," January 13, 2007

[131]FOXNews.com, "Rice won't rule out Force vs. Syria," October 19, 2005; Liz Sidoti, "Rice justifies Iraq policy doesn't rule out long stay," Seattle Times, October 19, 2005; Elise Labott, "Rice: U.S. will defeat insurgency, rebuild Iraq," CNN. com, October 19, 2005; USATODAY.com, "Rice won't rule out U.S. troops in Iraq in 10 years," October 19, 2005

[132]Condoleezza Rice, Interview on NBC's Today Show by Meredith Vieira, US State Department, September 12, 2007 www.state.gov/secretary/rm/2007/09/91991. htm; New York Post, "Rice: Iraq effort just beginning," September 13, 2007; Speaker Nancy Pelosi News Room- Press Releases, "Pelosi: The President's Iraq Plan is Recipe for an Endless War September 12, 2007; Carl Hulse, "Disappointment Democrats Map Withdrawal Strategy," New York Times, September 13, 2007; CNN.com, "Pelosi becomes first woman House speaker," January 5, 2007

[133]FoxNews.com, "Sen. Clinton Backs Husband After 'FOX News' Interview…," September 6, 2006; Ian Bishop, "Rice boils over at bubba," New York Post, September 26, 2006; CBS News, "Sen. Clinton Fires Back at Rice…, "September 27, 2006; MSNBC.com, "Sen. Clinton backs husband in terror hunt row," September 27, 2006

[134]USATODAY.com, "Rice challenges Clinton's of anti-terror record," September 26, 2006; FOX News.com, -Transcript: "Counterterror Experts Debate Clinton Claims on 'FNS", FNS with Chris Wallace, October 1, 2006, www.foxnews. com/story/0,2933,216964,00.html; Ian Bishop and Geoff Earle, "Hill joins bill in terror war," New York Post, September 27, 2007; White House, "President Bush welcomes President Karzai of Afghanistan…," September 26, 2006

[135]www.amazon.com/Because-He-Could-Dick-Morris/dp/0060784156; **Secretary Condoleezza Rice, "Interview by Sean Hannity," The Sean Hannity Show,** September 13, 2007 www.state.gov/secretary/rm/2007/09/92063.htm

CHAPTER 7

[136] "Newt Gingrich: Biography and Much More," Answers.com www.answers.com/topic/newt-gingrich; "Newt Gingrich: Biography," www.usembassy-amman.org.jo/wwwhgbio.htm

[137]John E. Yang, "House Reprimands, Penalizes Speaker," Washingtonpost.com, January 22 1997; Page A01; Thomas H. Moore, "Gingrich Wins A Squeaker,"CNN.com, January 7, 1997; Oreskes, "Ethics Committee Expected to Find Violations by Wright on Finances," New York Times, April 5, 1989; Robin Toner, "Texans' Acts Show They Want Wright to Stay On," New York Times, June 20, 1989; www.answers.com/topic/newt-gingrich; www.usembassy-amman.org.jo/wwwhgbio.htm

[138]www.pbs.org/wgbh/pages/frontline/newt/ vanityfair7.html; Jeffrey Bell, "DeLay, Red Statesman," Weeklystandard.com, April 25, 2005; Jacob V. Lamar "An Attack Dog, Not a Lapdog," TIME.com, April 03, 1989; Clifford Krauss, "The House Bank; Foley Proposes Using Outsider to Run House Services ..."New York Times, March 16, 1992; David M. Mason, "Time to Resolve the House Post Office Scandal," The Heritage Foundation, February 17, 1994; The Rush Limbaugh Show, "History of Scandals from 1979 to 2005," WABC, November 29, 2005

[139]Helen Dewar, "Parties Wrestle Over HMO Issue," Washington Post, July 24, 1998; Page A04; Jeffrey B. Gayner, "The Contract with America: Implementing New Ideas in the U.S." The Heritage Foundation, October 12, 1995

[140]"1994 Congressional Elections: An Analysis," Fairvote.org www.fairvote.org/reports/1995/chp3/gans.html; James Carney, "TIME This Week," CNN.com, June 24, 1996 www.cnn.com/ALLPOLITICS/1996/analysis/time/9606/24/carney.shtml

[141]CNN.com, "Gingrich Attacks Clinton On Lewinsky Matter," May 18, 1998

[142]CNN.com, "Record-breaking federal shutdown ends," January 6, 1996

[143]Baker Spring, "A Game Plan for Restoring America's Defenses," The Heritage Foundation, February 3, 1995

[144]John E. Yang and Helen Dewar, "Ethics Panel Supports Reprimand of Gingrich," Washington Post, January 18 1997; Page A01;**Glenn Simpson, Will Newt Fall?" Mother Jones,** July/August 1995 Issue

[145]R. Morris Barrett, "After The Coup: Can The Peace Hold?" CNN.com, July 24, 1997; CNN.com, "Apology for a Coup Attempt," July 23, 1997; *Kevin Merida,*

"Rep. Tom DeLay Showed His Strength and Hung Onto His GOP Post," Washington Post, July 25, 1997; Page D01

[146]Marc Sandalow, "Gingrich Takes Heat From GOP / Dismal showing at polls worries party ..." San Francisco Chronicle, November 5, 1998; CNN.com, "Gingrich stuns Washington by stepping aside," November 6, 1998

[147]Katharine Q Seelye, "The Speaker steps down; The overview; Facing a revolt, Gingrich won't..." New York Times, November 7, 1998; www.answers.com/topic/newt-gingrich; www.usembassy-amman.org.jo/wwwhgbio.htm

[148]CNN.com "Election '98" www.cnn.com/ELECTION/1998; Tony Karon, "How Jim Jeffords Changed the World," TIME.com, May 29 2001

[149]"Lame Duck Sessions," U.S. Senate Reference Home www.senate.gov/pagelayout/reference/four_column_table/Lame_Duck.htm; CNN.com, "Lott steps down as majority leader," December 20, 2002; Richard W. Stevenson and David Firestone, "For Lott, Complex Relationship With Bush Gets Trickier," New York Times, November 16, 2002

[150]retail politics - Definitions from Dictionary.com www.amazon.com/Winning-Future-Century-Contract-America/dp/0895260425; Michael McCord, "The New Hampshire Primary: Brief History," February 7, 2007

[151]www.amazon.com/Contract-Earth-Newt-Gingrich/dp/0452289920; Newt Gingrich, Interview by Tim Russert, "Meet The Press," NBC, May 20, 2007; MSNBC.com, "Sen. Chris Dodd & Newt Gingrich debate the war in Iraq," 'Meet the Press' transcript for May 20, 2007 www.msnbc.msn.com/id/18720045

[152]John 8. 1-11 (King James Version); Jake Tapper, "Gingrich admits to affair during Clinton impeachment," ABC News, March 9, 2007; Lloyd Grove, "Ever the Speaker," Washingtonpost.com, July 1, 2007; Page D01; John Nichols, "French Lesson for Republicans," The Nation, June 18, 2007

[153]Newt Gingrich, "Interview by Brit Hume," Special Report, FOX News', March 27; 2005; USATODAY.com, "Gingrich critical of bilingual education," March 31, 2007; ABC News, "Gingrich Decries Bilingual Education," March 31, 2007; Kasie Hunt, "Gingrich: Bilingual Classes Teach 'Ghetto' Language," Washingtonpost.com April 1, 2007; A05

[154]Fox News.com, "Newt Gingrich on Hillary's Health Care Plan," Hannity and Colmes, September 18, 2007

[155]'The Rush Limbaugh Show,' "What's Newt Talking About?" August 6, 2007; Steve Holland, "Gingrich: Republicans need clean break from Bush," Reuters, September

14, 2007; Washingtonpost.com, "Pessimism about the GOP's White House prospects," September 15, 2007; A04; USATODAY.com, "McCain brushes off Gingrich's criticism," July 24, 2007; Bill Sammon, "Newt Gingrich goes nuclear: May enter race to foil 'pygmies,'" Examiner.com, July 23, 2007 examiner.com/a-842080-Newt_goes_nuclear_ _May_enter_race_to_foil_pygmies.. 'The Rush Limbaugh Show,. "Newt Unloads on GOP Candidates," July 24, 2007

[156]FOXNews.com, "Gingrich jabs at GOP pursuing 2008 White House nod," July 24, 2007; Tim Graham, "Newt Gingrich Cited Bozell Column on 'Fox News Sunday," NewsBusters.org, February 20, 2007; Bill Sammon, "Newt Gingrich goes nuclear: May enter race to foil 'pygmies,'" Examiner.com, July 23, 2007

CHAPTER 8

[157]John McCain Biography - Biography.com www.biography.com/search/article.do?id=9542249; "John McCain: Biography," Answers.com www.answers.com/topic/john-mccain; www.merriam-webster.com/dictionary/jus sanguinis; www.merriam-webster.com/dictionary/ jus+soli

[158]The United States Constitution, Article One www.usconstitution.net/const.html www.law.cornell.edu/constitution/ constitution.articleii.html; USATODAY.com, "Schwarzenegger seeks to open path of power, February 22, 2004; John Broder, "Schwarzenegger Backs Amendment to Allow Immigrant Presidents," New York Times.com, February 23, 2004

[159]www.biography.com/search/article.do?id=9542249; www.answers.com/topic/john-mccain

[160]U.S. Senate Reference Home www.senate.gov/pagelayout/reference/three_column_table/Senators.htm

[161]Goldwater vs Religious Right www.liberalslikechrist.org/about/Goldwater.html; Barry Goldwater Biography and List of Works www.biblio.com/authors/705/Barry_Goldwater_Biography.html

[162]Barry Goldwater www.spartacus.schoolnet.co.uk/USAgoldwater.htm; www.biblio.com/authors/705/Barry_Goldwater_Biography.html

[163]Richard Davis, "The anatomy of a smear campaign," The Boston Globe, March 21, 2004; Jim Boyd, "For 'Gutter Politics,' Look to the Bush Camp," Star Tribune, February 20, 2004 www.commondreams.org/views04/0220- 07.htm; www.pbs.org/wgbh/pages/frontline/shows/ architect/rove/cron.html; www.biography.com/search/article.do?id=9542249; www.answers.com/topic/john-mccain

[164]Bob Cusack, "Democrats say McCain nearly abandoned GOP," TheHill.com, March 3, 2007; CNN.com, "McCain denies party switch and presidential run," June 2, 2001; Ben Macintyre, "McCain may leave Republican Party to fight Bush in 2004,"Free Republic, July 24, 2001

[165]David Postman, "McCain's theme: Bush was right on Iraq war," The Seattle Times, August 31, 2004; Jim VandeHei and Dan Balz, "Kerry Picks Edwards as Running Mate," Washington Post, July 7, 2004; Page A01; DemocracyNow, "Amy Goodman Questions John McCain on the Smear Tactics…," September 3, 2004 www.democracynow.org/2004/9/3/amy_goodman_questions_john_mccain_on

[166]Project Vote Smart, "Senator John Sidney McCain III - Voting Record," www.votesmart.org/voting_category.php?can_id=53270

[167]CNN.com, "McCain announces '08 bid on Letterman," March 1, 2007; CNN.com, "Time's 25 Most Influential Americans," April 21, 1997

[168]CNN.com, CNN Political Ticker, April 26, 2007 cnn.com/POLITICS/blogs/…/04/mccain- criticized-for-joking-about.html; ABC News, "John McCain to Murtha: 'Lighten Up,' 'Get a Life," April 26, 2007; FOXNews.com, "McCain Brushes Off Latest Criticism of His Sense of Humor," April 26, 2007; 'The Rush Limbaugh Show,' "We try to Praise Senator McCain," April 26, 2007

[169]The Rush Limbaugh Show, "Huckabee's Rollins Trashes Rush Instead of Debating Conservatism," WABC, December 21, 2007

[170]Charles Hurt, "Raising McCain," New York Post, May 19, 2007; 'Hannity and Colmes,' "Cursed by McCain! Sen. John Cornyn on Immigration Debate," FOXNews.com, May 22, 2007; Steve Holland, "Bush wants immigration battle resolved," Reuters, May 19, 2007; Telegraph.co.uk, "The Declaration of Alien Dependence," July 1, 2007

[171]Charles Babington and Shailagh Murray "Senate Supports Interrogation Limits," Washington Post, October 6, 2005; Page A01; CNN.com, "Senate ignores veto threat in limiting detainee treatment," October 6, 2005

[172] Brain Ross, Richard Esposito and Martha Raddatz, "CIA Bans Waterboarding in Terror Interrogations," ABCNews.com, September 14, 2007; Robert Windrem and Andrea Mitchell, "CIA officer fired after admitting leak," NBC News, April. 21, 2006; http://www.msnbc.msn.com/id/12423825/; Charlie Savage, "McCain fights exception to torture ban," The Boston Globe, October 26, 2005

[173]John Berman, "Sen. John McCain Re-Surges in Iowa," ABC News, September 12, 2007; Candy Crowley, "McCain hopes to reignite 'Straight Talk Express' magic," CNN.com, March 15, 2007

[174] **Ron Brynaert and Mike Sheehan,** "DNC slams McCain for 'pandering to far right' on MLK," The Raw Story, January 15, 2007;

[175] United States Constitution-Amendment 12, Ratified12/9/1803 www.usconstitution.net/xconst_Am12.html' www.law.cornell.edu/constitution/constitution.amendmentxii.html

CHAPTER 9

[176]Wellesley College News Releases www.wellesley.edu/PublicAffairs/PAhomepage/releasestoc.html; "Hillary (Rodham) Clinton Biography," Biography.com www.biography.com/search/article.do?id=9251306; Hillary Clinton - Excerpts.com www.excerpts.com/content/hillary-clinton.html

[177]The Rush Limbaugh Show, "No Coincidences with Clinton, Inc." WABC, July 30, 2007; Mark Leibovich, "In Turmoil of '68, Clinton Found a New Voice," New York Times, September 5, 2007 www.biography.com/search/article.do?id=9251306; www.excerpts.com/content/hillary-clinton.html

[178]George McGovern, Biography and Much More from Answers.com www.answers.com/topic/george-mcgovern; Mark Stricherz, "Ideas Primary colors," Boston Globe, November 23, 2003; Howard Fineman, "The Dovish Democrats," Newsweek March 3, 2003

[179]Jackie Judd and Ted Koppel, "Making Hillary Clinton an issue," PBS, March 26, 1992; Jay Nordlinger, "Two for the Price of One," The New York Sun, March 20, 2006; www.biography.com/search/article.do?id=9251306; www.excerpts.com/content/hillary-clinton.html

[180]www.nationalreview.com/comment/comment110600b.shtml; "Hillary Rodham Clinton," Britannica Online Encyclopedia www.britannica.com/EBchecked/topic/121809/Hillary-Rodham-Clinton

[181]Grace-Marie Arnett, National Review, September 2, 1996; findarticles.com/p/articles/mi_m1282/is_n16_v48/ai_18614086; Ralph R. Reilland, "Hillarycare Revisited," Pennsylvaniatownhall.com, patownhall.com/article/2381; www.biography.com/search/article.do?id=9251306; www.excerpts.com/content/hillary-clinton.html

[182]"First Ladies" Biographical Information www.firstladies.org/biographies/firstladies.aspx?biography=43; **Feminist Daily News,** "Hillary Clinton Condemns Taliban Abuses in U.N. Speech,"**March 5, 1999**; Carl Sferrazza Anthony, "Lady in Waiting," Washington Monthly, July-August 2003; Feminist Majority Report,

"Feminist Majority Joins European Parliament's Call to End Gender Apartheid in Afghanistan," Spring 1998

[183]Turkishdailynews.com, "Clinton: Hillary will 'be terrific in Senate' Russians ease opposition, February 17, 1999; Hun Sen, "And Hillary Clinton's potential senate run in New York State," Voice of America, February 17, 1999; CNN.com, "Potential candidate Hillary Clinton readies New York blitz, July 4, 1999; Christopher Matthews, "Clinton turns to Boxer for aid in Senate race," San Francisco Chronicle, February 18, 1999; Joyce Purnick, "Hillary Rodham Clinton News," The New York Times, August 27, 1998

[184]Adam Nagourney, "With Some Help, Clintons Purchase a White House," New York Times, September 3, 1999

[185]US Senate, "Opening Remarks Of Senator Hillary Clinton...," November 29, 2001; Feminist Daily News, "Hillary Clinton Hosts Forum for Afghanistan...," November 30, 2001; NewMax.com, "Hillary Clinton's 9/11 Cash Squandered," December 4, 2005; TIME, "Hillary Clinton, "New Hope For Afghanistan's Women,'" November 24, 2001

[186]NewsMax.com, "Hillary Clinton: Iraq war vote a mistake," November 29, 2005; Project Vote Smart – "Senator Hillary Rodham Clinton - Voting Record" www.votesmart.org/voting_category.php?can_id=55463; Manu Raju, Elana Schor and Ilan Wurman, "Few senators read Iraq NIE report," The Hill.com, June 9, 2007; CNN.com, "Clinton's defense of Bush surprises fellow Democrats," July 23, 2003; NewsMax.com, "Hillary Clinton: Iraq War Vote a Mistake," November 29, 2005

[187]Uruknet.info, "War News," December 18, 2006, www.uruknet.info/?p=29124; DAWN, "UK forces to stay, says Blair," December 18, 2006; Rye Brook, "Hillary: immediate Iraq withdrawal 'a big mistake,"FOXNews.com, November 21, 2005; US Senate, "Senator Hillary Rodham Clinton: National Security," November 29, 2005 clinton.senate.gov/issues/nationalsecurity/index.cfm?topic=iraqlette Kristen Lombardi, "Hillary Clinton Talks Iraq," Villagevoice.com, November 29, 2005

[188]James Gerstenzang and Nicole Gaouette, "Bush urges all sides to cool," Seattle Times, March 24, 2006; National Review Online, "The Bible And The Border," CBS News, May 16, 2006; Geoff Earle, "Swing Conservative," Washington Monthly, April 2005; USATODAY.com, "Clinton, Frist tout medical records bill," June, 16, 2005; U.S. Senate, Hillary Rodham Clinton, Senator for New York, August 9, 2005

[189]US Senate "Remarks of Senator Hillary Rodham Clinton on the Senate Floor on the Nomination of Judge Samuel Alito," January 25, 2006 http://clinton.senate.gov/news/statements/details.cfm?id=250765; Susan Jones, "Sen. Clinton Will Vote 'No' on Roberts," GOPUSA, September 23, 2005 www.gopusa.com/

news/2005/september/0923_clinton_roberts.shtml; Oyez: Bush v. Gore, 531 U.S. 98 (2000), U.S. Supreme Court Case Summary www.oyez.org/cases/2000-2009/2000/2000_00_949

[190]CNN Crossfire, "President Bush Tackles Medical Malpractice Reform," CNN. com, January 5, 2005; On the January 3, 2005 edition of Christian Broadcasting Network's The 700 Club, Reverend Pat Robertson; FindLaw Supreme Court Center: Supreme Court History supreme.lp.findlaw.com/supreme_court/supcthist.html

[191]Annee Kornblut, "Clinton Won Easily, but Bankroll Shows the Toll," New York Times, November 21, 2006; David Espo, "Senate GOP Foils Debate on Iraq Surge," CBS News.com, February 18, 2007; CNN.com, "Cheney: 'Self-appointed strategists' forcing withdrawal," April 3, 2007; Brian Naylor, "Senate Approves Timetable for Iraq Pullout," NPR, March 28, 2007

[192]Christopher Matthews, "Hillary Clinton turns to Boxer for aid in Senate race," San Francisco Chronicle, February 18, 1999

[193]Congress Ratings Improve: 26% Say Good or Excellent www.rasmussenreports. com/content/pdf/3556; Sasha Johnson and Paul Steinhauser, "Poll: 75 percent disapprove of Congress' performance," CNN.com, October 26, 2007; Paul Bedard, "Don't Count Russ Feingold Out Yet," CBS News, July 20, 2007; Randi Rhodes, "The Randi Rhodes Show," Air America Radio, n.d

[194]CNN.com, "Hillary Clinton in Whitewater focus," December 1, 1995; Dan Froomkin, "Whitewater Special Report," Washington Post, 2000 www-cgi.cnn. com/US/9512/whitewater/12-01/index.html; Bob Woodward, "A Prosecutor Bound by Duty," Washington Post, June 15, 1999; Page A01

[195]Raymond Hernandez, "Oddly, Hillary and, Yes, Newt Agree to Agree," New York Times, May 13, 2005

[196]Ana Marie Cox, "How Americans View Hillary, Popular but Polarizing," Time Magazine, August 19, 2006; Anne E Kornblut and Dan Balz, "Clinton Cites Lessons of Partisanship," Washingtonpost.com, October 10, 2007; Page A01; Bill Schneider, "Clinton-Obama tussle reveals some real issues," CNN.com, February 22, 2007; CNN.com, "Democrats worry Clinton could hurt party," August 12, 2007

[197]Kathryn Joyce and Jeff Sharlet, "Hillary's Prayer: Hillary Clinton's Religion and Politics," Mother Jones, September 1, 2007; 'The Rush Limbaugh Show,' "Democrats Pander to Christian Conservative on CNN Special," June 5, 2007; Dena Potter, "Falwell Acknowledges Clinton Comment," FOXNews.com,

September 24, 2006; Peter Wallsten, "Clinton could outdraw the devil," The Seattle Times, September 24, 2006

[198]Rush Interviews Karl Rove, 'The Rush Limbaugh Show,' August 15, 2007 rushlimbaugh.com/home/.../content/Rush_Interviews_Karl_Rove.guest.html; ABC News "Rove: Clinton Negatives Will Hurt Her," August 19, 2007; Karl Rove, Interview by David Gregory, Meet the Press, NBC, August 19, 2007, www.msnbc.msn.com/id/20302351/page; Frank Newport, Jeffrey M. Jones and Joseph Carroll, "Gallup Poll Review: Karl Rove's Assertions About Hillary Clinton," Gallup, August 22, 2007 gallup.com/poll/28477/Gallup-Poll-Review-Karl-Roves-Assertions-Abou

[199]FOX News.com, "Transcript: Laura Bush on 'FOX News Sunday' with Chris Wallace," October 28, 2007; Michael McAuliff, "Laura Bush won't vote for Hillary Clinton," New York Daily News, October 29, 2007; Media Matters, "Taking lead from Drudge, conservative echo chamber," December 18, 2007; CBS News, "Fox's Hannity Stays the Course With Bush," April 16, 2006 cbsnews.com/stories/2006/04/16/ap/entertainment/mainD8H170L02.shtml;_Randi Rhodes, "The Randi Rhodes Show," Air America Radio, n.d

CHAPTER 10

[200]The Carpetbagger Report, "Jeb Bush 'not ruling in or out' 2008 race," December 12, 2006; www.thecarpetbaggerreport.com/archives/9313.htmlNewsmax.com, "Mitt Romney-Jeb Bush for GOP Ticket in 2008?"October 30, 2006; Martin Frost, "Replacing Cheney Gives White House," FoxNews.com, February 14, 2007; Webster's universal College dictionary,1997 Edition; New York, Random House, Inc

[201]US CODE: Title 18,1385. www.law.cornell.edu/uscode/18/1385.html; Insurrection Act http://leahy.Senate.gov/issues/insurrectionAct/index.html; Frank Morales, "Bush Moves Toward Martial law," Toward Freedom, October 26, 2006; Public Law 109-364, the "John Warner Defense Authorization Act of 2007(H. R.5122)" http://www.bordc.org/threats/hr5122.php

[202]"Project for the New American Century"www.newamericancentury.org; Right Web, "Profile Project for the New American Century" rightweb.irc-online.org/profile/1535.html

[203]Thom Hartmann Radio Program, "Stack December 2006," December 29, 2006 thomhartmann.org/Web/stack0612.shtml

[204]Dana Milbank, com "Bush Disavows Hussein-Sept. 11 Link." Washingtonpost.com September 18, 2003; Josh Marshall, "'First time I met you,'" TheHill.com, July, 10, 2004   James Risen and David Johnston, "Threats and Responses: The

Hearing; F.B.I. Account Outlines..."New York Times, September 27, 2002; CNN.com, "9/11 commission faults U.S. intelligence," April 15, 2004; *Walter C. Uhler, "National Issues," The Free Press,* February 3, 2006; www.freepress.org/departments/display/20/2006/1770

[205]DefendAmerica News www, US Department of Defense, May 2003 defendamerica. mil/iraq/may2003/usviews050203.html; Interview with Vice-President, 'Meet the Press,' NBC, August 26, 2002; DefenseLink News, "Transcript, Secretary Rumsfeld Remarks to the Reserve," US Department of Defense, September 19, 2002

[206]White House, "Remarks by the President at New Hampshire Welcome Pease International Tradeport Airport," November 1, 2002; White House, "President Outlines Priorities," November 7, 2002

[207]White House, "President Bush Outlines Iraqi Threat," October 7, 2002; Wolf Blitzer, "Searching for the 'smoking gun,"CNN.com, January 10, 2003; CBS News, "U.N. 'Not Satisfied' With Iraqi Answers, Inspectors Find 'No Smoking Gun," June 9, 2003; Wendy S. Ross and Phillip Kurata, "White House, State Department Say Iraq Not Disarming as Required...," January 9, 2003

[208]BBC News, "Rumsfeld Foresees Swift Iraq War," February 7, 2003 White House, "President's Radio Address," February 8, 2003; Susan Page, "Confronting Iraq," USATODAY,April 1, 2003; www.democraticunderground.com/articles/05/05/11_wrong.htm

[209]DoD News Briefing, "Secretary Rumsfeld and Gen. Myers, US Department of Defense," February 12, 2003; http://www.defenselink.mil/transcripts/transcript.aspx?transcriptid=2636;   The Dubya Report, "Cakewalk," April 13, 2003 www.thedubyareport.com/iraq1.html

[210]Constitution for the United States of America www.constitution.org/constit_.htm; Article 1 - The Legislative Branch Section 8 - Powers of Congress

[211]Bill Frist, Senate Speech, March 7, 2003; White House, "Press Conference by the President," February 14, 2007; National Review Online, "Tom DeLay on Iraq," August 22, 2002, www.nationalreview.com/document/document082202.asp

[212]Bill Frist, "When War Is the Best Medicine," Washingtonpost.com March 16, 2003; Page B07; White House, "President Says Saddam Hussein Must Leave Iraq Within 48 Hours," March 17, 2003; US Department of Defense, "Veterans of Foreign Wars," March 11, 2003; Jake Tapper, "Iraq War's Architect Apologizes in Salary Scandal," ABC News, April 13, 2007

[213]BBC News, "Blair and Iraq weapons," September 29, 2004; MSNBC.com "Transcript for March 16, 2003 – 'Meet the Press,'; Nile Gardiner, "British and

European Responses to the Proposed U.S. Military Action Against Iraq," The Heritage foundation, April 1, 2002; BBC News, "Cheney warned over Iraq attack," March 12, 2002; "House of Commons (British government)" Britannica Online Encyclopedia www.britannica.com/EBchecked/topic/128885/House-of-Commons

[214]10 Downing Street, "Prime Minister Tony Blair Press Conference," March 25, 2003; Donald Runsfeld, Interview by George Stephanopoulos, This Week with George Stephanopoulos, ABC News, March 30, 2003; Linda Diebel, "Weight of the War Takes Toll on Bush," Common Dreams.org, March 28, 2003

[215]White House, "President Says Saddam Hussein Must Leave Iraq Within 48 Hours," March 17, 2003; Bill Frist, A Speech to American Israel Political Action Committee, March 31, 2003

[216]White House, "President's Message to the Iraqi People," April 10, 2003; White House, "An interview of President Bush by Tom Brokaw of NBC News aboard Air Force One," April 24, 2003; Vice President interview on 'Meet the Press,' NBC News, September 14, 2003

[217]White House, "President Bush Announces Combat Operations in Iraq Have Ended," May 1, 2003 www.state.gov/p/nea/rls/rm/20203.htm; White House, "President Bush, P.M. Howard Discuss Operation Iraqi Freedom, May 3, 2003

[218]FOX News, "Transcript: Donald Rumsfeld on Fox News Sunday with Tony Snow," May 04, 2003; U.S. Department of State, "Remarks After Interview With NBC's Meet the Press," May 4, 2003 www.state.gov/secretary/former/powell/remarks/2003/20166.htm; U.S. Department of Defense, "News Transcript: Presenter: Deputy Secretary of Defense Paul Wolfowitz, May 28, 2003 www.defenselink.mil/transcripts/transcript.aspx?transcriptid=2676

[219]USATODAY.com, "Saddam scientists' capabilities said to justify invasion," April 9, 2003; Vernon Loeb, "Rumsfeld Backs U.N. Resolution on Iraq,"Washingtonpost.com, September 11, 2003; Page A17

[220]FOXNews.com, "Bush WMD Joke Draws Criticism- You Decide 2004," March 26, 2004

[221]Walter Pincus and Dana Milbank, "Al Qaeda-Hussein Link Is Dismissed," Washingtonpost.com, June 17, 2004; CNN.com, "9/11 panel: Information on Iraq, al Qaeda welcome," June 20, 2004; Wayne Washington, "Bush puts distance on a Hussein link to 9/11," The Boston Globe, September 18, 2003; David E. Sanger, "Bush Reports No Evidence of Hussein Tie to 9/11," New York Times, September 18, 2003; Robert Burns, "Rumsfeld sees no link between 9/11 and

Iraq," Salon.com, September 16, 2003; White House, "Press Conference by the President," August 21, 2006

[222]Carol Lin, CNN Sunday Night, CNN.com, October 24, 2004 transcripts.cnn.com/TRANSCRIPTS/0410/24/snn.01.html

[223]DefenseLink News Transcript, "Remarks by Secretary of Defense Donald Rumsfeld to the Heritage Foundation," U.S. Department of Defense, May 17, 2004; Colin Powell, Interview on Meet the Press, NBC News, May 16, 2004

[224]CNN.com, "Bush insists Iraq, al Qaeda had 'relationship," June 17, 2004; BBC News, "WMD may never be found – Blair," July 6 2004; White House, "Press Conference by the President," August 21, 2006 www.whitehouse.gov/news/relea ses/2006/08/20060821.html; FoxNews.com, "CIA Director Tenet Resigns," June 03, 2004

[225]Martin Fletcher, "Hezbollah jumping on Hamas wagon? - Mideast/N. Africa,"Msnbc.com, July 12, 2006

[226]William Saletan "Should We Invade Syria?" Slate Magazine, August 23, 2002; Central Intelligence Agency (CIA) www.cia.gov; US State Department, "Opening Remarks by Secretary of State-Designate Dr. Condoleezza Rice," January 18, 2005, www.state.gov/secretary/rm/2005/40991.htm; IRIB News, "Ahmadinejad: Israel must be wiped off the map," October 26, 2005; CNN.com, "Iranian leader: Wipe out Israel," October 27, 2005 edition.cnn.com/2005/WORLD/meast/10/26/ ahmadinejad/index.html; US State Department, "U.S.-Japan Security Alliance," October 29, 2005; Human Rights, www.state.gov/g/drl/rls/hrrpt

[227]White House, "President's Address to the Nation," September 11, 2006 www. whitehouse.gov/news/releases/2006/09/20060911-3.html

[228]US State Department, "Briefing by Secretary of State Condoleezza Rice," January 12, 2006 www.state.gov/secretary/rm/2006/59083.htm; Michael Hirsh, "Diplo-Dancing With Iran," Newsweek.com, June 12, 2006; Maggie Farley, "Iran's President Refuses to Forgo Atomic Activities," Los Angeles Times, September 18, 2005; Treaty on the Non-proliferation of Nuclear Weapons (NPT) www.un.org/ Depts/dda/WMD/treaty; Maggie Farley, "U.N. Warns Iran to End Nuclear Work," Los Angeles Times, March 30, 2006; United States Department of State, "P5 + 1 Statement: Negotiations With Iran," July 12, 2006

[229]Seymour M. Hersh, "Annals of National Security: The Iran Plans," The New Yorker, April 17 2006

[230]Joint Chiefs of Staff "JCS Link"www.jcs.mil; CNN.com, "Pace leaving as Joint Chiefs chairman," June 8, 2007; Army.Mil, "General George Casey Discusses New

Army Chief of Staff Role," April 10, 2007 army.mil/-newsreleases/2007/04/10/26 10-general-george-casey-discusses-new-army

231Frank Morales, "Bush Moves Toward Martial law," Toward Freedom, October 26, 2006; www.leahy.senate.gov/arch2007.html

232John Negroponte, Interview by Andrea Mitchell, Nightly News with Brian Williams, NBC, April 19 2006; Reuters, "Bush nominates Negroponte, McConnell," January 5, 2007; Jim Lobe and Michael Flynn, "The Rise and Decline of the Neoconservatives," Right Web, November 17, 2006 rightweb.irc-online. org/rw/3713.html; Adam Zagorin and Elaine Shannon, "Behind Negroponte's Move," TIME.com

233Sheryl Gay Stolberg and Kate Zernike, "Bush Backs Away From 2 Key Ideas of Panel on Iraq," New York Times, December 8, 2006; John Hendren, "Tony Blair on Iraq: 'We Need to Act Urgently," ABC News, December 7, 2006

234Tim Shipman, "Neocons seek to justify action against Teheran," Telegraph, January 10, 2007

235Gary Leupp, "Frustrated with Bush, the Veep Urges Israel to Attack Iran," Counterpunch, May 26/27, 2007; Seymour M. Hersh, "Annals of National Security: Shifting Targets," The New Yorker, October 8, 2007; CBS News, "Reid: Cheney Is Bush's "Attack Dog", Senate Democrat Reacts After VP…"April 27, 2004

236Ewen MacAskill and Julian Borger, "Cheney pushes Bush to act on Iran," Guardian.co.uk, July 16, 2007; http://www.guardian.co.uk/international/ story/0,,2127081,00.html Philip Sherwell and Tim Shipman, "Bush Setting America up for War with Iran," Telegraph.co.uk, September 16, 2007

237Ewen MacAskill and Julian Borger, "Cheney pushes Bush to act on Iran," Guardian. co.uk, July 16, 2007; Philip Sherwell and Tim Shipman, "Bush Setting America up for War with Iran," Telegraph.co.uk, September 16, 2007

238Lt Col. Rick Francona, "Middle East perspectives: enemy of my enemy is my friend," MSNBC.com, August 16 2007; Lolita C. Baldor, "Gates: Diplomacy with Iran Progressing,"FOXNews.com, April 18, 2007 www.foxnews.com/wires/ 2007Apr18/0,4670,GatesIraq,00.html

239Ewen MacAskill and Julian Borger, "Cheney pushes Bush to act on Iran," Guardian. co.uk, July 16, 2007; Philip Sherwell and Tim Shipman, "Bush Setting America up for War with Iran," Telegraph.co.uk, September 16, 2007

[240]White House, "President Bush and German Chancellor Merkel Participate in Press availability," July 13, 2006; Jake Tapper, "After Sunglasses Gaffe," ABC News, June 14, 2006

[241]White House, "President Bush Nominates Rob Portman as OMB Director and Susan Schwab for USTR," April 18, 2006; Patrick Leahy United States Senator, "Press Archives-2007," www.leahy.senate.gov/arch2007.html; Thom Hartmann, The Thom Hartmann Show, Air America Radio, n.d.; Zogby international, "Zogby Poll: 52 % Support U.S. Military Strike Against Iran," October 29, 2007 http://www.zogby.com/news/ReadNews.dbm?ID=1379

[242]Ewen MacAskill and Julian Borger, "Cheney pushes Bush to act on Iran," Guardian. co.uk, July 16, 2007; Philip Sherwell and Tim Shipman, "Bush Setting America up for War with Iran," Telegraph.co.uk, September 16, 2007 White House, "Press Conference by the President," September 20, 2007

[243]FOXNews.com, "Ahmadinejad Blasts Israel, Denies Existence of Iranian ...," September 24, 2007; Hamish McDonald, "Cheney's tough talking derails negotiations with North Korea," smh.com.au, December 22, 2003; Fred Kaplan, "The new North Korea deal is surprisingly Clintonian", slate.com, February 13, 2007 ...

[244]**Colin L. Powell,** "Interview by Ted Koppel of ABC News," U.S. Department of State, April 24, 2004 www.state.gov/secretary/former/powell/remarks/31769.htm; White House, "Remarks by the Vice President at Bush-Cheney '04 Luncheon," September 22, 2003; Bone thugs n Harmony, Art of War, Ruthless Record "Let the Law End," 1997

[245]FOXNews.com, "Sen. Feingold Proposes Censuring Bush," July 22, 2007; Karl Rove," Interview by Rush Limbaugh," The Rush Limbaugh Show, WABC, August 15, 2007 http://www.rushlimbaugh.com/home/daily/site_081507/content/01125106.guest.html

CHAPTER 11

[246]Fox News.com, "Democrat Presidential Hopeful Sen. Dodd," "The O'Reilly Factor" August 03, 2007

[247]FOXNews.com, "Bill O'Reilly, Hurt Feelings in San Francisco," November 15, 2005

[248]Media Matters, "Olbermann on O'Reilly's "Fox security" threat ..."March 6, 2006; Media Matters, "Letter to Bill O'Reilly from David Brock," June 1, 2004 mediamatters.org/items/200406010003; Noel Sheppard, "Janeane Garofalo: 'Bush is a War Criminal...'"NewsBusters, September 22, 2007

[249]"Bill O'Reilly Biography," Biography.com www.biography.com/search/article.do?id=9542547; FOXNews.com, "Bill O'Reilly's Bio," April 29, 2004 www.foxnews.com/story/0,2933,155,00.html

[250]Bill O'Reilly, "The Sign Of The Cross," CNS News Commentary.com, November 16, 2001; Free Republic, "Red Cross surrenders: Bill O'Reilly declares victory in battle with…," November 16, 2001

[251]Peter Hart, "Hart: Fox's O'Reilly -- a Bush apologist," March 15, 2004 www.cjonline.com/stories/031504/opi_hart.shtml; March 18, 2003 edition of 'The O'Reilly Factor; June 2003 edition of 'The O'Reilly Factor'

[252]Bill O'Reilly, Interview on Fresh Air from WHYY, NPR, October 8, 2003

[253]Bill O'Reilly, "A Message for the Democratic Party," FOXNews.com, June 16, 2006

[254]March 2, 2006 broadcast of 'The Radio Factor,' Westwood One; Media Matters, "O'Reilly threatened radio show caller with…, March 3, 2006

[255]The Bill O'Reilly Factor,' "Bill Moyers, PBS and telling the truth," FoxNews.com, April 25, 2007; Bill O'Reilly, "Mano a Mano: Bill vs. George Clooney,"FOXNews.com, November 7, 2001

[256]December 9, 2004 broadcast of 'The Radio Factor,' Westwood One; Media Matters, "Bill O'Reilly attacked Media Matters." December 9, 2004; John Amato, "O'Reilly Sends FOX Security -- Threatens Police Action…" The Huffington Post, March 4, 2006; www.amazon.com/Oh-Really-Factor-Unspinning-Channels/dp/158322601X; Media Matters for America www.mediamatters.org

[257]The Post Chronicle, "David Letterman vs. Bill O'Reilly," January 6, 2006; Bill O'Reilly on the January 3 edition of CBS' Late Show with David Letterman; June 20, 2005 broadcast of 'The Radio Factor,' Westwood One; Media Matter, "Fbi should arrest the "clown" at air America radio for being traitors," June 22, 2005; The Thom Hartman Show, Air America Radio, n.d.; Fox News.com, "The 'Passion of the Christ," February 18, 2004; "The Passion of the Christ (film by Gibson)," Britannica Online … original.britannica.com/eb/topic-1005915/The-Passion-of-the-Christ

[258]Bill O'Reilly, "Stupidity & Selfishness," 'The O'Reilly Factor,'FOXNews.com, December 11, 2001; BBC News, "UN chief warns against Iraq attack," December 10, 2001; Bill O'Reilly, "Bill O'Reilly rips Kofi Annan," Fox News, December11, 2001 http://www.usasurviva/org/oreilly.html; CNN.com, "U.N., Kofi Annan Receive Peace Prize," October 12, 2001

[259] The O'Reilly Factor, "Corruption at the United Nations," FOXNews.com, May 22, 2003; "UN Office of the Iraq Program - Oil-for-Food" www.un.org/Depts/oip

[260] Bill O'Reilly, "The O'Reilly Factor Flash," BillOReilly.com, December 3, 2004 www.billoreilly.com/show?action=viewTVShow&showID=38; BBC News, "Rwanda: How the genocide happened," April 1, 2004

[261] CNN.com, "Bush nominates Bolton as U.N. ambassador," March 7, 2005; "Bolton speech at the Federalist Society forum" February 3, 1994; John Bolton, Interview by Bill O'Reilly, 'The O'Reilly Factor,' FOXNews.com, July 20, 2006; 'The O'Reilly Factor,' "Can the U.N. Save the Day in the Middle East,?" FOXNews.com, July 20, 2006; Charles Moore, "This is why there is slaughter in Darfur," Telegraph, September 26, 2006

[262] Newsmax.com, "Bill O'Reilly Says He'd Consider Presidential Run," November 13, 2003; "Bill O'Reilly For President -Democrats, Republicans, biased," May 28, 2007 www.city-data.com/forum/2008-presidential-election/88798-bill-oreilly-president.html; www.biography.com/search/article.do?id=9542547; www.foxnews.com/story/0,2933,155,00.html

CHAPTER 12

[263] Hannity and Colmes, "He's Ready! Rudy Giuliani Talks with Sean Hannity," FOXNews.com, February 06, 2007; Hannity and Colmes, "Mitt Romney Talks With Sean Hannity,"FOXNews.com, April 05, 2007; "The Sean Hannity Show Live Commentary," WABC, July-December 2007

[264] President Bush, Interview by Sean Hannity, Hannity and Colmes, FOXNews.com, November 01, 2006 www.foxnews.com/story/0,2933,226645,00.html; "The Sean Hannity Show Live Commentary," WABC, July-December 2007

[265] CBS News, "Giuliani Knocks Clinton's Petraeus Comment...," September 12, 2007; Sam Youngman, "Giuliani demands MoveOn's New York Times ad rate," The Hill.com, September 13, 2007; MoveOn.org: Democracy in Action www.moveon.org; Jake Tapper, "Ad Against Petraeus Strikes a Nerve," ABC News, September 10, 2007; Pete Hegseth, "MoveOn.org Calls Petraeus a Traitor," Weekly Standard, September 9, 2007; Michael Abramowitz and Jonathan Weisman, "Bush to Endorse Petraeus Plan," Washingtonpost.com, September 12, 2007; Page A01; "The Sean Hannity Show Live Commentary," WABC, July-December 2007

[266] Carl Hulse, "Disappointed Democrats Map Withdrawal Strategy," New York Times, September 13, 2007; HeraldTribune.com, "New York Times International Feed," September 13, 2007; White House, "President's Address to the Nation,"

January 10, 2007 www.whitehouse.gov/news/releases/2007/01/20070110-7.html;David Espo, "Senate Dems Fail to Cut Off War Funds," FOXNews. com, May 16, 2007; Shailagh Murray, "Reid Backs Iraq War-Funds Cutoff," Washingtonpost.com, April 3, 2007; A04; David M. Herszenhorn and Carl Hulse, "Bid to Cut Off Iraq War Funding Fails," New York Times, September 20, 2007; John Bresnahan, "Feingold Pushes Plan to Cut Off War Funds," Politico. com, February 1, 2007;Carl Hulse, "Democrats set to challenge Bush Iraq plan," New York Times, September 12, 2007

267 "Sean Hannity" www.hannity.com/index/bio; NewsMax.com, "NewsMax's Top 25 Radio Talk Show Hosts: 5. Sean Hannity," TALKERS magazine – Home www. talkers.com/main; FOXNews.com "Sean Hannity – Bio," May 17, 2007 www. foxnews.com/story/0,2933,1242,00.html

268 Laura Blumenfeld, "Soros's Deep Pockets vs. Bush," Washingtonpost.com, November 11, 2003; Page A03; FOXNews.com, "Soros Targets Bush - The Big Story w/ Gibson and Nauert," November 14, 2003; World Net Daily, "Soros blames U.S., Israel for anti-Semitism," November 11, 2003; cnsnews.com/ ViewPolitics.asp?Page=\Politics\archive\200312\POL20031; Judicial Watch .org, "Judicial Watch Probes Sale of Sleepovers in Lincoln Bedroom and Camp David," September 18, 2000; Jim Kuhnhenn, "Fundraiser's Legal Woes Dog Clinton Camp{Hillary's Hsu }," FreeRepublic.com, September 14, 2007; "The Sean Hannity Show Live Commentary," WABC, July-December 2007

269 New York Post, "The model of a major modern Democrat," November 2, 2006; FOXNews.com, "Obama: U.S. Troops in Afghanistan Must Do More Than Kill...," August 14, 2007; Jamie McIntyre, "Lawmaker says Marines killed Iraqis 'in cold blood," CNN.com, May 19, 2006; "The Sean Hannity Show Live Commentary," WABC, July-December 2007

270Shailagh Murray and Dan Balz, "Democratic Leadership Welcomes Lamont," Washingtonpost.com, August 10, 2006; Page A01; "The Sean Hannity Show Live Commentary," WABC, July-December 2007

271 Jeff Cohen, "Media and the Election,"Commindreams.org, November 22, 2004; "The Sean Hannity Show Live Commentary," WABC, July-December 2007; www.foxnews.com/story/0,2933,1242,00.html; www.hannity.com/index/bio

272 reddit.com/info/x50u/related CNN.com, "Iran's president says he won't insist on ground zero visit," September 20, 2007; Sarah Gerland, "New York to Ahmadinejad: 'No'," The New York Sun, - September 20, 2007

273Washington Times, "Ill will for Ahmadinejad," September 25, 2007; Washingtonpost.com, "President Ahmadinejad Delivers Remarks at Columbia University," September 24, 2007; Nahai Toosi, "Ahmadinejad questions 9/11,

Holocaust," USATODAY.com, September 25, 2007; "The Sean Hannity Show Live Commentary," WABC, July-December 2007

274 Cyberalerts, "CBS's Pelley: Ahmadinejad 'Friendly,' 'Incorruptible,' 'Modest'", September 25, 2007 www.mrc.org/cyberalerts/2007/cyb20070925.asp; Brad Wilmouth, "Colmes: Right Shouldn't Complain About 'Conservative' Ahmadinejad's Speech," NewsBuster, September 25, 2007; FOXNews.com "Ahmadinejad Blasts Israel, Denies Existence of Iranian...," September 24, 2007; BBC News "Iran president in NY campus row, September 25, 2007; Online NewsHour, "Ahmadinejad Continues U.S. Tour," PBS, September 25, 2007; New York Daily News, "Iran's president: I don't deny Holocaust," September 24, 2007; ABC News, "Ahmadinejad Goes Ivy, Will Speak at Columbia Despite Criticism," September 21, 2007; "The Sean Hannity Show Live Commentary," WABC, July-December 2007

275 Steve Holland "Gingrich: Republicans need "clean break" from Bush," Reuters, September 14, 2007; "The Sean Hannity Show Live Commentary," WABC, July-December 2007

276 David E. Sanger and Eric Lipton, "Bush Threatens to Veto Any Bill to Stop Port Takeover," New York Times, February 21, 2006; FOXNews.com, "Bush: Don't Worry," February 23, 2007; Gerry J. Gilmore, "England Discusses Port Security Issue on..." DefenseLink News, February 23, 2006

277 Habitat for Humanity Int'l www.habitat.org; "2007 Hannity Freedom Concert" www.hannityfreedomconcert.com; "The Sean Hannity Show Live Commentary," WABC, July-December 2007; www.foxnews.com/story/0,2933,1242,00.html; www.hannity.com/index/bio

278 Shmuley Boteach, "Why Jimmy Carter is not an anti-Semite," The Jerusalem Post, December 26, 2006; BBC News, "BBC on this day 4 1980: Reagan beats Carter in landslide,"; Diane Alden, "Jimmy Carter and the 40 Ayatollahs," Newsmax. com, October 30, 2002; "The Sean Hannity Show Live Commentary," WABC, July-December 2007

279 Hannity and Colmes, "What Was John Edwards Really Saying About Black Men.." FOXNews.com, October 01, 2007; "The Sean Hannity Show Live Commentary," WABC, July-December 2007

280 Media Matters – "Randi Rhodes tells Larry King to check Media..."August 10, 2006

281"The Sean Hannity Show Live Commentary," WABC, July-December 2007

282 Martina McBride, "Independence Day," Life # 9, RCA Records, 1994.

CHAPTER 13

[283] Air America Radio, airamerica.com; MSNBC.com, "Air America Radio files Chapter 11 - U.S. business," October 13, 2006

[284]Rick Klein and Susan Milligan, "Bush seems to shift on his grounds for dismissal," The Boston Globe, July 19, 2005; Dan Eggen, "Justice Department races to replace interim US attorneys," The Boston Globe, June 18, 2007; Warwick Sabin, "Senators question U.S. attorney appointment," Arkansas Times, December 28, 2006; Paul Kiel, "Specter: "I Do Not Slip Things In," TPM, February 6, 2007 tpmmuckraker.talkingpointsmemo.com/archives/002487.php

[285]**Jesse J. Holland, "**Ex-Bush Aide Says Again She Won't Appear," ABC News, July 17, 2007; Carl Tobias, "Heading off the constitutional showdown," TheHill.com, July 31, 2007; Patrick O'Connor, "Conyers Rejects Immunity Argument from Mier Lawyer," CBS News, July 17, 2007; Newsmax.com, *Harriet Miers* Defies *Subpoena*, Skips Hearing," July 12, 2007

[286] Crs report for Congress, Congress's Contempt Power, Scotusblog.com www.scotusblog.com/movabletype/archives/crs.contempt.report.pdf; MSNBC.com, "Bush orders Miers to defy House subpoena, July 12, 2007; cbs11tv.com, "White House Stonewalls Firings Probe," July 11, 2007; Laurie Kellman, "Bush Orders Miers Not to Testify," ABC News, July 12, 2007; The Randi Rhodes Show, Air America Radio, n.d; bc.edu/schools/law/lawreviews/bclawreview/.../49_3/04_geldert_web.pdfwww.merriam-webster.com/dictionary/executive+privilege; Wyatt Buchanan, "Pelosi promises congressional contempt charge for Harriet Miers, San Francisco Chronicle, July 22, 2007

[287] Will Dunham, "Bush pick for key Justice Department job withdraws," Boston.com, June 22, 2007; USATODAY.com, "Ex-Bush aide declines to testify on attorney firings," July 11, 2007

[288]Greg Palast, "U.S. Attorney resigns following Conyers' request for BBC documents," Catch Match, June 1, 2007 www.gnn.tv/articles/3124/Cage_Match; Greg Palast, "Election Issues," Free Press, June 2, 2007 www.freepress.org/departments/display/19/2007/2619; gregpalast.com/rove-pick-for-us-attorney-resigns-following-conyers%; CNN.com, "Deputy AG 'not fully candid,' ex-Justice aide testifies," May 28, 2007; The Randi Rhodes Show, Air America Radio, n.d; Warwick Sabin, "Senators question U.S. attorney appointment," Arkansas Times, December 28, 2006

[289] *Dan Eggen,* "Bush Authorized Domestic Spying," Washingtonpost.com, December 16, 2005; Page A01; Athan G. Theoharis, "The FISA File," The Nation, February 16, 2006 Ari Shapiro, "Ex-Justice Official: Spy Plan Sparked Threats to Quit," NPR, May 16, 2007

[290] Online NewsHour, "Democrats Seek Perjury Probe," PBS, July 27, 2007; Laurie Kellman and Lara J. Jordan, "FBI Chief Contradicts Gonzales Testimony," ABC News, July 27, 2007; USATODAY.com, "Democrats seek independent probe of Gonzales," July 26, 2007; Washingtonpost.com, "U.S. Senate Judiciary Committee Holds a Hearing on Wartime Executive Power and the NSA's Surveillance Authority," February 6, 2006; CNN.com, "White House insiders: Gonzales hurt himself before panel," April 23, 2007; Washingtonpost.com, "Gonzales Testifies Before House Judiciary Committee," May 10, 2007; USATODAY.com, "Senate panel questions Gonzales' credibility," July 24, 2007

[291] U.S. Senate, "Committee Hearing Sen. Patrick J. Leahy…" May 15, 2007; CNN.com, "Transcript-Gonzales Testimony Contradictory; White House Retorts Dems Playing Politics," Lou Dobbs this week," July 29, 2007; David Johnston and Scott Shane, "F.B.I. Chief Gives Account at Odds With Gonzales's," New York Time, July 27, 2007; CNN.com, "FBI director appears to contradict Gonzales' testimony," July 27, 2007; The Randi Rhodes Show, Air America Radio, n.d

[292] CNN.com, "Gonzales explains bedside meeting with ailing Ashcroft, July 24, 2007; Washingtonpost.com, "U.S. Senate Judiciary Commmittee Hearing on Oversight of the Department," July 24, 2007

[293] Iconoclast, "Seattle Post-Intelligencer: Sound Off," July 24, 2007; seattlepi.nwsource.com/soundoff/comment.asp?articleID=324923; U.S Senate, "Alberto Gonzalez Testify before the Senate Judiciary Committee," July 24, 2007; Michael Isikoff, "Gonzales Hangs On … But for How Long?" Newsweek, July 7, 2007; Barton Gellman, "Daschle: Congress Denied Bush War Powers in U.S." Washingtonpost.com, December 23, 2005; Page A04; Dan Eggen and Paul Kane, "Gonzales Hospital Episode Detailed," Washingtonpost.com, May 16, 2007; Page A01; Ari Shapiro, "Former Justice Deputy Describes Political Clash," NPR, May 15 2007; Laurie Kellman, "Cheney Blocked Official's Promotion," Commondreams.org, June 7, 2007; USATODAY.com, "Senate panel questions Gonzales' credibility," July 25, 2007; Context of 'March 10, 2004: Cheney Briefs Gang of Eight' Congressional; American Civil Liberties Union, "ACLU Letter to the Senate…"March 16, 2006 www.aclu.org/safefree/general/24623leg20060316.html; The Crypt's Blog, "Rockefeller says March 2004 'Gang of Eight' meeting was not as Gonzales described," Politico.com, July 24, 2007; CNN.com, "Gonzales explains bedside meeting with ailing Ashcroft, July 24, 2007

[294] White House, "President Bush: Information Sharing, Patriot Act Vital to Homeland Security," April 20, 2004; White House, "Press Conference of the President," January 26, 2006; The Randi Rhodes Show, Air America Radio, n.d

[295] Dana Milbank, "Maybe Gonzales Won't Recall His Painful Day on the Hill," Washingtonpost.com, April 20, 2007; Page A02; Online NewsHour, "Gonzales Appears Before Committee," PBS, April 19, 2007; New York Times, "Mr.

Gonzales's Never-Ending Story," July 29, 2007; The Crypt's Blog, "Rockefeller says March 2004 'Gang of Eight' meeting was not as Gonzales described," Politico.com, July 24, 2007

[296]MSNBC.com, "Gonzales denies pressuring Ashcroft on spying," July 24, 2007; Jay Newton-Small, "Gonzales Digs a Deeper Hole," TIME, July 24, 2007; Glenn Kessler, "No Coverup in Tillman Case, Rumsfeld Tells House Panel," Washingtonpost.com, August 2, 2007; Page A16; The Randi Rhodes Show, Air America Radio, n.d

[297]CNN.com, "FBI director appears to contradict Gonzales' testimony," July 27, 2007; Editorial, "Overprivileged Executive," - New York Times, July 11, 2007; Jake Tapper and Cindy Smith, "Hillary Clinton calls for Gonzales' Resignation," ABC News, March 13, 2007

[298]Brit Hume, on with E.D. Hill on Fox News Live, FOXNews.com, August 27, 2007; Scott Horton, "Graceful Exits... and the Other Kind," Harper's Magazine, August 27, 2007

[299]*Dan Eggen and Mike Allen,* "Ashcroft, Evans To Leave Cabinet," Washingtonpost.com, November 10, 2004; Page A01; CNN.com, "Bush attorney general pick is Alberto Gonzales," November 11, 2004; *Dan Eggen,* "Justice Dept.'s No. 2 to Resign," Washingtonpost.com, May 15, 2007; Page A01; *Dan Eggen,* "Third-in-Command at Justice Dept. Resigns," Washingtonpost.com, June 23, 2007; Page A04; The Randi Rhodes Show, Air America Radio, n.d

[300] Information Security Oversight Office (ISOO) www.archives.gov/isoo/index.html; Josh Gerstein, "Cheney Refused an Inspection for Security," The New Sun, June 22, 2007; NewsHour "Supreme Court to Hear Cheney's Energy Task Force Appeal," PBS, December 15, 2003; CNN.com, "Andersen admits destroying Enron docs," January 10, 2002; White House, "Press Briefing by Ari Fleischer," January 28, 2002; U.S. Government Accountability Office (U.S. GAO) www.gao.gov

[301]The Tampa Tribune, "Cheney Is His Own Dark Planet," June 27, 2007; Http://freedemocracy.blogspot.com/2007/06/maureen-dowd-vice-pre

[302]Ann Coulter, "If at first you don't succeed, lie, lie again," Townhall.com August 15, 2007; The Randi Rhodes Show, Air America Radio, n.d

[303]Al Franken's blog- Air America Radio www.airamerica.com/blog/342363; www.amazon.com/Lies-Lying-Liars-Tell-Them/dp/0525947647; Phil Hirschkorn, "Fox News loses attempt to block satirist's book,"CNN.com, August 22, 2003

[304]Russell Shorto, "Al Franken, Seriously," New York Times, March 21, 2004; "Al Franken: Biography," Answers.com www.answers.com/topic/al-franken

[305]Toby Harnden, "Bin Laden is wanted: dead or alive, says Bush," Telegraph.co.uk, September 18, 200; CNN.com, "Bush: bin Laden 'prime suspect,'" September 17, 2001; Jim Burns, "Cheney Wants bin-Laden's Head On Platter," CNSNews. com, September 16, 2001; ABC News, "Bush: Bin Laden Wanted Dead or Alive," September 17, 2001; White House, "Guard and Reserves- Define Spirit of America," September 17, 2001; Flicker.com. September 16, 2001 www.flickr. com/photos/firstlight/504477406; White House, "President Bush Holds Press Conference," March 13, 2002

[306]BBC News, "Comedian Franken makes Senate bid," February 15, 2007

[307]Thom Hartmann Radio Program, "Stack September 2007," September 27, 2007 thomhartmann.org/Web/stack0709.shtml; "The Thom Hartmann Program," Air America Radio http://airamerica.com/thomhartmanpage; "The Thom Hartman Show Live Commentary," Air America Radio, July-December 2007

[308]Thom Hartmann, "Talking Back To Talk Radio - Fairness, Democracy, and Profits," Commondreams.org, December 3, 2002; "The Thom Hartman Show Live Commentary," Air America Radio, July-December 2007

[309]Ben Faraji, "Deconstruction of the myth," Real Bay News, July 10, 2006; BBC News, "Halliburton bankrupts own units," December 17, 2003; "The Thom Hartman Show Live Commentary," Air America Radio, July-December 2007

[310]ThomHartmann.com, "Transcript: Last Election?" September 01, 2006 thomhartmann.com/index.php?...&task=view&id=414&Itemid=119; PBS, "American Experience-The Presidents- Richard M. Nixon," May 20, 1977; Constitution for the United States of America www.constitution.org/constit .htm; "The Thom Hartman Show Live Commentary," Air America Radio, July-December 2007

[311]Haider Rizvi "Rumsfeld Charged with Torture in French Court," CommonDreams. org, October 29, 2007; "The Thom Hartman Show Live Commentary," Air America Radio, July-December 2007

[312]John T. Woolley and Gerhard Peters, "Ronald Reagan: The President's News Conference," The American Presidency Project, August 12th, 1986 www. presidency.ucsb.edu/ws/print.php?pid=37733 CNN.com, "Maybe deficits do matter," February 15, 2006; Thomas M. Humbert, "Breach of Faith: The Tax Package," The Heritage Foundation, August 7, 1982; Edwin Meese III, "An Amnesty by Any Other Name," New York Times, May 24, 2006; Paul Krugman, "The Great Taxer," New York Times, June 8, 2004

[313]The Founding Fathers info home page. www.foundingfathers.info; www.amazon.com/What-Would-Jefferson-Thom-Hartmann/dp/1400052084; Freelibrary.com, "The revolutionary conservatism of Jefferson's small republics" www.thefreelibrary.com/The+revolutionary+conservatism+of+Jefferson's+small+republics-a0146; "The Thom Hartman Show Live Commentary," Air America Radio, July-December 2007

[314]PBS, "American Experience- The Presidents- John F. Kennedy," January 20, 1961 www.pbs.org/wgbh/amex/presidents/35_kennedy/psources/ra_inaug.html "Peace Corps" www.peacecorps.gov; PBS, "American Experience- The Presidents - Franklin D. Roosevelt, March 4, 1933 pbs.org/wgbh/.../presidents/32_f_roosevelt/psources/ps_inaugural1.html

[315]White House, "President's Remarks at Ask President Bush Event," July 9, 2004 www.whitehouse.gov/news/releases/2004/07/20040709-5.html; Jean-Marie Colombani, "War on Terrorism, September 11 Terrorist Attacks," *Le Monde,* September 12, 2001; From the November 2001 issue of *World Press Review* (VOL. 48, No. 11) "We Are All Americans" www.worldpress.org/specials/wtc/front.htm; "The Thom Hartman Show Live Commentary," Air America Radio, July-December 2007 www.thomhartmann.com/index.php?option=com_content&task=view&id=539&Itemid=113; Benjamin Wallace-Wells, "Mourning Has Broken,"Washington Monthly, October 2003; "The Great Depression" www.nps.gov/archive/elro/glossary/great-depression.htm

[316]Today on the Show, ThomHartmann.com, December 27 2007 thomhartmann.com/index.php?...&task=view&id=356&Itemid=116

[317]USATODAY.com, "Bush secures College majority,"December 19, 2000;Charles Babington, "Bush Claims Presidency as Gore Concedes," Washingtonpost.com, December 13, 2000; BBC News, "Americas- Gore speech in full," December 14, 2000; White House, "Remarks of Vice President Cheney and Senator Edwards in Vice Presidential Debate Veale Center," October 6, 2004; Adam Nagourney, "Campaign 2004," The New York Times, October 6, 2004; Susan Page, "Popular vote vs. the electoral vote," USA TODAY, November 6, 2000; CNN.com, "Bush carries Electoral College after delay," January 6, 2005; White House, "Remarks of Vice President Cheney and Senator Edwards in Vice…"October 6, 2004; Amy Lorentzen, "Cheney: Kerry Victory Will Lead to Another Terrorist Attack on US,"CommonDreams.org, *September 7, 2004;* "The Thom Hartman Show Live Commentary," Air America Radio, July-December 2007

[318]Thom Hartman, How to take back a stolen election, CommonDreams.org, November 29, 2004 thomhartmann.com/index.php?...&task=view&id=130&Itemid=123; Timothy Noah, "Faithless Elector Watch: Ask Doctor Faithless!"Slate.com, December 7, 2000; Common Ground Common Sense, "Tom Delay -

TRAITOR to the United States," April 17, 2006 commongroundcommonsense. org/forums/lofiversion/index.php/t54037.html CommonDreams.org, "Roberts Gave GOP Advice in 2000 Recount," July 21, 2005; "The Thom Hartman Show Live Commentary," Air America Radio, July-December 2007

[319]"U.S. Electoral College, Official - About the Electoral College" www.archives.gov/ federal-register/**electoral-college**/about.html

[320]Charles Babington, "Democrats Won't Try To Impeach President," Washingtonpost. com, May 12, 2006; Page A06; "The Thom Hartman Show Live Commentary," Air America Radio, July-December 2007

[321]Center for Voting and Democracy www.fairvote.org/irv/end_majority_rule. htm; "The Thom Hartman Show Live Commentary," Air America Radio, July-December 2007

[322]www.amazon.com/Fair-Game-Betrayal-White-House/dp/B000WJVK7G www. amazon.com/Surrender-Not-Option-Defending-America/dp/1416552847; David Edwards and Muriel Kane, "Bolton sees Bush administration's Iran diplomacy as appeasement,"The Raw Story, November 9, 2007; www.amazon. com/Day-Reckoning-Ideology-Tearing-America/dp/0312376960 amazon.com/ Independents-Day-Awakening-American-Spirit/dp/0670018368; "The Thom Hartman Show Live Commentary," Air America Radio, July-December 2007

CHAPTER 14

[323]MSNBC – "Chris Matthews Profile, Biography,"www.cnbc.com/ id/15838038;"Keith Olbermann at Hollywood.com www.hollywood.com/ celebrity/Keith_Olbermann/4031238

[324]Media Matters, "Hardball for the left, softball for the right" ... March 8, 2006; Think Progress, "Matthews to McCain: 'People Will Learn A …,"February 7, 2006

[325]Brad Wilmouth, "Olbermann Denies Liberal Bias, Insists in Politics He's 'Neutral'," Newsbuster.org, July 29, 2006; Media Research Center www.mediaresearch.org; Keith Olbermann, "**Olbermann: Bush, Cheney should resign,**" MSNBC, July 3, 2007; Countdown with Keith Olbermann, "Bush just playing us with 'troop withdrawal," MSNBC, September 4, 2007; Countdown with Keith Olbermann, "Countdown with Keith Olbermann' for July 26," MSNBC, July 27, 2007

[326]USATODAY.com, "Fox News calls Olbermann 'over the line,'"July 25, 2006; Countdown with Keith Olbermann, "The Worst Person in the World," MSNBC. com, September 15, 2006; CNN.com, "Producer sues O'Reilly for sexual harassment; he sues for…," October 14, 2004

[327] 'Countdown with Keith Olbermann' for March 3, 2006, MSNBC.com, March 6, 2006; Alex Koppelman, "The MSNBC maverick…,"Salon.com, September 11, 2006; Media Matters, "O'Reilly threatened radio show caller with "a little, March 3, 2006

[328] FOXNews.com, "Gingrich Jabs at GOP Pursuing 2008 White House Nod," July 24, 2007; NBC4.com, "Gingrich Sees Clinton-Obama For Democrats," July 30, 2007; Noel Sheppard, "Chris Matthews on "ToNight Show," NewsBuster.org, July 20, 2006

[329] Katrina Vanden Heuvel "Dean Takes on Big Media," CommonDreams.org, December 19, 2003

[330] "HardBall with Chris Matthews," MSNBC, February 9, 2003; "GE 2007 Annual Report: Our Businesses: Operating Segments, Divisions, Units" www.ge.com/ar2007/ob.jsp; CommonDreams.org, "Future of Iraq: The Spoils of War," January 7, 2007; Jason Linkins "Chris Matthews Imitates Vampires, Flunks Geography," The Huffington Post, December 26, 2007; The Randi Rhodes Show, Air America Radio, n.d

[331] Countdown with Keith Olbermann, "Have you no sense…,"September 25, 2006

[332] Countdown with Keith Olbermann, "DeLay's Delusion," MSNBC, March 26, 2007; Countdown with Keith Olbermann, "Condi goes too far," MSNBC, February 27, 2007; Countdown with Keith Olbermann, "Have you no sense…,"September 25, 2006

[333] Chris Matthews, "10th Anniversary of Hardball," MSNBC, October 4, 2007; Dan Froomkin, "Bush Deplores American Timidity," washingtonpost.com, October 12, 2007; Carl Campanile, "Impartial' Host Rips GOP," New York Post, October 6, 2007; History News Network, "Max Boot: Bush didn't start the Mideast Fire," July 5, 2006; Geoffrey Dickens, "Chris Matthews Makes Final Push For Anti-War Candidate…"NewsBusters, August 7, 2006

[334] Infowars.com, "Video Surfaces of Cheney, in 1994, Warning That An Invasion of Iraq," August 13, 2007; www.mediazine.net/view/dick_cheney_on_invading_iraq; journals.democraticunderground.com/top10/304; thenexthurrah.typepad.com/the_next_hurrah/2006/12/swearing_dick.html

[335] White House, "Address by the President to the Nation on the Way Forward in Iraq," September 13, 2007; Joe Biden, Interview by Chris Matthews, MSNBC Coverage of the President's Speech, MSNBC, September 14, 2007

[336] R. Jeffrey Smith, "Ex-Colleague Says Armitage Was Source of CIA Leak," washingtonpost.com, August 29, 2006; Page A06; Pete Yost, "New twist in CIA leak probe," Boston.com. April 8, 2006

[337] *Dana Milbank and Carol D. Leonnig,* "Democrats Demand Rove's Firing,"Washingtonpost.com, October 31, 2005; Page A04; ABC News, "Time Reporter Says He Learned Agent's Identity From Rove," October 31, 2005; MSNBC.com, "Libby: White House sacrificed him for Rove," January 23, 2007; Murray Waas, "What Now, Karl?" Village Voice, August 9, 2005 ; Peter Johnson and Mark Memmott, "'Time' reporter to testify; 'N.Y. Times' reporter jailed," USA TODAY, July 6, 2005; *CNN.com, "Jailed reporter reaches deal in CIA leak probe," October 28, 2005*

[338] CNN.com, "Former ambassador blames White House for leak," September 29, 2003; Joseph C. Wilson 4th, "What I Didn't Find in Africa," New York Times, July 6, 2003; Carol D. Leonnig, "At Libby Trial, Power Players Face Uncomfortable Spotlight…," Washingtonpost.com, January 15, 2007; Page A01; Dan Froomkin, "Miller's Big Secret,"Washingtonpost.com, September 30, 2005; Don Van Natta Jr., Adam Liptak and Clifford J. Levy, "The Miller Case: A Notebook, a Cause, a Jail Cell and a Deal," New York Times, October 16, 2005; Carol D. Leonnig and Amy Goldstein "Libby 'Told a Dumb Lie,' Prosecutor Says in Closing Argument,"Washingtonpost.com, February 21, 2007; A04; *Carlo Bonini and Giuseppe d' Avanzo, "Berlusconi Provided false Niger Yellowcake documents," watchingamerica.com, October 24, 2005*

[339] New York Times, "Bush Unsure If Leaker Will Be Caught," October 7, 2003; White House, "President Meets with Cabinet, Discusses National and Economic Security," October 7, 2003; Richard Benedetto, "Bush: CIA leak may not be traced," USATODAY.com, October 7, 2003; MSNBC.com, "Jury convicts Libby on four charges,"_March. 6, 2007

[340] Washingtonpost.com, "Bush Defends calling DeLay Not Guilty," December 17, 2005; Page A09; CNN.com, "Joseph Wilson: 'Karl Rove should be fired," October 31, 2005; Online NewsHour "A Closer Look at Lewis Libby," PBS, October 28, 2005; The Thom Hartman Show, Air America Radio, n.d

[341] Media Channel –Home www.mediachannel.org; Keith Olbermann, "**Olbermann: Bush, Cheney should resign,**" MSNBC, July 3, 2007

CHAPTER 15

[342] Larry King-CNN, www.cnn.com/CNN/anchors_reporters/king.larry.html

[343] CNN Programs –"Anchors/Reporters - Wolf Blitzer" www.cnn.com/CNN/anchors_reporters/blitzer.wolf.html

344The Pew Research Center, "V. Media Credibility Declines: News Audience; Increasingly Politicized," June 8, 2004 people-press.org/report/?pageid=838; Anthony Crupi, "FNC Remains Ratings Leader," May 2, 2006 http://www.mediaweek.com/mw/news/recent_display.jsp?vnu_content_id=1002426373;American Journalism Review, "The Secrets of Fox's Success," December 2006/January 2007 www.ajr.org/Article.asp?id=4236; David Bauder, "Fox News Decline," Bottom Line Communications, October 1, 2006 www.bottomlinecom.com/fox_news_decline.htm

345Richard Cheney, Interview by Larry King, 'Larry King Live,' CNN.com , May 31, 2005 www.cnn.com/2005/US/05/30/cheney.iraq; Paris Hilton, Interview by Larry King, 'Larry King Live,' CNN.com. June 28, 2007

346CNN.com, "Cheney: Talk of blunders in Iraq is 'hogwash," January 25, 2007; White House, " Interview of the Vice President by Wolf Blitzer, CNN "Situation Room," January 24, 2007 www.whitehouse.gov/news/releases/2007/01/20070124-3.html

347CNN.com, "Cheney: Congressional probe of attorneys' firings 'a witch hunt,' July 31, 2007

348CBS 60 Minutes, "McCain Discusses Iraq Market Visit, Arizona Senator Speaks Exclusively…," CBS News, April 4, 2007; Mike Hersh, "Escalation's Reality," AfterDowningStreet.org, March 29, 2007

349CNN.com, "McCain on CNN's 'The Situation Room,' March 28, 2007; Kim Gamel, "McCain visits Baghdad, hails security crackdown," The Boston Globe, April 2, 2007; Transcripts, CNN.com, March 27, 2007; transcripts.cnn.com/TRANSCRIPTS/0703/27/sitroom.01.html – edition.cnn.com/TRANSCRIPTS/0703/27/sitroom.02.html

350Transcript, CNN.com July 9, 2007 transcripts.cnn.com/TRANSCRIPTS/0707/09/sitroom.03.html; July 9, 2007 edition of the 'Situation Room,' CNN.com

351www.cnn.com/CNN/anchors_reporters/king.larry.html Cronyism

352Bone Thugs- n- Harmony, "How many of us have them," Art of War, Ruthless Records, 1997.

353Bone Thugs- n- Harmony, "How many of us have them," Art of War, Ruthless Records, 1997

354Bassey Ekpenyong, Voice of Freedom International ministries, 2007

[355]Bone Thugs- n- Harmony, "How many of us have them," Art of War, Ruthless Records, 1997; Mark 4. 39 (King James Version).

[356]Bone Thugs- n- Harmony, "How many of us have them," Art of War, Ruthless Records, 1997.

[357]Bryon McCane, Credits, Art of War, Ruthless Records, 1997.

[358]Bone Brothers, "What's Friends," Forever Young, Koch Records, 2005.

[359]Bone Thugs- n- Harmony, "Murder One," BTNH Resurrection, Ruthless Records, 2000
[360]Mark Excell, Voice of Freedom International ministries, 2007.

[361]Bone Thugs- n- Harmony, "Bone Bone Bone," Thug World Order, Ruthless Records, 2002

[362]Bone Thugs- n- Harmony, "How many of us have them," Art of War, Ruthless Records, 1997.

[363]Bone Thugs- n- Harmony, "Da Introduction," E. 1999 Eternal, Ruthless Records, 1995.

[364]Bone Brothers, "Real Life," Forever Young, Koch Records, 2005